Communities of Difference ~

Communities of Difference ∾

Edited by

Peter Pericles Trifonas

For my father,
Panayiotis,
who taught me that dreams and hope have no bounds . . .

Contents ∾

List of Contributors ~

Effie Balomenos is an artist and illustrator, a cultural critic, as well as a teacher of the visual arts. She has published in the area of aesthetic education and critical pedagogy and has illustrated a series of picture books that is being used in schools around the globe.

Blane R. Després is Assistant Professor of Technology and Education at the Okanagan University College. His interests are in the ethical use of technology for education and its role in teacher education.

Paulo Ghiraldelli Jr. is Professor of Philosophy and Education at the Universidade Federal de Peranà, Brazil. He is the editor of *Contemporary Pragmatism* and the *Encyclopaedia of Philosophy of Education*. He is also Visiting Professor in Philosophy at Oklahoma State University and has lectured widely in Europe and North America.

Henry A. Giroux is Waterbury Chair Professor at Pennsylvania State University. He is the author of numerous articles and books including *Channel Surfing*, *Counternarratives* and *The Mouse that Roared: Disney and the End of Innocence* (Rowman & Littlefield).

Carl Leggo is a poet and Associate Professor in the Department of Language and Literacy Education at the University of British Columbia in Vancouver, Canada, where he teaches courses in narrative research and writing. His poetry and fiction and scholarly essays have been published in many journals in North America and around the world. He is the author of two collections of poems, titled *Growing Up Perpendicular on the Side of a Hill* and *View from My Mother's House*, as well as a book about reading and teaching poetry, titled *Teaching to Wonder: Responding to Poetry in the Secondary Classroom*.

Robert Luke is a Curriculum Coordinator at the Special Needs Opportunity Windows (SNOW) Project, an initiative of the Adaptive Technology Resource Centre at the University of Toronto.

Darren E. Lund is Assistant Professor at the University of Calgary. Darren taught high school for 16 years and received a number of honors for his work in promoting diversity, including the first Alberta Human Rights Award (1987). He was named a Reader's Digest National Leader in Education (1996) and twice named Intercultural Educator of the Year, by the EF Institute for Cultural Exchange (1995) and the Intercultural Council the Alberta Teachers' Association (2000). He is Past President of the Alberta Association for Multicultural Education, and his work has been published in the *Canadian Journal of Education, Teaching Education, Alberta Journal of Educational Research, Interchange,* and *Journal of Educational Thought.*

Peter McLaren is Professor in the Division of Urban Schooling, Graduate School of Education and Information Studies, University of California, Los Angeles. He is the author and editor of more than 35 books on topics ranging from critical ethnography and the sociology of education to critical social theory and critical pedagogy. His most recent books include Che Guevara, Paulo Freire, and the Pedagogy of Revolution (Rowman & Littlefield, 2000); Life in Schools (4th ed.) (Allyn & Bacon, 2002); and Marxism Against Postmodernism in Educational Theory (edited with D. Hill, M. Cole, & G. Rikowski) (Lexington Books, 2002). Professor McLaren lectures worldwide on the politics of liberation. His works have been translated into 17 languages.

Vera Nincic is a doctoral candidate at the Ontario Institute of Study in Education, University of Toronto. She is currently writing a dissertation on the academic uses of information and communication technologies by non-native English-speaking graduate students and working as the Assistant Editor of the Handbook of Virtual Learning Environments (Kluwer).

Jason Nolan is Scholar in Residence with the Knowledge Media Design Institute and Senior Fellow with the McLuhan Program in Culture and Technology, both at the university of Toronto. He is coeditor of the International Handbook of Virtual Learning Environments. His research interests include collaborative virtual environments, wikis and blogs, the digital divide, and Dracula and virtuality.

Trevor Norris is a Ph.D. student in the Department of Theory and Policy Studies at OISE/UT. His interests center around philosophy and education as a way to rethink community and the ethical subject beyond neoliberalism.

Carlo Ricci is Assistant Professor at Nippising University. Before joining Nipissing as an assistant professor, Ricci was teaching English at a secondary school for the Peel District School Board and he was also teaching part-time at the University of Toronto. Ricci's research interests include: the erosion of democracy in our education system and advocating for its revitalization, teaching literacy using the spirit of Paulo Freire's pedagogical assumptions, Democratic Education, Critical Theory and the negative impact of standardized testing.

Peter Pericles Trifonas teaches Cultural Studies in Education at the Ontario Institute for Studies in Education/University of Toronto. He has taught at schools and universities in North America and Europe. His books include *The Ethics of Writing: Derrida, Deconstruction, and Pedagogy, Revolutionary Pedagogies, Pedagogies of Difference,* and *Ethics, Institutions, and the Right to Philosophy* with Jacques Derrida.

Joel Weiss, after 34 years as a faculty member at The Ontario Institute for Studies in Education, took early retirement to concentrate on major writing projects. He is the

Senior Editor of the *Handbook of Virtual Learning Environments*, being prepared for Kluwer Academic Publishers, and, is writing a different type of research book, *Research Wisdom*. He is The Founding Editor of Curriculum Inquiry, and recently published in TCRecord, with Robert Brown, "Telling Tales Over Time: Constructing and Deconstructing the School Calendar."

John Willinsky is Pacific Educational Press Professor of Technology at the University of British Columbia. Postmodernism, postcolonialism, literacy, critical theory, and technology are among his major areas of interest. His most recent books are *Technologies of Knowing* and *Learning to Divide the World: Education at Empire's End*.

Communities of Difference:
A Preface to a Knowledge of
Ourselves as Another ⌇

Now, more than ever, there is a obligation to recognize the presence of infinite possibilities and multiple horizons of alterity that destabilize the grounding of subjectivity in communities of difference. This responsibility highlights the problem of exposing or creating locations within communitarian-based cultures that still occupy the colonized space of traditional knowledge archives and are at the same time alterior to the logic of the status quo.[1] If so, how and where are gestures toward the spaces of these new locations enacted as communities of difference by which we define the difference of ourselves as another?

The inside and outside borders of any cultural spaces we define according to the age-old concept of community open up the material locations within which theory and praxis are renewed through the syncretic nature of subjectivity as a condition of impossibility fueled by a global vision of a shared community running rampant today. The idea of global citizenship nurtures the idea of a communal proclivity of the autotelic Subject and produces the call for a leveling of difference in what Jacques Derrida has called the cosmopolitical point of view. In relation to culture, language, and technology, the alterity of subjectivity and systems of representation in communities of difference are conjoined and yet render their unique in the difference of themselves by the forces of globalization. Otherness is present yes, but with a debt and duty to the historicity of what has gone before. The cosmopolitical defines communities of difference through the necessity of marking the interior and exterior limits of culture through language and the rise of other technologies of representation. The logic of the cosmopolitical within the notion of communities of difference broaches the question of human rights and education. It asks us to rethink the certainty of knowledge as a philosophical project of genealogical excavation in relation to social justice and educational equity. The ethical problem of who can, should be, or is capable of determining the propriety of the formal location of inquiry—the space and place of the cultural–institutional indexicality marking the public paths of difference, its entrances and exits—is a flash point of conflict. Pedagogy is always already implicated in the perennial question of democracy and discipline, of knowledge, difference, otherness, social justice, and the right to education for each and every subject and citizen.

The moment of questioning the nature or community directly addresses the academic responsibility of educational institutions and by extension those who teach, work, and live *in* and, perhaps, *for* them, as the teaching body *(le corps eneignant)*,[2] to value difference. What does this mean exactly? To say that a pedagogical institution, and those who are a part of it, are it, possess total and unabiding and hence *irresponsible and unaccountable* control of the intellectual domain they survey is to surmise a legacy of exclusion. There is no space left to welcome another. It is a question of affinity and openness toward embracing the difference of the Other without giving way to hesitance or reservation, empirical qualification and moral judgment, let alone indignation.

The question of a "proper domain" of the question of rights, of institutions, of community and difference—of propriety and domination, appropriation, expropriation, of property, participation, ownership and fairness, and therefore of law, ethics, and ultimately, of social justice—brings us back to the connections between culture and knowledge. It extends the problem of democracy and *democraticity*, governance and governmentality, of the responsibilities and principles relating to the formation and formativity of a system of public education on an international scale. It is a matter of locating the axiomatic difference of these terms, the difference of their axiomaticity, and their interrelatability, within a hospitable space and place that only an open concept of community can entreat them to because there is difference. Concept excavation as a genealogy of difference eventually leads to a productive recognition of alterity. That is, an ethical expansion of thought and thinking without limitations or borders.

The heterogeneous scope of this impossible territory wherein the struggle over difference and human rights occurs, after Immanuel Kant and his "risky" envisioning of the cosmopolitical condition: a hypothetical situation of geo-global interconnectivity or "mondialization" having an "inter-national or inter-state dimension"[3] and related to the question of the *emanation* and diaspora of the *polis* and *politeia as a way of life*. The idea of the cosmopolitical solidifies the problem of a universal history or "the link among the cities, the *poleis* of the world, as nations, as people, or as States."[4] However, we cannot in good conscience subscribe to the constellations of a panoptic vision of an "abstract universalism"[5] that strangles difference in the name of a general culture of homogeneous communities. Kant postulated the cosmopolitical as an organic global synthesis of cultures and subjects upon which a template for writing the blueprint of any and all institutions *to come* can be. In many ways, the vision still guides us and the pedagogical imperatives of today's educational and social institutions. Interrogating the modality of this desire for sameness demands a rethinking of the future of thinking and works toward illuminating and transforming rather than dismissing or deriding the historicity of "philosophical acts and archives."[6] In questioning the ground of institutions and the reason of their institutionality with respect to the formation of subjectivity, engages the real-world effects produced by the performative force of epistemological discourses and their responsibility as instances of founding and therefore of foundation. The notion of communities of difference arise from an anti-utopian thrust, contrary to the ideal of a natural universalism of thought and action uniting thinking and subjectivity in the image of the global citizen. It enables us to link the problem of human rights and difference with the Kantian conception of a cosmopolitical point of view and community in a positive rather than a negative way. We must remember that knowledge and knowing are articulated by the continual reaggregation of the logic of the letter, the terms of its reading as production and reproduction, and the domain of its archive. The problem of how to go about securing both private and public "access to this language and culture, first and foremost by means of education,"[7] involves, more or less, the working-out of the problems of community and difference central to answering the question of academic privilege (who has the right to knowledge?) and the power of location (how? and why?).

The pedagogical onus on an affable (simple, crude, vulgar) modality of cultural production and reproduction without the complexity of resistance or complications of difference fixes the parameters of an institutional ethic of response and responsibility. But this reduction of the frame of reference to categorical imperatives that willfully ignore the limitations and boundaries of a project of repeating the historicity of Western education occurs only if and when the cosmopolitical nature of difference as a source for community is not taken into account. It would be wrong to ignore the diversity within the composition of difference and to cull a universal difference without diversity. The emanation of the cosmopolitical view is a gathering of multiplicity in communities of difference that articulate the ethical terms of a responsibility to acknowledge the profundity of difference, the unimaginable manifestation of many parts and partners, nations, states, and peoples whose materiality comprises and cannot but exceed the conceptual totality of its essence, These aspects are not unrelated insofar as such ethico-qualitative judgments require an identification of who would have the privilege and opportunity of participation regarding curricular decisions about the future of the right to education, and why. The global diaspora of subjectivity is the open ground of a *democracy-to-come*, with a *pedagogy-to-come*, and the potentially diverging paths of its filiations, friendships, what is held close, in affinity, to the spirit and the heart, not the mind.

Kant's ethical universalism, and its Eurocentric bias, can be used in a novel way by turning it toward the question of human rights, community, and difference to mobilize the cosmopolitical as a viewpoint *not only* for reconceptualizing the "eternal becoming"[8] of being-in-the-world, *but as a new approach to realizing the impossible futures of a "progressive institutionality" to come and the unforeseeability of its educational methods and apparatus.* This does not simply mean a securing of the opportunity for freedom in thinking and teaching; neither does it defer pedagogically, nor ethically, to the teaching of thinking without reference to the tradition of Western episteme, however it may be defined in curricular terms. The notion of the cosmopolitical reawakens and resituates the Eurocentrism of the concept and its implications for reinscribing the "horizon of a new community"[9] of the question and the impossibility of the question that teaches the Other to question the sources of the Self and the Other through meditations on difference. This may sound strange to those who envision and portray deconstruction as a *destruction* of Western metaphysics, its institutions and its teachings. All Western ideas about education *predict* a trajectory of thinking along a "teleological axis"[10] with respect to the epistemologico-cultural ideal of the "infinite progress" of Being and the temporal procession of beings toward perfectability, achievable or not. Anything else "would be nothing but a novel"[11] given the inseparability of the European epistemological tradition from the notion of the universal, "a plan of nature that aims at the total, perfect political unification of the human species *(die vollkommen bürgerliche Vereinigung in der Menschengattung)*."[12] Any social or cultural institution is founded on memory and the material conditions of its working-out as a dynamic tradition of theory and practice, philosophy and action. Communities are predicated *on taking memory and its differences into account*: accounting for the causality of its effects, its bias, its exclusions, rendering an account of what makes memory, disrupts it, constructs its limits, openings, how and why it favors. It mobilizes a thoroughly Western conceit and philosophical project directed toward the pragmatic rectification of Being as presence and the sending of itself forward in time toward the infinity of progressive becoming.

We have to accept the reality of the forces of globality and cosmopolitanism and yet safeguard the right to difference. A critique—coming down on one side or the other—of efficacy is not at all useful, but a misleading endeavor seeking an ethical refuge in the evaluative power of a binary form of metaphysical reasoning pitting "the good" against "the bad," "essentialism" against "antiessentialism," "Eurocentrism" against "anti-Eurocentrism," and so on. The endwork of such a critical task that freely places blame or adjudicates value for the sake of a castigation or rejection of worth is performed too quickly and easily. Its decisions are rendered by and appeal to the dictates of a universalist conception of "reason" and its demotic (and not at all democratic) corollary of "common sense" to construct the ideologico-conceptual grounds of what is "good" and what is "bad." The judgmental edifice of its *either/or* rationale presumes a lack of interpretative complexity, a plainness of truth that is totally transparent and obvious to everyone, a clear-cut and unarguable judgment made with no fathomable case to be made for the possibility of opposition or exemption to the rule of law. One life-world. One reality. One Truth. The metaphysical value of this ethic of perception and its monological model of representation determines the non-oppositional grounds of truth. Conditional and definitive limits thereby demarcate the freedom of what it is possible to know and to think and what it is possible to say without offending the much guarded sensibilities of "reason" and "good taste"— however their values might be constructed and articulated—as the ideals of commonly held responses to cultural institutions and practices. Difference is abdicated in favor of a community of shared interpretative responsibility and the unethical hegemony of its "majority rules" attitude that bids one to erect barriers against diversity, "to see and talk about things only as they are or could be." The priority of clarity as an ethical prerequisite of a "responsible response" is, without a doubt, everything when the analytical imperative is *nothing but* an exercise of choosing sides. There is a more productive approach.

The ethical impetus of the "postcolonial," "anticolonial," or even the "neocolonial" moment as it is called by Gayatri Chakravorty Spivak begins with a philosophical nod to what is, for Derrida, the performative legacy of the institutions and models of "Greco-European memory."[13] Addressing the textual composition of this epistemic and cultural genealogy of Western knowledge, Kant's discourse on the cosmopolitical is only one example of a host of writings by philosophers who possess the temerity to have made such audacious and largely accurate statements about the dominance of "the guiding thread *(Leitfaden)* of Greek history *(griechische Geschichte)*"[14] with respect to explaining the unfolding of the Reason of Being within communities across space and over time. The axiomaticity of this logic directed at excluding an "Other" from the fundamental (pure) archive of its heritage would be only natural from a philosophical perspective of human historicity that narcotizes the productive value of difference and thus denies the validity of allowing for the possibility of a heterogeneous opening to a world community from a cosmopolitical point of view. As Derrida says, "One encounters [its Eurocentric axiology] again and again, intact and invariable throughout variations as serious as those that distinguish Hegel, Husserl, Heidegger, and Valéry."[15] But of course there is a difference in what Kant proposes by way of a vision of the world from a cosmopolitical point of view and its universal enactment in the form of a "Society of Nations" despite the emphasis he places upon Greek philosophy and history, because it attempts to *sublate*, to synthesize and at the same time keep the tensions of the values of cultural difference in an amicable and moral unification of humanity worked out, more or less, along with the trajectory of the "teleological axis of this discourse [that] has become the tradition of European modernity."[16] The concept of nature, and specifically the "unsociability *(Ungeselligkeit, Unvertragsamkeit)*"[17] of human being *by nature*, is actually the means to a salvation "through culture, art and artifice *(Kunst)*, and reason, to make the seeds of nature grow."[18] And Kant truly believes in the potentially unifying power of this "natural or originary state of war among men"[19] (in Kant's time there could literally only be a state of war *among men*). Because of the propensity of subjective (cultural) differences to force antagonisms, territoriality, and conflict, there is only one possible solution that "resembles a novel-like story yet isn't one, that which in truth is but the very historicity of history, is the ruse of nature."[20] And here we may be amazed (or not) by the implications of the Kantian vision.

For Kant, violence—and its threat to the security of human *Dasein*—is the catalyst that allows nature "to aid reason and thereby put philosophy into operation through the society of nations"[21] we forge under the auspices of global security and nations united. This is a troubling thesis, holding together the logic of the cosmopolitical community of global proportions around the concept of alterity as productive tension. On the one hand, peace achieved through the danger of violence is not really a peace made at all. It is a provisional state of human entropy with respect to the appeasement of the tensions of difference and the possible uprising of transgressions and aggressions against subjective alterity that depends on the ethico-philosophical essence of the cosmopolitical covenant of being. The condition of peace represents the satiating of a reaction to nullify the difference of difference. On the other, a peace compelled by the dark side of the human spirit is perhaps the only *possible and natural* peace that could be rendered effective or legislated under circumstances within which no other decision or action is acceptable, viable, or defensible given the alternative of violence. This of course begs the question of the constitutive force of community—whatever that *ideal* may entail as an affective identification of a subjective sense of belonging, a *being-at-home-in-the-world with others*—and the responsibility of its opening-up of the Self unto the difference of the Other. When these two states or conditions of existence, peace (community) and violence (war), are placed in direct opposition to each other, the ethical choice is clearly delineated by the power of a humanistic appeal that is made to a *universal* and hence *moral will* denying the propriety of any transgression of subjectivity at all costs, even if this means suppressing human rights and freedoms for "the greater good." Community, then, is a matter of instilling and practicing a homogeneous concept of culture, a *general* culture whose model of a collective intersubjectivity acts as a unified resistance to the threat of alterity. The promoting of common points of recognition and identification within the ideologico-philosophical consciousness of its constituents in order to defy or suppress the propensity for violence against the threat of difference—or at the very least to quell the performativity of the desire to do so—establishes the psychic and figural ground for the foundations of friendship and belonging. Playing by the determinative ethics of these rules of consensus in the name of community and commonality, and also of communication, reduces the Other to the Same and minimizes the potential of a subjective resistance to the inclusion of contrariety within the sphere of a closed system of shared associations. This illusion of unity masks the radical violence of alterity and softens the risk of its provisional acceptance by replacing the shock of its reality with the comforting image of a single, harmonious group, a majority without difference. *They is Us.* The correlation of subjectivity relieves the discord of diversity because one has to inhere and adhere to the fundamental agreements of a consensual state of abstract universalism to be part of the general yet specific culture of a community *I am We.* An ethical and philosophical contrition of sorts must be achieved in this case by the subject to ensure the manifestation of a "responsible response" that is itself a coming to peace of the Self with the avowable laws of a community and its effacing of difference. If we consider the Eurocentrism of the reasoning put forward for pursuing a universal alliance of humanity from the cosmopolitical view, and its prefiguring of new models of global gathering and world institutions like the United Nations and UNESCO, we cannot avoid addressing the ethico-philosophical focus of such an idea aimed at rearticulating the notion of community after the multiplicity of difference as communities of difference.

Notes

1. Derrida, "Of the Humanities and the Philosophical Discipline," in *Surfaces* Vol. VI.108, 1996, pp. 1–40.
2. See Jacques Derrida, "Où commence et comment finit un corps enseignant," in *Du droit à la philosophie* (Paris & Galilée, 1990) 111–153.
3. Derrida, "Of the Humanities and the Philosophical Discipline," 2.
4. Ibid.
5. Ibid.
6. Ibid.
7. Ibid.
8. The "Roundtable Discussion" on Jacques Derrida's "Des humanités et de la discipline philosophiques"/"Of the Humanities and Philosophical Disciplines" in *Surfaces* Vol. VI.108 (v.1.0A-16/08/1996), 5–40 involved Hazard Adams, Ernst Behler, Hendrick Birus, Jacques Derrida, Wolfgang Iser, Ludwig Pfeiffer, Bill Readings, Ching-hsien Wang, and Pauline Yu. All further quotations from this text are comments made by Derrida. The page references are from the website version of the text, found at http:// tornade.ere.umontreal.ca/guedon/Surfaces/vol6/derrida.html. This endnote refers to a quotation from page 3.
9. Ibid., 3.
10. Ibid.
11. Derrida, "Of the Humanities and the Philosophical Discipline," 2.
12. Ibid., 2.
13. Ibid., 4.
14. Ibid., 3.

15. Ibid.

16. Ibid.

17. Immanuel Kant cited in Derrida, "Of the Humanities and the Philosophical Discipline," 3.

18. Derrida, "Of the Humanities and the Philosophical Discipline," 3.

19. Ibid.

20. Ibid.

21. Ibid.

Acknowledgments ❧

I would like to thank the contributors to this collection: Effie Balomenos, Blane Després, Paulo Ghiraldelli, Henry Giroux, Carl Leggo, Darren Lund, Robert Luke, Peter McLaren, Vera Nincic, Jason Nolan, Trevor Norris, Carlo Ricci, Joel Weiss, John Willinsky. It is indeed rare to find educators and thinkers who are very committed and dedicated to social justice and community. This book would not have been possible without their inspiration, vision, and boundless friendship.

Part 1 ~

Culture, Difference, Community

Chapter 1 ∼

The War Against Children and the Shredding of the Social Contract

Henry A. Giroux

I begin with two quotes that I believe signal the presence of another war somewhat removed from the Iraqi conflict, a war being waged on the domestic front that feeds off the general decay of democratic politics and reinforces what neoliberals cheerfully call the death of the social. This war is ostensibly aimed against "big government," which is really a war against the welfare state and the social contract itself—this is a war against the notion that everyone should have access to decent education, health care, employment, and other public services. The first quote comes from Debbie Riddle, a current Texas state representative. The second quote comes from Grover Norquist, the president of the Americans for Tax Reform and arguably Washington's leading right-wing strategist.

> Where did this idea come from that everybody deserves free education? Free medical care? Free whatever? It comes from Moscow. From Russia. It comes straight out of the pit of hell.[1]
>
> My goal is to cut government in half in twenty-five years, to get it down to the size where we can drown it in the bathtub.[2]

As these quotes suggest, Norquist and his ilk target some parts of government for downsizing a little more energetically than others. They are most concerned to dismantle the parts of the public sector that serve the social and democratic needs of the nonaffluent majority of the American populace. The parts that provide "free" service and welfare to the privileged and opulent minority and dole out punishment to the poor are reserved from that great domestic war tool, the budgetary axe. Democracy has never appeared more fragile and endangered in the United States than in this time of civic and political crisis. This is especially true for young people. While a great deal has been written about the budget busting costs of the invasion and occupation of Iraq and the passing of new antiterrorist laws in the name of "homeland security" that make it easier to undermine those basic civil liberties that protect individuals against invasive and potentially repressive government actions, there is a thunderous silence on the part of many critics and academics regarding the ongoing insecurity and injustice suffered by young people in this country, which is now being intensified as a result of the state's increasing resort to repression and punitive social policies at home and war abroad. The "war" on working-class youth and youth of color, in particular, is evident not only in the disproportionate numbers of such youth who provide the fodder in Iraq and Afghanistan for Bush's preventive war policy, it is also evident in the silent war at home, especially since the Iraqi war and the war against terrorism are being financed from cuts in domestic funding on health care, children's education, and other public services. The recent war with Iraq will change the way the United States relates to the rest of the world as well as how it addresses the most pressing problems Americans face in their everyday lives. It would be a tragic mistake for educational critics either to separate the war in Iraq from the many problems Americans face at home or fail to recognize how war is being waged by this government on multiple fronts.

The war against terrorism is part and parcel of the war against democracy at home. Slavoj Zizek claims that the "true target of the 'war on terror' is American society itself—the disciplining of its emancipatory excesses" (Zizek, 2003).[3] George Steinmets argues that the current state of emergency represents a new shift in the mode of political power and regulation. He claims that:

> The refocusing of political power on the level of the American national state has been most evident in the area of U.S. Geopolitical strategy (unilateralism and preemptive military strikes), but much of the new regulatory activity has focused on the state apparatus itself and the "domestic" level of politics, with the creation of a huge new government agency (the department of Homeland Security), transformations of the legal system (e.g., secret trials and arrests, indefinite detentions), and intensified domestic surveillance: first with the 2001 USA Patriot Act, which dramatically relaxed restrictions on search and seizure; then with the Total Information Awareness program, which collects and analyzes vast amounts of data on private communications and commercial transactions; and most recently with the proposed domestic Security Enhancement Act of 2003. (Steinmetz, 2003)[4]

Both observations are partly right. The Bush "permanent war doctrine" is not just aimed at alleged terrorists or the excesses of democracy, but also against disposable populations in the homeland, whether they be young black men who inhabit our nations' poorest neighborhoods or those unemployed workers who have been abandoned by the flight of capital as well as all levels of government. The financing of the war in Iraq is buttressed by what Vice President Dick Cheney calls the concept of "never ending war." This is a concept that declares permanent war as a continuous state of emergency and brings into play a fundamentally new mode of politics. In a commencement speech given recently at the U.S. Military Academy, Cheney provides a succinct outline of the permanent war concept:

> The battle of Iraq was a major victory in the war on terror, but the war itself is far from over. We cannot allow ourselves to grow complacent. We cannot forget that the terrorists

remain determined to kill as many Americans as possible, both abroad and here at home, and they are still seeking weapons of mass destruction to use against us. With such an enemy, no peace treaty is possible; no policy of containment or deterrence will prove effective. The only way to deal with this threat is to destroy it, completely and utterly.[5]

The apocalyptic tone of his comments do more than cover up the fictive relationship between Iraq and 9/11; it also serves to legitimate a bloated and obscene military budget as well as economic and tax policies that are financially bankrupting the states' budgets, destroying public education, and plundering public services. The U.S. government plans to spend up to $400 billion to finance the Iraqi invasion and the ongoing occupation, while it allocates only $16 billion to welfare programs that cannot possibly address the needs of over 34.8 million people who live below the poverty line, many of them children, or the 75 million without health insurance, or the millions now unemployed because of diminished public services and state resources. While $723 billion dollars (estimated at a trillion over a ten-year period) are allocated for tax cuts for the rich, state governments are cutting a total of $75 billion in health, welfare benefits, and education. Many states such as California, with a $38.8 billion dollar budget gap, are implementing "drastic cuts in public school services and the withholding potentially life saving medicine from seriously ill patients."[6] Oregon has cut back on the school year and cut out extracurricular activities. Many states are laying off crucially needed police, fire, and health workers. Massachusetts has laid off hundreds of solely needed public school teachers. Many states such as New York and Pennsylvania have cut back on crucial basic programs such as medical services to seriously ill individuals, programs for the disabled, and prescription drug benefits for the poor.

The sheer inhumanity the Bush administration displays toward the working poor and children living below and slightly above poverty level can be seen in the decision by Republicans in Congress to eliminate from the 2003 tax bill the $400 child credit for families with incomes between 10,000 and 26,000 dollars. The money saved by this cutback will be used to pay for the reduction on dividend taxes. As a result, as Bill Moyers observes, "[Twelve] million children are punished for being poor, even as the rich are rewarded for being rich."[7] Bush's tax cuts are an insult to any viable notion of social justice. For instance, according to the Citizens for Tax Justice, "the top 1 percent of Americans—those making over 335,000 a year or more—will get, on the average, tax breaks worth $103,899," while the bottom "20 percent—those making under $16,000—will get all of $45 over the four-year period."[8]

As engaged intellectuals, academics and students need to connect these multiple attacks on the poor and much-needed public services to an expanded political and social vision that refuses the cynicism and sense of powerlessness that accompanies the destruction of social goods, the corporatization of the media, the dismantling of workers' rights, and the incorporation of intellectuals. Against this totalitarian onslaught, educators need to develop a language of critique and possibility, one that connects diverse struggles, uses theory as a resource, and defines politics as not merely critical but also as a transformative intervention into public life. We need a language that relates the discourse of war to an attack on democracy at home *and* abroad, and we need to use that language in a way that captures the needs, desires, histories, and experiences that shape people's daily lives. Similarly, as democratic institutions are downsized and public goods are offered up for corporate plunder, those educators who take seriously the related issues of equality, human rights, justice, and freedom face the crucial challenge of formulating a notion of the political suitable for addressing the urgent problems now facing the twenty-first century—a politics that as Zygmunt Bauman argues "never stops criticizing the level of justice already achieved and seeking more justice and better justice."[9]

As the federal government is restructured as a result of right-wing assaults by the Bush administration, it has dramatically shifted its allegiance away from providing for people's welfare, protecting the environment, and expanding the realm of public good. As a result of such a shift, the social contract that provides for social provisions against life's hazards and that lies at the heart of a substantive democracy has been nullified. As the social contract is shredded by Bush's army of neoliberal evangelicals, neoconservative hard-liners, and religious fundamentalists, government relies more heavily on its militarizing functions giving free reign to the principle of rational security at the expense of public service and endorsing property rights over human rights. A spreading culture of fear in an age of automated surveillance and repressive legislation has created a security state that gives people the false choice between being safe or free. As a result, constitutional freedoms and civil liberties are compromised as the FBI is given the power to siege the records of library users and bookstore customers, the CIA and Pentagon are allowed to engage in domestic intelligence work, and the PATRIOT Act allows people to be detained indefinitely in secret without access to either lawyers or family members. Under such circumstances, as Arundhati Roy argues, "the fundamental governing principles of democracy are not just being subverted but deliberately sabotaged. This kind of democracy is the problem, not the solution."[10] The shadow of authoritarianism becomes increasingly darker as society is organized relentlessly around a culture of fear, cynicism, and unbridled self interest—a society in which the government promotes legislation urging neighbors to spy on each other and the president of the United States endorses a notion of patriotism based on moral absolutes and an alleged mandate to govern, which, if John Ashcroft is to be believed, comes directly from God (with a little help, of course, from Jeb Bush and the U.S. Supreme Court).

Increasingly, we are told by President Bush, John Ashcroft, Dick Cheney, and others that patriotism is now legitimated through the physics of unaccountable power and unquestioned authority, defined rather crudely in the dictum "Either you are with us or with the terrorists."[11] Such absolutes, of course, have little respect for difference, dissent, or for that matter democracy itself. Politics in this instance has much less in common with public engagement, dialogue, and democratic governance than with a heavy reliance on institutions that rule through fear and, if necessary, brute force. The devaluation of politics and the depolliticization of public engagement in the United States has taken an ominous turn in light of the ongoing militarization of language, public space, and everyday life. Communities are now organized around fear rather than civic courage, compassion, or democratic values. Increasingly, power is being used by the Bush administration to promote, what Sheldon Wolin calls, "empire abroad and corporate power at home,"[12] increasingly mediated and legitimized through the rhetoric of war, fear, and antiterrorism.

As Ulrich Beck has argued, the language of war has taken a distinctly different turn in the new millennium.[13] War no longer needs to be ratified by Congress since it is now waged by various government agencies that escape the need for official approval. War has become a permanent condition adopted by a nation-state that is largely defined by its repressive functions in response to its powerlessness to regulate corporate power, provide social investments for the populace, and guarantee a measure of social freedom. The concept of war occupies a strange place in the current lexicon of foreign and domestic policy. It no longer simply refers to a war waged against a sovereign state such as Iraq, nor is it merely a moral referent for engaging in acts of national self-defense. The concept of war has been both expanded and inverted. It has been expanded in that it has become one of the most powerful concepts for understanding and structuring political culture, public space, and everyday life. Wars are now waged against crime, drugs, terrorism, even obesity, among a host of alleged public disorders. Wars are not declared against foreign enemies but against alleged domestic threats. The concept of war has also been inverted in that it has been removed from any concept of social justice—a relationship that emerged under President Lyndon Johnson and that exemplified in the war on poverty. War has become a metaphor for legitimating a zone of power in which the national security state displaces its more democratic role (social, egalitarian, peaceful, and democratic). As Susan Buck-Morss observes:

> The US national security state is a war machine positioned within a geopolitical landscape. It must have a localizable enemy for its power to appear legitimate; its biggest threat is that the enemy disappears. But given a war, even a Cold War, and now given an ill-defined yet total "war on terrorism," the declared "state of emergency" is justification for suspending the rights and freedoms of citizens. It justifies arresting and holding individuals without due process. It justifies killing and bombing without oversight or accountability. It justifies secrecy, censorship, and a monopoly over the accumulation and dissemination of information. All of these state practices are totalitarian, of course.[14]

Under the reign of the national security state, war is now defined almost exclusively as a punitive and militaristic process. This can be seen in the ways in which social policies are now criminalized so that the war on poverty is now a war against the poor, the war on drugs is now a war waged largely against youth of color, and the war against terrorism is now largely a war against immigrants, domestic freedoms, and dissent itself. In the Bush, Perle, Rumsfeld, and Ashcroft view of terrorism, war is individualized as every citizen becomes a potential terrorist who has to prove that he or she is not dangerous. Under the rubric of emergency time that feeds on government-induced media panics, war provides the moral imperative to collapse the "boundaries between innocent and guilty, between suspects and non-suspects."[15] War provides the primary rhetorical tool for articulating a notion of the social as a community organized around shared fears rather than shared responsibilities and civic courage. War is now transformed into a slick, Hollywood spectacle designed to both glamorize a notion of hypermasculinity fashioned in the oil fields of Texas and fill public space with celebrations of ritualized militaristic posturing touting the virtues of either becoming part of "an Army of one" or indulging in commodified patriotism by purchasing a new Hummer. Of course, this corrupt version of patriotism excludes certain class and racial minorities who can buy their participation in it.

War as a spectacle combines easily with the culture of fear to divert public attention away from domestic problems, define patriotism as consensus, and further the growth of a police state. The latter takes on dangerous overtones not only with the passage of the PATRIOT Act and the suspension of civil liberties, but is also evident in the elimination of those laws that traditionally separated the military from domestic law enforcement and offered individuals a vestige of civil liberties and freedoms. The political implications of the expanded and inverted use of war as a metaphor can also be seen in the war against "big government," which is really a war against the welfare state and the social contract itself—that is, a war against the notion that everyone should have access to decent education, health care, employment, and other public services. Of course, while the war against big government has been relegated to a knee-jerk political slogan by Republicans and conservative Democrats alike, one has to search far and wide to hear a peep out of this group about the threat that big corporations pose to democracy or, for that matter, an articulation of what the role of responsible government might actually be. One of the most serious issues to be addressed in the debate about Bush's concept of permanent war is the effect it is having on one of our most vulnerable populations, children, and the political opportunity this issue represents for articulating a language of both opposition and possibility.

The War Against Children and the Politics of Neoliberalism

Wars are almost always legitimated in order to make the world safe for "our children's future" but the rhetoric belies how their future is often denied by the acts of aggression put into place by a range of ideological state apparatuses that operate on the precepts of a war footing. This would include the horrible effects of the militarization of schools, the use of the criminal justice system to redefine social issues such as poverty and homelessness as violations of the social order, and the subsequent rise of a prison-industrial complex as a way to contain disposable populations such as youth of color who are poor and marginalized. Under the rubric of war, security, and antiterrorism, children are "disappeared" from the most basic social spheres that provide the conditions for a sense of agency and possibility, as they are rhetorically excised from any discourse about the future. The "disappearing" of children is made more concrete and reprehensible with the recent revelation that the three children between the ages of 13 and 15 are being held without legal representation as enemy combatants in possibly inhumane conditions at the military's infamous Camp Delta at Guantanamo Bay, Cuba. One wonders how the Bush administration reconciles its construction of a U.S. Gulag for children with their fervent support of family values and the ideology of compassionate conservativism.

The Bush administration's aggressive attempts to reduce the essence of democracy to profit making, shred the social contract, elevate property rights over human rights, make public schools dysfunctional, and promote tax cuts that will limit the growth of social programs and public investments fail completely when applied to the vast majority of citizens, but especially so when they are applied to children. And yet, children provide one of the most important referents for exposing and combating such policies. President Bush and his administrative cronies are redefining the nature of the social contract so as to remove it from the realm of politics and democracy. In doing so, Bush and his followers are not only consolidating their political power, they are also pushing through harsh policies and regressive measures that cut basic services and public assistance for the poor, sacrificing American democracy and individual autonomy for the promise of domestic security, and allocating resources and tax breaks to the rich through the airline bail-out and regressive tax cuts. Bush's rhetoric of "permanent war" and antiterrorism has done more than create a culture of fear and a flood of jingoistic patriotism, it has also covered up those neoliberal tax polices for the rich that are part of the war waged against public goods, the very notion of the social, and those marginalized by class and race. As Jeff Madrick observes:

> Narrow politics, of course, can partly account for the Bush administration's tax proposals. The tax cuts disproportionately benefit the wealthy, which, after all, is Bush's natural political constituency. But Bush's policies may, in fact, be explained by another, more radical agenda. Extensive tax cuts will require Congress to limit the growth of social programs and public investment and undermine other programs altogether. If that is your vision of the best direction America can take, the strategy makes some sense. So, we were wrong about how dividend tax cuts stimulate growth, you can almost hear the Bush advisers thinking. No problem. Rising deficits will inevitably force Congress to starve those "wasteful" social programs. The prospective high deficits may even make it imperative to privatize Social Security and Medicare eventually. Social spending is the problem, goes the argument, not tax cuts.[16]

Starving social programs and destroying public institutions have their most immediate effects on children, especially those who are poor, lack adequate resources, and who are trapped in a cycle of impoverishment and structures of inequality. Making visible the suffering and oppression of young people cannot help but challenge the key assumptions of "permanent war" policies designed to destroy public institutions and prevent government from providing important services that ameliorate ignorance, poverty, racism, inequality, and disease. The well-being and future of youth offer a crucial rationale for engaging in a critical discussion about the long-term consequences of current policies, especially those driven by neoliberalism, an issue I address below in more detail.

As society is defined through the culture, values, and relations of neoliberalism, the relationship between a critical education, public morality, and civic responsibility as a condition for creating thoughtful and engaged citizens is sacrificed all too willingly to the interest of finance capital, corporate greed, and the logic of profit making. Under the auspices of neoliberalism, citizens lose their public voice as market liberties replace civic freedoms and society increasingly depends on "consumers to do the work of citizens."[17]

Similarly, as corporate culture extends even deeper into the basic institutions of civil and political society, there is a simultaneous diminishing of non-commodified public spheres—those institutions such as public schools, churches, noncommercial public broadcasting, libraries, trade unions, and various voluntary institutions engaged in dialogue, education, and learning—that address the relationship of the self to public life and social responsibility to the broader demands of citizenship as well as provide a robust vehicle for public participation and democratic citizenship. As Edward Herman and Robert McChesney observe, such non-commodified public spheres have played an invaluable role historically "as places and forums where issues of importance to a political community are discussed and debated, and where information is presented that is essential to citizen participation in community life."[18] Without these critical public spheres corporate power often goes unchecked and politics becomes dull, cynical, and oppressive.[19] But more importantly, in the absence of such public spheres it becomes more difficult for citizens to challenge the neoliberal myth that citizens are *merely* consumers and that "wholly unregulated markets are the sole means by which we can produce and distribute everything we care about, from durable goods to spiritual values, from capital development to social justice, from profitability to sustainable environments, from private wealth to essential commonweal."[20] As democratic values give way to commercial values, intellectual ambitions are often reduced to an instrument of the entrepreneurial self, and social visions are dismissed as hopelessly out of date. Public space is portrayed exclusively as an investment opportunity, and the public good increasingly becomes a metaphor for public disorder, that is, as any notion of the public becomes synonymous with disrepair, danger, and risk, for example, public schools, public transportation, public parks, and so on. Within this discourse, anyone who does not believe that rapacious capitalism is the only road to freedom and the good life is dismissed as either a crank or worse. Hence it is not surprising to read an editorial in *The Economist*, in which youthful critics of capitalism are dismissed with the nasty claim that "Dwelling too long on their bogus concerns is apt to rot the intellect."[21]

In the absence of such public spaces, it has become much easier for advocates of neoliberalism to eliminate the most basic social provisions of the welfare state, weaken the power of unions, enhance the influence of corporate power over all aspects of daily life, wage war on the environment, leave citizens isolated and disarmed in the face of a worldwide culture of insecurity and fear, and wage class and racial warfare against the poor, immigrants, and people of color. Academics must address all of these issues as part of a pedagogy of responsibility and a politics of commitment. But what is most alarming as a result of the spread of neoliberalism is the way in which the social contract that connects adult responsibility to the welfare of youth and a belief in the future has been ruptured. Traditionally, the liberal, democratic social contract has been organized around a commitment to fairness, justice, generosity, and an insistence that government plays a vital part in providing an infrastructure of support and security with respect to health care, housing, and education as well as those basic services that address both the opportunities and the hazards in people's lives. The social contract provides the conditions for a safe, healthy, and educated life as well as crucial safeguards against sickness, growing old, and unemployment. Not only is the social contract foundational for any viable and inclusive democracy but also, and most importantly, for providing a decent future for generations of young people.

With the election of the George W. Bush as the president of the United States, the forces of neoliberalism have become more intensified as the social contract has been revoked and youth are removed from the inventory of democratic values and political, ethical, and social concerns. On almost every political, economic, cultural, and educational front, the market forces of privatization, deregulation, finance capital, and capital accumulation are radically altering the national and global landscape, and the effect on young people has been devastating.

Youth now constitute a crisis that has less to do with improving the future than with denying it. This lack of concern for the health, rights, and quality of children's lives provides the ideological and structural coherence that underlies neoliberal capitalism and its various expressions both at home and globally. The devaluation of children runs through various government policies that have shaped the last two decades. Increasingly, children are subject to a contradiction in the larger social order that reveals not only the social Darwinian impulse of a society that wants to abandon anyone who is not viable economically (either as a producer or consumer) and consigns the less technologically viable to low-wage, unskilled work, but also discloses the degree to which American society has lapsed into a kind of barbarism measured by the growing refusal to pay attention to the needs of its children. The contradiction is most evident in the ongoing suppression of children's rights, the repression of their voices, and their growing status as either being a threat or as simply disposable in the neoliberal equation. In this context, children are viewed as unfit to be free agents and utterly infantalized, reduced to being completely dependent on adults.[22] Yet, when adult society wants to punish children, they are treated as adults and subject to the most brutal machinations of the criminal justice system, including incarceration in adult prisons and the possibility of having the death penalty imposed on them. Child killing has become so integrated into public policy that there was barely a whimper of protest when Cruz Bustamante, currently a leading democratic candidate (no less) in the 2003 California race for governor, suggested that he would "cast a vote with a tear in my eye to execute 'hardened criminals' as young as 13."[23]

Youth are banished from the concerns of the moral community because they are viewed as disposable and unproductive, and their fate is not unlike that of the new poor who under the reign of neoliberalism are banished from visibility as they are removed from the discourse of deprivation to the language of depravity. Zygmunt Bauman's comments about the poor in present-day society extend to those youth in whom society has chosen not to invest. He observes:

> While banishing the poor from the streets, one can also banish them from the community of humans, from the world of ethical duty. This is done by rewriting the story from the language of deprivation to that of depravity. The poor supply the "usual suspects" rounded up to the accompaniment of public hue and cry whenever a fault in the habitual order is detected. The poor are portrayed as lax, sinful and devoid of moral standards. The media cheerfully cooperate with the police in presenting the sensation-greedy public lurid pictures of the crime-, drug- and sexual promiscuity-infested "criminal elements" who find their shelter in the darkness of mean streets.[24]

Many academics are once again engaging the sphere of the political, though they are not rallying around youth as a referent for thinking about the future. The future and its relationship to democracy has become a matter of great urgency for many academics because of the intensified threat posed by the Bush administration to civil liberties, unilateral aggression against Iraq, or the issue of globalization. Unfortunately, while a great many academics have entered into a public debate around the role of the United States in world affairs, the invasion of Iraq, and the ongoing repression of civil liberties, they have had almost nothing to say about how these issues affect young people. Youth rarely figure into any of the public conversations about the curtailing of civil rights and liberties, the dismantling of big government services, the rise of the security state, and the profound changes that are driving globalization and U.S. imperialism.

Outside of the contributions of Ed Herman, Noam Chomsky, Senator Robert Byrd, and a few others notwithstanding, there is almost no mention of children in debates about empire, war, and foreign policy. For example, the moral quality of U.S. foreign policy is rarely invoked in reference to the enormous suffering and deaths it has imposed on the children of Iraq as a result of the U.S. bombing in 1991 and the sanctions imposed after the war. During the 1991 war, Iraq lost a substantial part of its electrical grid, which powered equipment in its water and sewage plants. Of the 20 electric generating plants over 17 were either damaged or completely destroyed. One consequence was the breakdown of water, sewage, and hospital services and the spread of various water contaminated diseases such as dysentery. Anupama Roa Singh, one of the country directors for UNICEF, has claimed that over half a million Iraqi children under the age of five have died since the imposition of UN sanctions over a decade ago. The BBC reported in 1998 that 4,000–5,000 children in Iraq were dying every month from treatable diseases that are spreading because of bad diets, and the aforementioned breakdown of the public infrastructure. Against this murderous reality, it becomes more difficult to mount a convincing humanitarian argument for the current U.S. intervention in Iraq not only because it's clear that the murder and suffering of the children of Iraq will be intensified as a result of the war and the occupation, but also because it undercuts any moral discourse that the United States uses to defend its efforts to "liberate" and "rebuild" Iraq. In an impassioned speech before the U.S. Senate, Senator Robert Byrd raised this issue with incisive clarity. He perceptively noted "I must truly question the judgment of any President who can say that a massive unprovoked military attack on a nation which is over 50% children (under the age of 15) is 'in the highest moral traditions of our country'."[25] Bush's talk about the moral and democratic imperative to promote regime change, eliminate the axis of evil, and bring freedom to Iraq (and any other country the United States opposes) strikes a cruel and hypocritical note in light of the role the United States has played in the past in the death of over a half a million children in Iraq. And would it not be the same population—the people the Bush administration wants to free—who will pay the ultimate price for the current invasion and occupation by the United States. A recent study, "The Impact of War on Iraqi Children," published before the U.S. occupation of Iraq claimed that children under 18—13 million in all—are "at a grave risk of starvation, disease, death and psychological trauma," and that they are worse off now than they were just before the outbreak of war in 1991.

According to a study published by the United Nations Children's Fund, the recent U.S. invasion "has worsened the health hazards, disrupting clean water supplies, damaging sewage systems and halting rubbish collections."[26] During the recent war, 8,000 civilians were killed along with over 30,000 troops, most of whom were conscripted teenagers. In the aftermath of the war, as the respected journalist, John Pilger observes, the "biggest military machine on earth, said to be spending up to $5 billion-a-month on its occupation of Iraq, apparently cannot find the resources and manpower to bring generators to a people enduring [punishing high] temperatures . . . almost half of them children, of whom eight percent, says UNICEF, are suffering extreme malnutrition."[27]

Astonishingly, government officials are willing to not only ignore the suffering that war brings to the most vulnerable populations, but also defend the slaughter of children as politically expedient. For instance, Madeleine Albright, former U.S. secretary of state under Bill Clinton, appeared on the news program, "60 Minutes," on May 12, 1996 and was asked the following question by the show's host, Leslie Stahl: "We have heard that a half a million children have died [because of sanctions against Iraq]. I mean that's more children than died in Hiroshima. And—you know, is the price worth it?" Albright responded: "I think this is a very hard choice, but the price—we think the price is worth it." How might the parents of Iraqi children feel about this type of cruel political expediency? Does regime change mean that Iraqi civilians, especially children, should be targeted as part of a military and political strategy? Does the liberation of Iraq by Bush and the neocon warriors justify dropping cluster bombs and uranium-tipped shells on defenseless populations or, for that matter, securing oil fields but allowing the wholesale looting of a Iraq's national treasures while doing very little to provide basic services such as electricity and fresh water?

The moral insensitivity and inhumanity that underlie U.S. policy toward Iraq cannot be reduced simply to the expediency of its antiterrorism campaign or its need to seize Iraq's rich oil reserves. The roots of this indifference to the rights and needs of children, if not human life in general, must be understood within the larger framework of neoliberalism. As both an economic policy and political strategy, neoliberalism refuses to sustain the social wage, destroys those institutions that maintain social provisions, privatizes all aspects of the public good, and narrows the role of the state to being both a gatekeeper for capital and a policing force for maintaining social order and racial control. As an economic policy, neoliberalism allows a handful of private interests to control all aspects of society, and defines society exclusively through the privileging of market relations, deregulation, privatization, and consumerism. As a political philosophy, neoliberalism construes profit making as the essence of democracy and provides a rationale for a handful of private interests to control as much of social life as possible to maximize their financial investments. Unrestricted by social legislation or government regulation, market relations as they define the economy are viewed as a paradigm for democracy itself. Central to neoliberal philosophy is the claim that the development of all aspects of society should be left to the wisdom of the market. Similarly, neoliberal warriors argue that democratic values be subordinated to economic considerations, social issues be translated as private problems, part-time labor replace full-time work, trade unions be weakened, and everybody be treated as a customer. Within this market-driven perspective, the exchange of capital takes precedence over social justice, the making of socially responsible citizens, and the building of democratic communities. Neoliberalism not only separates politics from economic power, destroys the public sector, and transforms everything according to the mandates of the market, it also obliterates public concerns and cancels out the democratic impulses and practices of civil society by either devaluing or absorbing them within the logic of the market. This is what Milton Friedman, the reigning guru of neoliberalism, means in *Capitalism and Freedom* when he argues that "The basic problem of social organization is how to co-ordinate the economic activities of large numbers of people."[28] There is no language here for recognizing antidemocratic forms of power, developing nonmarket values, or fighting against substantive injustices in a society founded on deep inequalities. Hence, it is not surprising that Friedman can argue without irony that he does not "believe in freedom for madmen or children."[29] Nor should it be surprising that under neoliberalism children are considered valuable only in the most reductive economic terms.

More recently, the debate about neoliberalism has been linked to narrowing of public debate brought on, in part, by the concentration of power in the hands of a relatively few corporations that now control the media. Monopoly capital is increasingly linked to not only inequality, the war against big government, and the abrogation of the social contract but also to the weakening of civil liberties and basic freedoms, though little has been said by academics and journalists about how neoliberalism has impacted youth and how neoliberal policies are related to the ongoing war against young people. While the official discourse about highjacking civic freedoms drapes itself in the mantle of national security, secrecy, and patriotism, the repressive policies that underlie the rhetoric have been alive and well long before the terrorists attacks on September 11. The short list includes the Palmer raids of the 1920s, the internment of Japanese Americans during the World War II, the McCarthy hysteria of the 1950s, or the illegal FBI domestic counter-intelligence program (COINTELPRO), conducted between 1956 and 1971, whose sole purpose was to "neutralize" politically dissident groups such as the antiwar and civil rights movements in addition to the Black Panthers. These are powerful examples of how repression has rarely been on the side of either security or justice, but what must be added to this often cited historical record are the various modes of repression that youth have been experiencing since the 1980s.

As the social contract between adult society and children disappears, the old ideology that saw youth as an investment and source of democratic renewal has given away increasingly to pure repression. For instance, children, especially youth of color, are increasingly portrayed as a danger to society and an element to be monitored and contained. The consequences of such views when translated into social policies can be seen in the intensified application of profiling, especially among urban youth, the widespread use of random drug testing of public school students, physical searches, and the increased presence of police and the application of zero tolerance laws in the schools. As the state is increasingly reconfigured as a conduit for the criminal justice system, it withdraws from its liberal role of investing in the social and now punishes those young people who are caught in the downward spiral of its economic policies. Punishment, incarceration, and surveillance have come to represent the role of the new state. One consequence is that the implied contract between the state and citizens is broken, and social guarantees for youth as well as civic obligations to the future vanish from the agenda of public concern. Crucial issues such as homelessness, poverty, and illiteracy among youth are now viewed as individual pathologies rather than as social problems and young people who have to bear the burden of these effects are now blamed for these social issues and treated as criminals rather than as victims, let alone investments in the future. Children have become the enemy within. Characterized largely through a public rhetoric of fear, control, and surveillance, children appear alien, removed from the social contract, and divorced from institutions capable of protecting their rights. Daytime talk show hosts such as Sally Jesse Raphael and Jerry Springer offer endless images of kids out of control—narcissistic, selfish, violent, immoral, and drug addicted—and public policy reinforces these images by suggesting that the only way to deal with kids is to severely discipline them, even if this means incarcerating them at record levels and in some cases putting them to death. For a third of all minority youth, the future holds the disturbing possibility of either "prison, probation, or some form of supervision within the criminal justice system."[30] Until the recent recession, states were spending more on prison construction than on higher education. Paul Street states that in Illinois, for every "African-American enrolled in [its] universities, two and a-half Blacks are in prison or on parole. . . . [While] in New York . . . more Blacks entered prison just for drug offenses than graduated from the state's massive university system with undergraduate, masters, and doctoral degrees combined in the 1990s."[31]

Under such circumstances, repressive practices cannot be simply linked to the war on terrorism. On the contrary, repressive policies and practices are reinforced and extended through an appeal to national security, but the roots of such undemocratic actions lie in the spreading of neoliberalism and its transformation of the democratic state into the corporate state, and political power largely into a force for domestic militarization and repression. Engaging the relationship between repression and the war on young people expands opportunities on the part of critics and activists for understanding the current attack on civil liberties as part of a broader crisis over the political and ethical importance of the social sphere and the possibility of upholding, if not struggling, over the very idea of a democratic future both nationally and internationally. With few exceptions, debates about globalization also seem to take place in a world without young people. And, yet, the massive changes prompted by globalization have had a profound affect on many of the world's 2.9 billion children.

In a new world order marked by deregulation, acceleration, free-flowing global finance, trade, and capital, short-term gains replace long-term visions. The search for markets and profits are now buttressed by highly destructive and sophisticated military technologies that work in conjunction with new global information systems that overcome the burden of geographical distance while creating ruling elites that no longer feel either committed or obligated to traditional notions of place, whether they be towns, cities, states, or nations. Reality TV with its social Darwinian logic supplies the fodder for high television ratings as it provides global audiences with models of social justice repackaged as laws of nature and citizenship as an utterly privatized affair. Neoliberal globalization widens the gap between both the public and the private, on the one hand, and politics and economic power on the other. Globalization now signals the retreat of nation-states that once played a significant role in ameliorating the most brutal features of capitalism. As the nation-state abdicates its traditional hold on power,[32] it is being replaced by the national security state engaged in both fighting the alleged threats from domestic terrorism—signaled by an over-the-top racial profiling and anti-youth repression—and external terrorism largely manifested in the most blatant forms of racism and xenophobia directed at Arab and Muslim populations and immigrants.

The consequences of neoliberal globalization can be seen not only in growing inequalities worldwide in income, wealth, basic services, and health care, but also in substantial increases in the exploitation and suffering of millions of young people around the globe. The fallout is easy to document. As globalization and militarization mutually reinforce each other as both an economic policy and as a means to settle conflicts, wars are no longer fought between soldiers but are now visited upon civilians and appear to have the most detrimental effects on children. Within the last decade, 2 million children have died in military conflicts. Another 4 million have been disabled, 12 million have been left homeless, and millions more have been orphaned.[33]

Increasingly, children are being recruited, abducted, or forced into military service as lighter weapons enable children as young as 12 to be trained as effective killers. But the fruits of modern warfare not only enable children to kill, they also result in the killing of them, especially through the proliferation of landmines, which are estimated to kill 8,000–10,000 children each year. The International Committee on the Red Cross estimates that "some 110 million land mines threaten children in more than 70 countries" and that they are chillingly effective: "82.5 percent of amputations performed in ICRC hospitals are for land mine victims."[34]

As the leading supplier of arms in the world, the United States bears an enormous responsibility for fueling military conflicts throughout the globe. As reported in the Congressional Research Service, a division of the Library of Congress, American manufacturers in 2000 signed contracts for just under $18.6 billion in weapon sales, with sales going primarily to developing countries. Empire in this instance is not simply about the power pretensions of an imperial presidency, it is also about neoliberal policies that feed corporate profits through the selling of arms that largely cripple and take the lives of children. Hence, it should come as no surprise to learn that in the age of empire, domestic markets even in the United States are no longer at a safe remove from the scorched earth policies and consequences of arms manufacturers. For instance, the United States ranks worst among industrialized nations in the number of children killed by guns, with over 50,000 American youth killed since 1979. Globalization is not only about the emergence of new technologies, the consolidation of corporate power, and the flow of financial capital, it is also about the intersection of profits and militarization—and the killing and maiming of poor children at home and abroad. Under such circumstances, it makes more sense for Left critics to address the issue of globalization and Bush's "Axis of Evil" moralism by exposing the administration's hypocrisy in promoting the conditions for military conflict all over the globe. In spite of what the cheerleaders for neoliberalism claim, globalization is not simply about creating "free trade" and opening markets. In actuality, it refers to "advancing . . . corporate and commercial interests"[35] through the internationalization of armed conflict and globalization policies fueled by the incessant need for profits whatever the human costs.

The division of labor and exploitation promoted through neoliberal globalization has given new meaning to Manuel Castells's pronouncement that the primary labor issue in the new information age "is not the end of work but the condition of work."[36] The search for cheap labor, the powerlessness of children, and the 120 million children who are born poor each year creates fertile conditions for multinational corporations to gain significant profits through the hiring of children, largely in developing countries. The International Labor Office estimates that 120 million children between the ages of 5 and 14 are compelled to work full time, often under harsh and inhumane conditions, and that if part-time work is included the figure reaches 250 million.[37] Children are engaged in a variety of forms of labor ranging from domestic servants and shoe production to brick making and agricultural work. Many children are either injured or killed on the job, with the number of annual injuries estimated at 70,000. Not all children are exploited by being paid substandard wages for their work, the most unfortunate, and generally the most destitute, are forced into bonded slavery in order to pay off their family loans or are sold outright on the market by their families in the hopes of bringing in additional income. Many of these children are forced into prostitution, domestic service, or put on the streets as beggars. Prostitution, in particular, has become a substantial growth market fueled by the globalization of child pornography rings that are largely circulated through the Internet and other global circuits of power such as organized sex tours. While the figures on this illicit trade are difficult to establish, it has been estimated by the Center for Protection of Children's Rights that more than a million children enter into prostitution each year, many with or contracting HIV. Child prostitution is also on the rise in the United States, with an estimated 100,000–300,000 children exploited through prostitution and pornography.[38] In spite of the virtual crisis that children are facing all over the world with respect to the violation of their rights and their bodily dignity, the United States has refused to both address critically the myriad ways in which it contributes to turning innocent children into victims through policies that strip countries of their public services, resources, and revenue while at the same time declining to ratify a number of international treaties designed specifically to improve the quality of life for the world's children. The message that is unabashedly put forth by the Bush administration about children both at home and abroad is that it has little regard for the bodies and minds of young people. This message is reinforced by a market-driven politics that suggests that young people under the command of neoliberalism do not even merit a commitment to human rights, social justice, health care, environmental protection, or minimal social provisions. How else to explain the refusal of the Bush administration to sign or ratify the United Nations Convention on the Rights of the Child (passed in 1989), the small arms treaty, and the land mines treaty? Or, for that matter, the Bush administration's opposition to the Kyoto Protocol on climate change, the International Plan for Cleaner Energy, the protocol for the Biological Weapons Convention, and the International Covenant on Economic, Social and Cultural Rights.[39]

Intellectual Responsibility and Civic Courage

If we are to think our way to a future different from the insensate scenario of unlimited warfare that has been prescribed for us, then culture needs to imagine alternative forms that are not even dreams at present—produced for a public that extends beyond the initiates, and "political" in the sense of relevant to worldly affairs—with confidence that a truly unforced cultural project will be free of both the fundamentalist intolerance and the commercial libertinism that, from partial perspectives, are now so feared.[40]

As a public sphere that both prepares youth for the future as well as shapes it, higher education is deeply implicated in how it relates to broader social, political, and economic forces that bear down on youth. As the subject and object of learning, youth provide faculty and administrators with a political and moral referent for addressing the relationship between knowledge and power, learning and social change, and values and classroom social relations as they bridge the gap between the diverse public spheres that youth inhabit and the university as a site of socialization and political engagement. The overwhelming presence of middle- and upper-class youth in the university raises important questions about the role of higher education in furthering and reproducing those divisions of labor between the rich and the poor that are made visible not only in the class and racial imbalances of most student populations, but also in a range of social relations outside of the university. Educators would do well in their own classrooms and teaching to address how higher education furthers forms of class, racial, and gender divisions resonate with dominant modes of exclusion and discrimination that are accentuated under the auspices of neoliberalism. Surely, if educators have a responsibility to fight against those forces that undermine the university's claims to providing a quality education for all students, they would have to address the increasing corporatization of university life and its effects on the university as a democratic public sphere. For instance, they might want to address the role of neoliberalism in raising tuition rates, deepening the fiscal crisis of the state, contributing to massive fiscal cuts in funding higher education, and the growing exploitation of adjuncts and graduate students in a growing number of universities and colleges.

One of the challenges that academics face as engaged intellectuals centers around recovering the language of sociality, agency, solidarity, democracy, and public life as the basis for creating new conceptions of pedagogy, learning, and governance. Part of this effort demands creating new vocabularies, experiences, and subject positions that allow students to become more than they are now, to question what it is they have become within existing institutional and social formations, and "to give some thought to their experiences so that they can transform their relations of subordination and oppression."[41] Samir Amin rightly argues that it is the absence of social values such as generosity and human solidarity that "reinforce[s] submission to the dominating power of capitalist ideology."[42] And, yet it is precisely through a focus on the obligations of adult society to young people that such values become concrete and persuasive. It is often difficult for adults and students to dismiss the suffering of young people as a matter of individual character or to reduce their plight to the realm of the family or private sphere, the depoliticizing strategy of choice used by social conservatives and neoliberals. The plight of children provides a powerful entry into public consciousness. Young people offer a compelling referent for a pedagogy of disruption, social criticism, and collective change because their suffering and hardships offer the pedagogical promise of both a public hearing and a potent social category to connect a range of issues and problems that are often addressed in isolation, a subtle way of identifying grievances without inquiring into their social and political roots. More than any other group, they provide a credible referent for challenging the moralisms and policies of conservatives while simultaneously opening up the possibility to create new ethical discourses, modes of agency, and forms of advocacy. Young people are one of the few referents left for reclaiming a future that does not imitate the present, a future that makes good on the promise of new models of human association and pedagogy based on democratic values and a radical transformation of the existing inegalitarian structures of political power and economic wealth. A social analysis of the crisis of youth is not only important for its own sake, but also because it points to much broader analysis in that the various forms of oppression that young people experience directly undermine the dominant and traditional justifications for class, racial, sexual, and gendered divisions in society. For instance, the long neglected discussion of class becomes more visible and poignant when analyzing the inhumane and class-specific effects underlying George W. Bush's economic stimulus policies, which offers huge tax cuts for the rich while driving the United States into deficits and debts that will cut several viable public services and social programs for many children in addition to saddling the next generation "with nothing but a mountain of debt."[43] While it is crucial for educators and others to make clear that Bush's budget policies will do little to help the poor, elderly, homeless, and disabled, such criticism becomes more powerful when children are included as a crucially affected population. In this instance, it is important to shed light on the fact that the effects of the tax cuts for many children will be devastating—with over 50,000 kids eliminated from after school programs, 8,000 homeless young people cut from vital education programs, and over 33,000 children dropped from child care. It is difficult to ignore the effects these cuts are having on children while at the same time using children as a referent to talk about class warfare in the broader sense. For example, public discussions about Bush's handling of the economy is often shrouded in a statistical language that adds little social gravity to an economic policy that has resulted in over 5.6 million young people unemployed as of 2003, with the youth unemployment rate is some cities such as Wichita, Kansas reaching as high as 50 percent. The same can be said about Bush's occupation of Iraq. Bush talks about building schools in Iraq, but does nothing to prevent public school systems in the United States from shortening the school year, laying off many needed teachers, dropping programs in music and art, or providing much-needed financial resources to rebuild the decaying physical infrastructures of a school system largely built in the 1950s. How might an analysis of the state of today's youth be used to raise questions about the ethical, political, and economic priorities of a country that spends more on beauty products than on education.[44] What does it say about a political system that neither calls into question such shameful priorities nor does anything to challenge them?

Young people provide a crucial lens through which hegemony can be analyzed, compassion mobilized, and politics engaged beyond local interests and national boundaries. That is, hegemony in this instance does not simply refer to the ideologies, discourses, or images that represent young people or position them in particular ways, but also to the way in which they actually experience the different modalities of power and powerlessness as an empirical reality within particular class and racial formations marked by deep inequalities of power within and across national boundaries.[45]

Young people are born into the existing social order and cannot be blamed so easily for the conditions of poverty, racism, and daily violence that produce inadequate health care, education, and housing for the most defenseless and least powerful of its inhabitants. The oppression of young people is crucial for public intellectuals to address because it is the fundamental lie at the heart of neoliberalism and its falsely "utopian" notion of the future.

Academics, activists, parents, and others should consider making children the focus of renewed critical discussion about the long-term consequences of current policies and social practices because they provide a powerful referent for decoding and understanding the suffering of others. They invoke compassion and cause moral unease making it possible to reassert the importance of the social sphere, civic engagement, political imagination, and a culture of questioning.[46] Focusing on the social position of children opens up an ethical and political space for oppositional forces to translate private troubles into public considerations and public considerations into private concerns, particularly as progressives grapple with questions of politics, power, social justice, and public consciousness. The plight of young people must play a central role in rearticulating the promise of critical citizenship and reaffirmation of a social contract that embraces and affirms democratic values, practices, and identities while challenging the limitations of those individualizing relations and identities produced by neoliberalism. Making visible the suffering and oppression of young people cannot help but challenge the core ideology of neoliberalism.

Educators need a new language in which young people are not detached from politics but become central to any transformative notion of pedagogy conceived in terms of social and public responsibility. The growing attack on youth in American society may say less about the reputed apathy of the populace than it might about the bankruptcy of old political languages and orthodoxies and the need for new vocabularies and visions for clarifying our intellectual, ethical, and political projects, especially as they work to reabsorb questions of agency, ethics, and meaning back into politics and public life. In the absence of such a language as well as the social formations and public spheres that make democracy and justice operative, politics becomes narcissistic and caters to the mood of widespread pessimism and the cathartic allure of the spectacle. In addition, public service and government intervention is sneered upon as either bureaucratic or a constraint upon individual freedom. Any attempt to give new life to a substantive democratic politics suggests that educators address the issue of both how people learn to be political agents and what kind of educational work is necessary within what kind of public spaces to enable people to use their full intellectual resources to critique existing institutions and struggle to make the operation of freedom and autonomy possible for as many people as possible in a wide variety of spheres. As critical educators, we are required to understand more fully why the tools we used in the past feel awkward in the present, often failing to respond to problems now facing the United States and other parts of the globe. Educators face the challenge posed by the failure or absence of oppositional discourses and the disorganization of dissent to bridge the gap between how society represents itself and how and why individuals fail to understand and critically engage such representations in order to intervene in the oppressive social relationships they often legitimate. Progressives need a language adequate to the demands a global public sphere. They need to understand how the local affects the global public sphere and in turn is affected by those larger forces that constitute a global public. Most importantly, they need a language that goes beyond identity politics, rises above criticism, and addresses the conditions necessary for salvaging the most radical dimensions of diverse traditions that refuse to cover up the inequities of domination while also recognizing the ongoing struggle of negotiating "between the real and the ideal, hence, at least potentially in protest against the societies and power structures in which they emerge."[47] We need a new language for expressing global solidarity as well as an understanding of the political and pedagogical strategies necessary to create a global public sphere where such solidarities become possible.

At a time when civil liberties are being destroyed, massive tax cuts are being given to the rich, public services destroyed, the nation squanders its resources in maintaining military control of Iraq, and public institutions and goods all over the globe are under assault by the forces of a rapacious global capitalism, there is a sense of concrete urgency that demands on the part of academics new modes of resistance and collective struggle buttressed by rigorous intellectual work, social responsibility, and political courage.

As theorists such as Pierre Bourdieu, Noam Chomsky, Howard Zinn, Arundhati Roy, and Edward Said have reminded us, intellectuals have a special responsibility to use their talents to uncover the imposed silence of normalized power, to create the conditions for a culture of questioning around crucial social issues, and to present alternative narratives that both make dominant power accountable and offer alternative strategies of intervention that make realizable democratic views of the future. In part, this means not only offering a critical analysis of representations that service dominant power and legitimate the status quo, but also making visible those issues that exist outside of dominant discourses and the social conditions that produce them. As intellectuals, academics need to make public the experiences of those whose voices are either excluded from public debate or when they are heard rarely carry any sort of authority.

Academics need to connect their work to a larger public and assume a measure of responsibility in naming, struggling against, and alleviating human suffering. This suggests working with others to produce knowledge in a variety of public spheres that can address those forms of social suffering, relations of power, and cultural formations such as media concentrations that pose a threat to democracy. Academics need to reject the cult of professionalism and assume the role of citizen scholars, which means as Edward Said points out, maintaining "a kind of coexistence between the necessities of the field and the discipline of the classroom, on the one hand, and of the special interest that one has in it, on the other, with one's own concerns as a human being, as a citizen in a larger society."[48] Such a recognition places a particularly important demand upon academics who increasingly depoliticize the very possibility of politics as they retreat into the most arcane discourses, specializations, or simple moral indifference to the outside world. Academics cannot collapse politics into a dehistoricized, text-centric pedagogy that "approaches the social world as if it was a text and reduces the role of the intellectual to a mere reader of texts."[49]

One imperative of a critical pedagogy is to offer students opportunities to become aware of their potential and responsibility as individual and social agents to expand, struggle over, and deepen democratic values, institutions, and identities. This suggests helping students unlearn the presupposition that knowledge is unrelated to action, conception to implementation, and learning to social change. Knowledge, in this case, is about more than understanding, it is also about the possibilities of self-determination, individual autonomy, and social agency. Rather than consolidate authority, academics need to make it accountable, tempering a reverence for power and authority with a deep distrust of its motives and effects. Academics need to reclaim not only their intellectual courage but a sense of ethical responsibility. Connecting academic work to social change should not be summarily dismissed either as partisan or burdensome. Arundhati Roy has argued that there are times in a nation's history when its political climate makes it imperative for intellectuals to take sides. Given the assault being waged by the Bush administration on public services, the welfare state, the environment, workers, civil rights, and democracy itself, I believe that this is a crucial time in American history for academics to make their ideas and voices felt in the struggle to reclaim democracy from the market fundamentalists, powerful corporate interests, and evangelical neoconservatives.[50] Pierre Bourdieu insightfully suggests that the time is right for intellectuals to assume responsibility for creating an international social movement that would exercise real influence on transnational corporations, nation-states, and nongovernmental agencies.[51] According to Bourdieu, neoliberalism in its current forms is so ruthless in its destruction of public goods, everyday social protections, meaningful labor, and the environment that it is bringing together academics, workers, students, farmers, consumers, and activists into new alliances.

Intellectuals—academic and nonacademic alike—have a special responsibility to enable the conditions for such protests to offer opportunities for new social actors and constructive modes of collective action and political intervention leading to new social policies, rather than allowing protests to degenerate into what Alain Touraine has called the politics of "pointless denunciations."[52] Intellectuals at all costs must fight against the mythic assumption of the neoliberal order that there are no alternatives and in doing resist the slide into cynicism and apathy with a new political language and vision, one marked by a discourse of critique and possibility. Such a discourse must move beyond analyzing only the crushing effects of domination, recognizing "that individual and groups [be regarded] as potential actors and not simply as victims who are either in chains or being manipulated."[53] At stake here is the need not only to combat a debilitating cynicism but to also capture the complexity of relations of power and resistance and to recognize that there are multiple sites of engagement where social actors can provide individual criticism and engage in the arduous task of mobilizing social movements. For instance, the antiwar movement, anti-sweatshop activism, Living Wage Campaigns, and global justice movements have brought together a number of students across the country who are creating alternative campus media to get their voices heard in order to both reach other students and to affect larger public discourses. Increasingly such students are reaching out to other groups such as trade unionists in building wider alliances. Progressive academics need to provide financial and intellectual support for these publications and forms of social activism not only because students represent an important political movement for social change, but also because they cannot allow conservative organizations like the Collegiate Network and the Leadership Institute to pour money into a network of campus newspapers in order to push a generation of college students toward the Right and away from broader progressive alliances. And this is only one instance of where such resistance can be acknowledged and supported politically and pedagogically.

The time has come for intellectuals to distinguish caution from cowardice and recognize that their obligations extend beyond deconstructing texts or promoting a culture of questioning. These are important pedagogical interventions, but they do not go far enough. We also need to link knowing with action, learning with social engagement and this suggests addressing the responsibilities that come with teaching students to fight for an inclusive and radical democracy by recognizing that education is not just about understanding, however critical, but also provides the conditions for addressing the responsibilities we have as citizens to others, especially those future generations who will inherit our mistakes. It is also crucial for educators to recognize that matters of responsibility, social action, and political intervention do not simply develop out of social critique but also forms of self-critique. Hence, the relationship between knowledge and power, on the one hand, and scholarship and politics, on the other, should always be self-reflexive about its effects, how it relates to the larger world, and what it might mean to take seriously matters of individual and social responsibility when it comes to addressing those forms of human suffering that are produced by inequalities that undermine any viable democracy. Neoliberalism not only places capital and market relations in a no-mans land beyond the reach of compassion, ethics, and decency, it also undermines those basic elements of the social contract in which self-reliance, confidence in others, and a trust in the longevity of public institutions provide the basis for modes of individual autonomy, social agency, and critical citizenship. The struggle is part of a broader struggle over education, power, and democracy in which young people are seen as the most valuable resource for ensuring that an inclusive and just society will help guarantee them a future of justice, dignity, and security.

Notes

1. Cited by Bill Moyers on NOW, aired on May 2003.
2. Cited in Robert Dreyfuss, "Grover Norquist: 'Field Marshal' of the Bush Plan," *The Nation* (May 14, 2001). Available on-line: http://www.thenation.com/doc.mhtml?i= 20010514 &s=dreyfuss, p. 1.
3. Slavoj Zizek, "Today Iraq Tomorrow . . . Democracy?" *In These Times* (May 5, 2003), p. 28.
4. George Steinmetz, "The State of Emergency and the Revival of American Imperialism; Toward an Authoritarian Post-Fordism," *Public Culture* 13:2 (Spring 2003): 329.
5. Dick Cheney cited in Sam Dillon, "Reelections on War, Peace, and how to Live Vitally and Act Globally," *The New York Times* (June 1, 2003), p. 28.
6. Bob Herbert, "Oblivious in DC.," *The New York Times* (June 30, 2003). Available online: http://www.nytimes.com/2003/06/30/opinion/30HERB.html.
7. Bill Moyers, "Deep in a Black Hole of Red Ink," Common Dreams News Center (May 30, 2003). Available on-line: www.commondreams.org/views03/0530-.

8. Cited in Editorial Comment, "Bush's sleights of Hand," *The Progressive* (July 2003), p. 8.

9. Zygmunt Bauman, *Society Under Siege* (Malden, MA: Blackwell, 2002), p. 54.

10. Arundhati Roy, *War Talk* (Boston: South End Press, 2003), p. 34.

11. President George W. Bush, Address to Joint Session of Congress, "September 11, 2001, Terrorist Attacks on the United States."

12. Sheldon Wolin, "Inverted Totalitarianism: How the Bush Regime is Effecting the Transformation to a Fascist-Like State," *The Nation* (May 19, 2003), p. 13.

13. Ulrich Beck, "The Silence of Words and Political Dynamics in the World Risk Society," *Logos* 1:4 (Fall 2002): 1.

14. Susan Buck-Morss, *Thinking Past Terror: Islamism and Critical Theory on the Left* (London: Verso Press, 2003), pp. 30–31.

15. Ulrich Beck, "The Silence of Words and Political Dynamics in the World Risk Society," p. 3.

16. Jeff Madrick, "The Iraqi Time Bomb," *The New York Times Magazine* (April 6, 2003), p. 50.

17. These ideas are taken from Benjamin R. Barber, "Blood Brothers, Consumers, or Citizens? Three Models of Identity–Ethnic, Commercial, and Civic," in *Cultural Identity and the Nation State* ed. Carol Gould and Pasquale Pasquino (Lanham: Rowman and Littlefield, 2001), p. 65.

18. Edward S. Herman and Robert W. McChesney, *The Global Media: The New Missionaries of Global Capitalism* (Washington and London: Cassell, 1997), p. 3.

19. I address this issue in Henry A. Giroux, *Public Spaces, Private Lives: Democracy Beyond Beyond 9/11* (Lanham: Rowman & Littlefield, 2002).

20. Barber, "Blood Brothers, Consumers, or Citizens? Three Models of Identity—Ethnic, Commercial, and Civic," p. 59.

21. Editorial, "Capitalism and Democracy," *The Economist* (June 28 to July 4, 2003), p. 13.

22. Zygmunt Bauman provides the same sort of analysis in analyzing the state of the poor under neoliberalism He argues the poor are excluded and often charged with the guilt of their exclusion, and thus seen as dangerous and a threat to society. See Zygmunt Bauman, *Work, Consumerism and the New Poor* (Philadelphia: Open University Press, 1998), especially chapter 5, "Prospects for the Poor," pp. 83–98.

23. Cited in Mike Davis, "Cry California," Common Dreams News Center (September 4, 2003). Available on-line: http://www.commondreams.org/views03/0903-.

24. See Bauman, *Work, Consumerism and the New Poor*, p. 93.

25. U.S. Senator Robert Byrd, "Reckless Administration May Reap Disastrous Consequences," Senate Floor Speech, February 12, 2003. Available on-line: http://www.commondreams.org/views03/0212-.

26. Published by the BBC, "Child Sickness 'Soars' in Iraq," June 9, 2003. Available on-line: http://www.commondreams.org/headlines03.

27. Cited by Bill Moyers on NOW, aired on May 2003.

28. Milton Friedman, *Capitalism and Freedom* (Chicago: University of Chicago Press, 2002-reprint), p. 12.

29. Ibid., p. 33.

30. Steven R. Donziger, ed., *The Real War on Crime: The Report of the National Criminal Justice Commission* (New York: Harper Perennial, 1996), p. 101.

31. Paul Street, "Race, Prison, and Poverty: The Race to Incarcerate in the Age of Correctional Keynesianism," *Z Magazine* (May 2001), p. 25.

32. Peter Marcuse is right to argue that the state under neoliberal globalization does not lack power, it abdicates state power. See Peter Marcuse, "The Language of Globalization," *Monthly Review* 52:3 (July–August 2000). Available on-line: http://www.monthlyreview.org/700marc.htmome or fail to recognize how war is being waged by this government on multiple fronts.

33. Cited in Editorial Comment, "Bush's sleights of Hand," *The Progressive* (July 2003), p. 8.

34. Jane Sutton-Redner, "Children in a World of Violence," *Children in Need Magazine* (December 2002). Available on-line: http://childreninneed.com/magazine/viole.

35. Robert W. McChesney, "Global Media, Neoliberalism, and Imperialism," *Monthly Review* (March 2001), p. 16.

36. Manuel Castells, *End of Millennium, III* (Malden, MA: Blackwell, 1998), p. 149. Of course, while Castells is right about the conditions of labor, he underemphasizes the huge surplus of labor around the world. This is made clear in another ILO report that states that about a quarter of the labor force around the world is unemployed and a third underemployed.

37. This information from the International Labor Office is available on-line—http://usilo.org/ilokidsnew/ILOU/101.htmland_racial warfare against the poor, immigrants, and people of color. Academics must address all of these issues as part of a pedagogy of responsibility and a politics of commitment. But what is most alarming as a result of the spread of neoliberalism is the way in which the social contract that connects adult responsibility to the welfare of youth and a belief in the future has been ruptured. Traditionally, the liberal, democratic social contract has been organized around a commitment to fairness, justice, generosity, and an insistence that government plays a vital part in providing an infrastructure of support and security with respect to health care, housing, and education as well as those basic services that address both the opportunities and the hazards in people's lives. The social contract provides the conditions for a safe, healthy, and educated life as well as crucial safeguards against sickness, growing old, and unemployment. Not only is the social contract foundational for any viable and inclusive democracy but also, and most importantly, for providing a decent future for generations of young people.

38. End Child Prostitution, Child Pornography, and the Trafficking of Children for Sexual Exploitation (ECPAT), *Europe and North America Regional Profile*, issued by the World Congress Against Commercial Sexual Exploitation of Children, held in Stockholm, Sweden (August 1996), p. 70.

39. For an extensive record of such treaty and protocol refusals on the part of the Bush administration, see Richard Du Buff, "Mirror Mirror on the Wall, Who's the Biggest Rogue of All?" *ZNet* (August 7, 2003). Available on-line: Znetupdates@Zmail.zmag.org.

40. Susan Buck-Morss, *Thinking Past Terror: Islamism and Critical Theory on the Left* (London: Verso Press, 2003), p. 10.

41. Lynn Worsham and Gary A. Olson, "Rethinking Political Community: Chantal Mouffe's Liberal Socialism," *Journal of Composition Theory* 19:2 (1999): 178.

42. Samir Amin, "Imperialization and Globalization," *Monthly Review* (June 2001): 16.

43. Bob Herbert, "The Money Magnet," *The New York Times* (June 23, 2003), p. A27.

44. Fathali MMoghaddam, "Health, Beauty, and Seniors," *Health and Age* (July 4, 2003). Available on-line: http://www.healthandage.c.

45. The wonderful distinction between hegemony lite and hegemony from which I have developed this idea comes from Kate Crehan, *Gramsci, Culture, and Anthropology* (Los Angeles: University of California Press, 2002), pp. 202–207.

46. This theme is developed with great care in Martha C. Nussbaum, "Compassion & Terror," *Daedalus* (Winter 2003), pp. 10–26, especially p. 12.
47. Susan Buck-Morss, *Thinking Past Terrorism*, pp. 103–104.
48. Edward Said, "On Defiance and Taking Positions," *Reflections On Exile and Other Essays* (Cambridge: Harvard University Press, 2001), p. 501.
49. Carol A. Stabile and Junya Morooka, " 'Between Two Evils, I Refuse to Choose the Lesser,' " *Cultural Studies* 17:3 (2003): 338.
50. See Arundhati Roy, *Power Politics* (Cambridge, MA: South End Press, 2001).
51. Pierre Bourdieu and Gunter Grass, "The Progressive Restoration: A Franco-German Dialogue," *New Left Review* 14 (March–April 2002): 63–67.
52. Alain Touraine, *Beyond Neoliberalism* (London: Polity, 2001), p. 50.
53. Ibid., p. 33.

Chapter 2 ~

Tackling Difference in the Conservative Heartland of Canada[1]

Darren E. Lund

Sometimes life's pivotal educational moments reveal themselves in unexpected situations. Like many other white mainstream Canadians, I have grown up virtually oblivious to an invisible bubble of white privilege, attending to instances of inequity and racism mainly for the purposes of telling inappropriate racist jokes. In 1987, however, during my first year of teaching high school in Red Deer, Alberta, Canada, a group of students in one of my nonacademic English classes at Lindsay Thurber Comprehensive High School opened my eyes to the potential for educators to work with students toward challenging racism and tackling issues of difference in school settings.

These unlikely student leaders initiated the formation of Students and Teachers Opposing Prejudice (STOP). For almost two decades it has remained a popular and viable school program, and has been widely recognized for leadership in innovative approaches to challenging racism and other forms of discrimination (Alberta Human Rights and Citizenship Commission, 2000; Canadian Race Relations Foundation, 2001). My own experience as the group's advisor for several years has led me to seek a deeper understanding of the group's success, and to engage in further research to guide other teacher and student activists who wish to form coalitions to address social justice concerns.

Countering a Lack of Attention to Student Activism

A review of current educational research literature in this country reveals a number of problematic features on the broad topic of education for diversity, equity, and social justice. First, there are relatively few detailed analyses of student social action projects in Canadian schools aside from anecdotal summaries of a few particular programs or activities (e.g., Berlin and Alladin, 1996; Cogan and Ramsankar, 1994;

Smith and Young, 1996). This dearth of academic attention to successful school-based activist programs suggests that the work of practitioners is either undiscovered or undervalued by the research community. In either case, there is a clear gap in the field that will only be filled through closer engagement with the activist educational community.

Further, there is limited academic interest in young people in general. Apart from standardized surveys of student attitudes on diversity issues (e.g., Griffith and Labercane, 1995; Kehoe, 1994), students are infrequently engaged in meaningful ways in educational research on social justice. This lack of scholarly attention to students seems a significant oversight in a discourse that ostensibly places their education at its center. My research with a range of student activists in this field responds directly to this observation (2003) and to a growing conservative backlash toward "youth" culture in general; Giroux (1996) notes that "youth as a self and social construction has become indeterminant, alien, and sometimes hazardous in the public eye, a source of repeated moral panics and the object of social regulation" (p. 11). He proposes a "radical democracy" involving challenges to traditional hierarchies in schools through power sharing. To this end, he calls for a "redistribution of power among teachers, students, and administrators [to] provide the conditions for students to become agents in their learning process [;] it also provides the basis for collective learning, civic action, and ethical responsibility" (p. 129).

STOP's proactive model of teacher–student activism on issues of difference has somehow initiated just such a collective response to social injustice in a relatively conservative community. In a potentially volatile social climate, STOP continues to engage students, teachers, parents, administration, other school staff, government, media, and community agencies in a collective effort to challenge racism and other discrimination. Ironically, some of the resistance we face in our work comes from within the teaching profession itself.

Countering the Conservatism of Teachers

Some scholars have characterized teaching as a traditionally conservative profession with practitioners who typically resist change and innovation (e.g., Fullan and Hargreaves, 1992; Solomon, 1995). This internal resistance during times of political conservatism can especially hinder progress in social justice education (Apple, 1993). In a survey of over 1,000 teachers across Canada, Solomon and Levine-Rasky (1996) uncover the dimensions of educators' resistance to multicultural and antiracist education. They assert that, given the "depoliticized and uncritical framework of teacher education institutions, the relative lack of self-awareness and 'race' consciousness that teachers demonstrate is rationalized" (p. 11). Indeed, they find that educators consistently seek to avoid contentious issues, and specifically that "denial and reluctance to name the problem of racism and thus the need for an antiracist pedagogy remains a most tenacious obstacle" (p. 12). My own experience as a longtime teacher and activist confirms these generalizations about many teachers, but I also recognize the tremendous potential of a small number of informed and committed activists to make a serious impact on conservative school settings.

Countering Hate in the Community

In the past decade's conservative political climate, any student or teacher activism in schools around diversity issues seems almost revolutionary. The initial frenzy of national media interest in our STOP group was likely due to our region's unfortunate widespread reputation for extremist hate group activity, worth reviewing briefly here. Our first school-wide STOP meeting attracted almost 200 students along with local media. Within a week the group was featured in a story on a national television news broadcast, giving the students' efforts a sense of social urgency.

Our program's exposure began a progressive movement in a community that had long languished in the Canadian national spotlight for racist extremism. Red Deer, our small city of about 70,000 in the heart of Canada's "Bible belt" in the province of Alberta (north of Montana) had been etched already onto the collective Canadian psyche; media coverage of Terry Long, Canadian leader of the Aryan Nations group, then running a "white power" training camp at the nearby town of Caroline, was intense. Long had also posted a classified advertisement in the local daily newspaper promoting a prerecorded "hate hotline" for over a year. Red Deer also hosted the trial and subsequent appeals of teacher James Keegstra, an unrepentant Holocaust denier convicted in 1985 for promoting hatred in his high school social studies classes at the nearby town of Eckville. Now the media had a story with an ironic twist—the enthusiastic students in STOP were actively opposing anti-Semitism and other forms of bigotry.

Instead of ignoring contentious issues or engaging in fruitless confrontations with extremists, the members of STOP took proactive steps within the community to counter this extremism. Students who admitted they had often found school assignments lacking relevance to their lives had become active agents in their own education. When Provost, a town about an hour east of Red Deer, endured a publicized cross-burning at a hate rally, STOP members arranged their own transportation and volunteered a weekend to work with students there. Our students knew that in the early 1980s, two homes in Red Deer had been targets of cross-burnings (Kinsella, 2001). Together the students shared ideas and resources in a collective effort to counter-hate groups. One idea they implemented was to organize a school-wide Human Rights Awareness Week, featuring noon hour forums with antiracist "skinhead punks" from SHARP (Skinheads Against Racial Prejudice), the president of the World Sikh Organization, a former university professor from Iran (then a caretaker at our school), and the chair of the Alberta Human Rights Commission.

Countering the Canadian Denial of a Racist Past (and Present)

Complicating the current discourse on diversity is a pervasive notion that Canada has always stood for harmony and acceptance; evidence exists that this is a profound distortion. The assumed absence of racism in Canada is refuted by a long history of discriminatory government and corporate policies and practices. As STOP continues to find, this denial of racism and reluctance to name specific instances often creates barriers to addressing problems as they arise in schools and communities. As one local historian notes, my home province has also struggled with an undercurrent of hatred:

> A darker side of Alberta that is not commonly part of the outsider's perception, having
> been largely overlooked by both academic and popular historians, is a semblance of the
> Ku Klux Klan mentality—a religious and racial bigotry that penetrated society far
> beyond the Ku Klux Klan membership and which emerged during Alberta's formative
> years when its foundation Anglo-Saxon stock felt its racial purity threatened by a wave
> of non-Anglo-Saxon immigrants. (Baergen, 2000, pp. 11–12)

Even the obvious actions of contemporary racist hate groups in Alberta and elsewhere in Canada are downplayed, though their recent resurgence "has become increasingly visible, and increasingly violent . . . [and] has grown to become a significant social problem" (Kinsella, 2001, pp. 4–5). This growth is compounded in Alberta by its hidden discriminatory past, the influence of which is felt in current public discourse against the French language, immigration, and homosexuals. Baergen (2000) agrees, noting that, "Alberta continues to struggle with heavy historical baggage in its quest to overcome racism" (p. 284). Moreover, racist perspectives have long permeated mainstream Canadian society as well.

Since European settlers began arriving, systematic discrimination has been practiced against individuals and groups based on racist ideologies and ethnocentric views about the primacy of British cultural norms, beginning with the colonization of Aboriginal peoples. Official government policies, formulated and implemented with popular public support, served to entrench, among other examples, racial segregation in schools, forced assimilation of Aboriginal Canadians, racialized immigration restrictions, anti-Semitism, the mistreatment of Chinese immigrant railway workers, and the displacement and internment of Japanese-Canadians (Baergen, 2000; Boyko, 1995; Henry et al., 1995; Walker, 1985). For various reasons, such unsavory aspects of Canadian history have been excluded, distorted, or downplayed in virtually all current social studies school materials, and by many in political and administrative positions.

For several years there has been strong public debate in Canada about the value of any form of multicultural education, and indeed, of the concept of multiculturalism itself (e.g., Bissoondath, 1994; Gairdner, 1991). Such arguments may be decoded as little more than a transparent desire for entrenching the status quo and denying legitimate concerns around diversity and equity issues. Borrowing from Willinsky's (1998) critique of similar arguments by American critics of multiculturalism, I concur that their call for unification under traditional values "does little to honor the history of a nation tragically built out of racial division" (p. 398).

Indeed, others have noted our national tendency toward white-washing our racist past. Boyko (1994) observes: "Canadians are often guilty of ignoring or warping our past while sanctimoniously feeling somewhat removed from, and superior to, countries struggling with racial problems and harbouring histories marked by slavery or racial violence" (p. 15). As STOP has shown, it is more instrumental to our understanding of effective pedagogical responses to racism to acknowledge specific sources and manifestations of racism in Canada, as painful as these may be to face; following Boyko's timely advice, "let us look truthfully at our past, admit our mistakes, atone for our crimes, and celebrate our progress" (p. 15). Atonement may represent the most promising way to initiate national healing that Archbishop Desmond Tutu insists is a necessary prerequisite to social justice reform (in Wiwa, 2001).

Countering Extremism Through Education

The STOP group and I have periodically confronted significant resistance to our efforts. When the national head of the Simon Wiesenthal Centre in Toronto traveled to Red Deer about a decade ago to present STOP with a "Courage to Remember" 40-poster series on the Holocaust, the response from the extremist fringe was immediate. Long, the national Aryan Nations leader, made the front page of the local newspaper decrying the Holocaust as a hoax, while an item on the national award was buried in the local section. Meanwhile, numerous cars in the school's parking lot were littered with KKK brochures, and STOP continued to receive revisionist "historical" evidence and pseudo-scientific studies in the mail. I received a personal letter from Long himself, seeking access to a student audience. The following year, the disgraced teacher Keegstra wrote me a three-page diatribe accusing me of cowardice and imploring me to turn from my "Talmudic masters" and face the "truth" about Jews.

STOP never responds personally to extremists, likening it to choosing to wrestle with a pig; one would likely end up getting dirty, and besides, the pig enjoys it! Rather, in this case, STOP laminated the Holocaust posters and donated them to the school district for use by all teachers. STOP also purchased additional archival material on the Holocaust from the U.S. National Archives, and often shares these resources with the local museum. Student interest led STOP to organize an annual Holocaust Awareness Symposium in conjunction with the Calgary Jewish Centre. Since 1994, actual survivors of Nazi concentration camps have spoken to thousands of high school students in the region.

STOP's mandate is to educate rather than confront but it often responds to contentious local issues. For example, when a Sikh man was denied entry into Red Deer's Royal Canadian Legion meeting room because he was wearing unauthorized "headgear" (his turban), STOP members wrote compelling letters to the parties involved and to the media. STOP also invited the victim to address a group of about 300 high school students to shine light on Sikh faith. It is illustrative of an instance where a group effectively used "intercultural sharing" in the struggle to name and confront specific examples of institutional racism, naturally bridging an apparent schism between the multicultural and antiracism supporters reported by some researchers (e.g., Kehoe, 1994; McGregor and Ungerleider, 1993). It makes sense to avoid simplified bipolar constructions or positions that deny the complexity of school-based activism.

Other STOP activities have included ambitious awareness campaigns on violence against women, including white ribbon campaigns, speakers and videos, and culminating in the organizing of the city's inaugural "Take Back the Night" event, now an annual civic tradition. To address the discrimination faced by gay and lesbian students in the high school, STOP formed the province's first Gay/Straight Alliance program (Kennedy, 2000). STOP's concerted lobbying of the provincial government assisted with the expansion of human rights protection.

Other specific student and teacher activism has included interrogation of school policies and curriculum materials, presentations to government officials, drama presentations to children, organizing literature and art contests, mounting local protests, international human rights advocacy, and public debates with political leaders on government policies (Lund, 1993, 1998). In the examples described above, students and teachers have taken decisive action on specific community issues of racism and discrimination in complex ways that respond to community backlash while overlapping apparently conflicting conceptual distinctions in the academic literature.

STOP's efforts have been rewarded with several national honors, most recently the 2001 Award of Distinction from the Canadian Race Relations Foundation. In 1999 STOP won a national Harmony Award of Distinction, and in 1998 a National Race Relations Award from the Canadian Federation of Municipalities. But perhaps the most exciting recognition for our group's members happened when the California hard rock band "Rage Against the Machine" (www.ratm.com) voted STOP their "March 2000 Freedom Fighter of the Month"!

Engaging Students and Teachers in Educational Research

Clearly, the inclusion of student voices in formulating social justice pedagogy does not simply mean co-opting a student or two to sit on an adult-driven committee or project. An exciting challenge for the STOP program and other activist groups I have studied has been to allow meaningful ways of engaging students in a collaborative sharing of the responsibility for bringing about substantive change in schools and communities. By allowing their traditionally silenced voices to be heard, educators, activists and researchers expose themselves to some risk, and inevitable conflict and debate. But as Hargreaves (1996) insists,

> There are other voices worth articulating, hearing, and sponsoring as well as those of teachers. In the present context of reform and restructuring, perhaps the time has come to bring together the different voices surrounding schooling—students with teacher; teachers with parents—and risk cacophony in our struggle to build authentic community. (p. 16)

Instead of framing this potentially raucous dialogue as discordant, I prefer to describe it as an ongoing composition that does not necessarily require perfect harmony.

When young people's concerns surrounding social justice are attended to by academics, their insights into issues of racism and other discrimination can be revelatory. SooHoo (1995) proposed a model of activism with young people, and describes her collaborations with students as a "syncopated rhythm." For all of the challenges that emerge, her work suggests that such collaborative research efforts hold tremendous potential for enacting social justice ideals in the most relevant ways for students in schools. Our intentional engagement of young activists as respected participants in research answers this timely call and signals an overdue acknowledgment of their significant roles as activists and informants in this area.

Despite the effusive language of empowerment and emancipation from many critical theorists, what is often missing in current literature on social justice education is a tangible link to practice in schools and education faculties. Ladson-Billings (1995) notes that because theory development and practice do not happen separately from one another, there is a "synergistic and dynamic relationship that exists between the two. Practitioners are not merely waiting for scholars to develop theory before they begin to try new approaches to pedagogy. True, theory informs practice, but practice also informs theory" (pp. 752–753). As more educators build activist coalitions with their students and colleagues, a simultaneous growth in the academic interest in their social justice projects can reflexively inform both research and theorizing in a reciprocal relationship.

Conclusion

As those involved with the STOP program have been discovering for almost two decades, educators and students can collaboratively explore, incorporate, and refine social justice principles through their school-based activism around issues of difference. It is time that more academics in this field opened their research models to respectful collaboration. Darling-Hammond (1996) highlights the reciprocal benefits of engaging teachers in research, noting that it is "a powerful way of learning about both teaching and research. It can improve the responsiveness of research to the realities of teaching while also developing the kind of thinking good teachers must engage in" (p. 12). This helps create a broader clientele for many types of pedagogical knowledge—both personal and professional—that teachers and researchers produce in developing social justice pedagogy.

My current research with a range of student and teacher activists is confirming what I have long suspected as I engaged in social justice activism within the STOP program: the benefits of collaborative research activities can be reaped by both teacher and student activists, some of whom help to shape and focus the research questions from the outset. Together we can continue to engage in a valuable conversation on our own understandings around our racialized identities, and on the complexity of activism, especially in conservative school and community settings. If, in the quest to make schools and communities more equitable, teachers and students are afforded more such opportunities to "roll up their sleeves" and participate in educational research and activism themselves, all parties stand to reap the rewards.

Note

1. Portions of this manuscript appear in revised form in Lund (2001), and are used with the kind permission of the publishers. I acknowledge the generous support of my research by fellowships from the Social Sciences and Humanities Research Council of Canada, the Alberta Teachers' Association, and the Killam Trusts.

References

Alberta Human Rights and Citizenship Commission. (2000). *Tools for Transformation: Human Rights Education and Diversity Initiatives in Alberta*. Edmonton, AB: Government of Alberta.

Apple, Michael W. (1993). *Official Knowledge: Democratic Education in a Conservative Age.* New York: Routledge.

Baergen, William P. (2000). *The Ku Klux Klan in Central Alberta.* Red Deer, AB: Central Alberta Historical Society.

Berlin, Myrna, and Ibrahim Alladin. (1996). "The Kipling Collegiate Institute Story: Towards Positive Race Relations in the School." In *Racism in Canadian Schools*, ed. Ibrahim Alladin. Toronto: Harcourt Brace, pp. 136–165.

Bissoondath, Neil. (1994). *Selling Illusions: The Cult of Multiculturalism in Canada.* Toronto: Penguin.

Boyko, John. (1995). *Last Steps to Freedom: The Evolution of Canadian Racism.* Winnipeg, MB: Watson & Dwyer.

Canadian Race Relations Foundation. (2001). *CRRF 2001 Best Practices Reader.* Toronto, ON: Author.

Cogan, Karen, and Steve Ramsankar. (1994). *Alex Taylor Community School: A Quarter Century of Programs and Promises.* Edmonton, AB: Alex Taylor School.

Darling-Hammond, Linda. "The Right to Learn and the Advancement of Teaching: Research, Policy, and Practice for Democratic Education." *Educational Researcher* 25:6 (1996): 5–17.

Fullan, Michael, and Andy Hargreaves (eds.). (1992). *Teacher Development and Educational Change.* Bristol, PA: Falmer Press.

Gairdner, William D. (1991). *The Trouble with Canada.* Toronto: General Paperbacks.

Giroux, Henry A. (1996). *Fugitive Cultures: Race, Violence, and Youth.* New York: Routledge.

Griffith, Bryant, and George Labercane. (1995). "High School Students' Attitudes Towards Racism in Canada: A Report on a 1993 Cross-Cultural Study." In *Multicultural Education: The State of the Art, Report #2*, ed. Keith A. McLeod. Winnipeg, MB: Canadian Association of Second Language Teachers.

Hargreaves, Andy. "Revisiting Voice." *Educational Researcher* 25:1 (1996): 12–19.

Henry, Frances, Carol Tator, Winston Mattis, and Tim Rees. (1995). *The Colour of Democracy: Racism in Canadian Society.* Toronto, ON: Harcourt Brace.

Kehoe, John W. "Multicultural Education vs. Anti-Racist Education: The Debate and the Research in Canada." *Social Education* 58 (1994): 354–358.

Kennedy, Cameron. "New Student Group Fights Anti-gay Bias at Local High School." *Red Deer Advocate*, November 20, 2000.

Kinsella, Warren. (2001). *Web of Hate: Inside Canada's Far Right Network* (2nd ed.). Toronto, ON: HarperCollins.

Ladson-Billings, Gloria. (1995). "Multicultural Teacher Education: Research, Practice, Policy." In *Handbook of Research on Multicultural Education*, ed. James A. Banks and Cherry A. McGee Banks. New York: Macmillan, pp. 36–51.

Lund, Darren E. (1993). "The Evolution of STOP—Students and Teachers Opposing Prejudice." In *Multicultural Education: The State of the Art National Study, Report #1*, ed. Keith A. McLeod. Winnipeg: Canadian Association of Second Language Teachers, pp. 26–45.

Lund, Darren E. "Social Justice Activism in a Conservative Climate: Students and Teachers Challenging Discrimination in Alberta." *Our Schools/Our Selves* 9:4 (1998): 24–38.

Lund, Darren E. "Promoting Human Rights in the Conservative Heartland of Canada: A Practical/Theoretical Approach to School-Based Activism." *Journal of Intergroup Relations* 28:2 (2001): 63–72.

Lund, Darren E. "Educating for Social Justice: Making Sense of Multicultural and Antiracist Theory and Practice with Canadian Teacher Activists." *Intercultural Education* 14 (2003): 3–16.

McGregor, Josette, and Charles Ungerleider. (1993). "Multicultural and Racism Awareness Programs for Teachers: A Meta-Analysis of the Research." In *Multicultural Education: The State of the Art National Study, Report #1*, ed. Keith A. McLeod. Winnipeg: Canadian Association of Second Language Teachers.

Smith, Jan, and Jon Young. (1996). "Building an Anti-Racist School: The Story of Victor Magel School." In *Multicultural Education: The State of the Art National Study, Report #4*, ed. Keith A. McLeod. Winnipeg, MB: Canadian Association of Second Language Teachers.

Solomon, R. Patrick. "Beyond Prescriptive Pedagogy: Teacher Inservice Education for Cultural Diversity." *Journal of Teacher Education* 46 (1995): 251–258.

Solomon, R. Patrick, and Cynthia Levine-Rasky. "When Principle Meets Practice: Teachers' Contradictory Responses to Anti-Racist Education." *Alberta Journal of Educational Research* 42 (1996): 19–33.

SooHoo, Suzanne. (1995). "Emerging Student and Teacher Voices: A Syncopated Rhythm in Public Education." In *Critical Multiculturalism: Uncommon Voices in a Common Struggle*, ed. Barry Kanpol and Peter McLaren. Westport, CT: Bergin & Garvey, pp. 89–101.

Walker, James W. S. (1985). *Racial Discrimination in Canada: The Black Experience*. Ottawa, ON: Canadian Historical Association.

Willinsky, John. "The Educational Politics of Identity and Category." *Interchange* 29 (1998): 385–402.

Wiwa, Ken. (2001). "The Apostle of Forgiveness." *The Globe and Mail*, May 5, 2001.

Chapter 3 ~

Our Political State in an Age of Globalization*

John Willinsky

For as long as there have been public schools in the West, with their flagpoles and colored maps on the wall, the nation has functioned as an educational apparatus for positioning people, for teaching the young and old not only who's who, but who-belongs-where. If we have indeed entered into a new, postimperial age of globalism, then it may be a good time to contemplate not only possible futures for the nation, but for considering our educational responsibilities in directing that future toward what has always been promised in the name of the nation, namely the right to join together in the making of a better world. I want to consider the schools are to do with this idea of the *nation*. What is to be made of this critical juncture of multinational, transnational, and post-national globalism? Among recent signs of a the shift are the debates of the United Nations that weigh human rights against national rights, which challenge the UN's traditional protection of national interests. Canada's Foreign Minister Lloyd Axworthy has commissioned an international study on how to begin thinking beyond the nation in protecting human rights: "Our take has been that since the end of the cold war we have to focus on the individuals, on the people. That is as much in the charter as sovereignty."[1]

The nation may still stand as the fundamental demarcation of geographical space, the primary organization of place. But the end of the Cold War has meant that the nation is no longer *the* domino in the only game in town. The nation is no longer the primary ideological unit, to stand as friend or foe, in the great struggle against evil. Global forces connect the world in a virtual and literal sense that pays little heed to national borders. It makes less sense, then, to think of the nation as defining who people are, how they live, and where they belong. For some, like John Tomlinson of Nottingham Trent University, it may well seem that globalization "weakens the cultural coherence of all nation-states, including economically powerful ones."[2] Yet I would hold that this sense of cultural coherence within the nation has always been a questionable state (forgive the pun). What this increased transnational flow of people, capital, and goods does enable us to do is to call this assumed coherence, and the unnecessary damage it does, more forcefully into question.

So let us not allow this seeming loss of national distinctions cause us to go misty-eyed. Let us be both educational and ethical opportunists here. We must ask how we can steer this ever-so-slight turning away from the nation toward some greater good for, in the first instance perhaps, the transnational young who are trying to find themselves in our schools. We can seek to correct the educational excesses that would closely link national identity to race, culture, and gender.[3] We can teach the young about holding the democratic nation to its promises, challenging its shortcomings, and supporting its ongoing civil and political experiment in public deliberation. This means drawing the young into a concern for the experiment they are living out, giving them a sense of responsibility, not for living out national destinies but for improving, on a local and global level, how people live and work together. It means teaching them how to hold the nation responsible for principles that extend beyond fostering the nation and nationalism.[4]

Now, such educational optimism may seem a trifle unwarranted. After all, I do read the papers. The headlines are regularly haunted by spectacles of ethnic nationalism. And I know that we are a long way from separating how we view nationality through the lens of race, culture, and gender, a long way from allowing that everyone has an equal and unequivocal claim to being *here* in that national sense.

I

We need to start somewhere, and I am proposing that we begin by reducing the emphasis on the nation as defining what is inherently common to us all, so that we can see it more fully as a civil and political device for working with and through differences. This is no small step, given that only a couple of decades ago, the distinguished social theorist Ernest Gellner could define nationalism as "the principle of homogeneous cultural units as the foundations of political life, and of the obligatory cultural unity of rulers and ruled" and that, as such, was inherent in "the condition of our times."[5]

Nationalism was neither natural state nor a "precondition for social life." Gellner held that it was driven by industrialization, which created a "national imperative" of cultural homogeneity. Such homogeneity was necessarily supported by national school systems that ensured a common language and sensibility. Such grand theories of national identity and unity are exactly what our students must test against the experience of their own neighborhoods, as well as within the global economies that dress, feed, and amuse them. They need to see how the nation has a history of stumbling badly over these assumptions of cultural coherence.

In the case of Canada, for example, they could well turn to the work of Sunera Thobani, in Women's Studies at Simon Fraser University. She has found that "historically, the Canadian state has contended with the conflicting interests of preserving 'whiteness' of the nation while simultaneously ensuring an adequate supply of labor."[6] And if that was then, what now, given that race has been ostensibly removed from this country's immigration policies, and voting privileges have, since World War II, been extended to immigrants from China and India, as well as to the aboriginal peoples? "Canadian nation building," Thobani finds, "relies in no small measure upon the construction of immigrants, in general, and immigrant women in particular, as one of the most potent threats to the nation's prosperity and well-being" (ibid.). This may well be an era of globalization, but we clearly have much to do in setting our ideas of the nation in order.

In this spirit, I have an educational proposal to make that calls the very idea of the nation into question. The proposal is all about advancing the nation's civil and democratic qualities: *First, we need to study with students how the original promise of the modern nation, as a free association of equals, is the point of a continuing economic, social, and philosophical struggle, even as the nation's status is changing in the face of globalization. Second, we need to explore with students various means of advancing this democratic experiment, not only with the nation-state, but at the global and local levels at which we now live.*

This rethinking of the nation with students could begin with how the modern nation-state has long been pulled in two directions: (1) ethnic (the nation as a source of cultural identity) and (2) civil (the nation as a form of voluntary political association). The goal here is not necessarily about striking a balance between the nation as shared destiny and political engagement, as the two ideas can easily work against each other. If democracy really did require this ethnic nationalist sense of a shared culture and a common set of values among its citizens (beyond a commitment to democratic processes), as Princeton political philosopher Amy Gutman makes clear, then it would be far less of a democracy, with far less hope of teaching us about ourselves and each other through deliberation and debate/[7](1999, p. 11). Rather, the democratic state was founded, at least in its formal political sense, on a minimal principle of association, based on an Enlightenment concept of a common humanity, with people committed to working out together ways of advancing their varying and common interests.

Certainly, the United States, to take a nearby example, was launched in the spirit of a political union rather than an ethnic nation. The country's initial public offering, otherwise known as the *Declaration of Independence*, refers to "nation" but once, and only when it speaks of how unworthy King George III is as head of a civilized nation. The Declaration speaks rather of "the political bands" that "connect" one people to another, held together by the self-evident truths of people's fundamental equality and their unalienable rights: "That to secure these rights, Governments are instituted among Men, deriving their just powers from the consent of the governed." This sense of the state, as a secular banding together of people interested in securing their rights, needs to guide our educational efforts, which must ultimately equip the young to judge the great shortfalls in securing the rights and to pursue a just power that derives from the consent of the governed.[8]

This secular, civil model of the nation has often been lost to its standing as a "spiritual principle," in the words of historian Ernest Renan. In his lecture "What Is a Nation?" given at the Sorbonne in 1882, Renan was, even then, concerned with stripping the nation of its metaphysical claims. He points to how critical "forgetting" and "historical error" are to the "creation of a nation" especially given that national unity is "always affected by means of brutality."[9] Renan goes on to reject the commonly assumed national principles of a shared race, language, and religion, only to accept, as a good historian should, perhaps, that the nation is "the outcome of the profound complications of history" (p. 18). "It presupposes a past," he adds, "it is summarized, however, in the present by a tangible fact, namely consent, the clearly expressed desire to continue a common life" (p. 19). In the face of the nation's "spiritual principle," he still looks for how its continuing existence reflects, in effect, "a daily plebiscite" (ibid.). Similarly, he holds the nation up as a love object, as "one loves the house that one has built and that one has handed down," even as he attempts to distance himself from its racial and cultural basis (ibid.). But how possible is that, you might well ask, given the horrendous associations of nation and race that burned through too much of the twentieth century, even as nations failed terribly to protect all of those who found themselves living within their borders.

Yet students also need to appreciate how this spirit of ethnic nationalism also proved an effective instrument against colonialism and the subjection of minority cultures within existing nations. Historian Partha Chatterjee, speaking of India's struggles against British imperialism, points out that "here nationalism launches its most powerful, creative, and historically significant project: to fashion a 'modern' national culture that is nevertheless not Western."[10] Still, Chatterjee allows, "the dominant elements of its self-definition, at least in post-colonial India, were drawn from the ideology of the liberal-democratic state" (p. 10), even as he offers a vision what comes after the triumph of this nationalism in India: "The critique of nationalist discourse must find for itself the ideological means to connect the popular strength of the people's struggles with the consciousness of a new universality."[11]

In a postcolonial Canada, both the Aboriginal peoples, as I've already indicated, and the Quebecois have called on a self-defining nationalism to fight for previously denied rights within the larger nation. Pierre Elliot Trudeau, among this nation's greatest prime ministers and another of this country's recent losses, was drawn, as a Quebecois, into politics to fight a Quebec nationalism that he saw as the enemy of a liberal democratic tradition. As it turned out, of course, Trudeau managed to hold the spirit of Quebec separatism at bay through a questionable political mixture: suspending civil liberties during the War Measures Act in 1970 while going on to make the country officially bilingual and multicultural and instituting a national Charter of Rights and Freedoms.

Although Quebec's future is by no means settled, students here might well appreciate how Trudeau sought to counter ethnic nationalism by strengthening a rights-based civil state. More importantly, and encouragingly for my proposal, this civil strategy has been on the rise on a global scale in recent years. Although ethnic bloodshed persists in Israel, Sri Lanka, and elsewhere, the decline in violence over the last decade, Gurr argues, points to gains in political and civil solutions to the question of what defines the nation. This channeling of ethnic disputes into national political processes—the persistence of terrorist and guerilla actions notwithstanding—has taken place among newly democratic governments in Europe, Asia, and Latin America, as they formally recognize and guarantee political and cultural rights to minorities within their borders. This, for me, holds important lessons about the changing nation-state. In far fewer instances is the nation defining itself as an ethnic unit.[12]

The historical lessons that need honing concern how the nation's best hopes for equal participation and unalienable rights have repeatedly fallen short of the promise, even as the nation may well have made small incremental steps toward that goal. Students also need to understand how this vision of humanity's basic equality has not always been a part of what was and continues to be taught in school. Students need to see how the schools' critical role in shaping how we perceive who-belongs-where by nationality, and their own textbooks, as well as earlier ones still sitting perhaps in the school's bookroom, form a fine starting point for understanding how we need to reset our understanding of the nation, setting it back on a civil path as an association of equals.[13]

II

After this all-too-brief historical look at the nation-state, and before going on to consider my second educational principle, which concerns how schools can support greater civil and political deliberation among students, I want to offer a critical interlude. For I can readily see four likely objections to my educational focus on the nation, namely that (1) I am undemocratically assuming a particularly Western approach to the nation-state, (2) the nation-state is already a dead concept, (3) the nation should be set aside in favor of cosmopolitanism, and finally (4) that this whole concern with the nation-state is simply educationally irrelevant today.

Consider this effort to reposition the nation-state as a free and reasoned association of rights and responsibilities. If this is to be all about respecting differences, then what of the charge that such faith in reason and democracy is a Western ploy to sustain its once and fading dominance? Are these national ideals better abandoned as a failed experiment? This is not simply about rejecting Western thinking on the nation. It is misleading and plain arrogant to imagine, Amartya Sen, the Nobel–prize winning economist has recently pointed out, that reason is strictly a Western ideal. He attacks the idea of setting a selective, singular set of "Asian values," in favor of discipline and order, against "Western values" of liberty and reason.[14] He goes on to argue that "once we recognize that many ideas that are taken to be quintessentially Western have also flourished in other civilizations . . . we need not begin with pessimism, at least on this ground, about the prospects of reasoned humanism in the world" (ibid.). Having rejected the West's exclusive hold on reason, we are left to explore how ideas of nation can work within the logic of democratic and deliberative processes.[15]

This brings me to a second concern, which is that the nation is already a lost cause and we had best just get over it. Such is the view, for example, of Mohammed Bamyeh, of New York University and editor of a journal of "transnational and transcultural studies." He holds in his critique of the new imperialism, that "the final victory of capitalism everywhere means . . . that the capitalist state has lost its mission and meaning."[16] Bamyeh places his faith in grassroots "organized voluntaristic interventions" and a "nascent 'global civil society'."[17] Similarly, Bernardo Gallegos argues that, in the case of Mexico and the United States, the nation can be "a disabling discursive category" that leads to the "erasure of indigenous identities" while he calls for a reconception of social space and arrangements, pointing to the indigenous Zapatista movement in the southern Mexican State of Chiapas as an example.[18]

It is clear that this is an age of new politics that upsets old ways of understanding the nation. As Anne-Christine Habbard, deputy secretary general of International Federation of Human Rights, has explained, these politics mean that "ours is a new planetary citizenship, reflecting the fact that decisions have migrated from the state level. Voting for national representatives, an old expression of citizenship, achieves nothing, because they have scant power."[19] There is no question that decisions of considerable consequence are increasingly taking place on the global stage, often behind the closed curtains of the WTO, IMF, and major financial interests. Even the president of the World Bank, James D. Wolfensohn, knows enough to declare that "something is wrong when the richest 20 percent of the global population receive more than 80 percent of the global income."[20] The question then is what to do in the face of a problem of such enormous scope. How can we, to further quote bank President Wolfensohn, "make globalization an instrument of opportunity and inclusion—not fear"? (ibid.). In the face of such a question, rather than simply joining in the chorus railing against the death of the nation and the rise of globalization demons, it may be far more helpful, I am suggesting, to identify what in our own work stands some chance of furthering opportunity and inclusion, whether we are bank presidents, teachers, or university professors.

I think it hasty to write off states as "large deadly vacuities," as Bamyeh does.[21] I think its time, following Gallegos, to reconceptualize the social space and arrangements of the nation. Let us at least turn to the state's school systems and universities to see if we can prepare the young and ourselves better for working in conjunction with grassroots organizations to foster a more civil society at every level. Civility cannot simply happen at the global level; it has to be civil all the way down. I see this as an opportunity for the schools and universities to sharpen the state's political focus, to help it bring public reason to bear on questions of local and global interests. This is about the capitalist state having a mission and meaning. We have to see how our work as educators can do more to expand, if not restore, the scope of the public sphere within national democratic processes.[22]

In this way, I open myself to a third possible objection with my seemingly parochial concern with the nation. To the contrary, I am advocating that we gain some critical distance on how education divides up the world. This seems to me a first step in paying greater allegiance, as Martha Nussbaum holds we should, to humanity's reason and moral capacity.[23] This distinguished philosopher at the University of Chicago is best known for having so thoughtfully kept the ancient wisdom of the Greeks vital in such works as the *Fragility of Goodness* and *Love's Knowledge*. More recently, however, she has published the more prosaically entitled, *Women and Human Development: The Capabilities Approach*.[24] This book finds her far from the Parthenon, sitting on the ground in rural Bihar in northeastern India observing for herself how well the Adithi literacy program is working in improving the lot of women. She actively solicits our participation in supporting the worldwide growth of women's education as a humane response to the forces of globalization by which we are otherwise profiting by in many ways.

Nussbaum has also called elsewhere for the introduction of a cosmopolitan rather than a nationalist education, in which we learn to see ourselves as citizens of the world, moved by the universal values of a common humanity.[25] Her provocative rejection of national patriotism has given rise to considerable debate over whether we can so easily turn away from our national commitments, given that there is no larger state to be a citizen of, nor any apparent agreement over which shared values provide a basis for such a common cause.[26] Yet we need not choose between nation and world in our allegiances, she holds against her dichotomizing critics; we need to overcome that particular chauvinism that mars the political stature of the nation by recognizing that what links me to my neighborhood links me to humanity at large.

How then are we to do a better job of honoring that principle of cosmopolitanism, whether within our own families and neighborhoods or among those that exist in seemingly distant lands? The problem, as Nussbaum identifies it, is that "we think of people from China as our fellows the minute they dwell in a certain place, namely the United States, but not when they dwell in a certain other place, namely China."[27] The term "Chinese" (and "Asian," for that matter) acts as a blended racial, cultural, and national designation that we need to critically analyze with students. These labels of "other" by another are one of the primary social legacies of imperialism, which each of us continues to live through.[28]

I have now arrived at the fourth (but never final) objection to this concern with redressing the nation, which is about whether I need to simply *get real*. For you may well be shaking your heads over how I am so totally missing the Big Education Issue of the Day, which is, of course, raising educational standards in the schools. (It is so *not* reducing the schools' spirit of nationalism.[29]) If I am not talking about ways of improving test scores, whether through incentives, vouchers, privatization, or computers, then I am not talking to parents, teachers, administrators, politicians, or anyone else who has a hope of influencing the schools.

In the face of such concerns, I would still ask that with this paramount concern that more students learn more in every grade, we give some consideration to what it is they are going to learn more about. There are lessons, I am suggesting, that we have long taught about the nation and nationality that do not serve our students well. If we are going to raise the standards for more students, then let us also reflect on what they learn and how it contributes to the world they are going to inherit. If those raised standards are intended to improve the quality of life, then let us consider the implications of what students learn and practice, whether in social studies, information technologies, or language arts, for democratic participation on a local, national, and global level. Otherwise, to go on assuming that the principal educational goal is to raise students' test scores seems to sell what we do in classrooms, not to mention the students themselves, vastly short.

Professors of education have a responsibility, I would hold, to find ways of extending the public conversation about education so that it continues to include a concern with what we are learning and how that learning contributes to this changing world. Schools everywhere have long reinforced this concept of a singular national identity with the world neatly divided into color-coded nations, each with their own characteristics, currencies, and customs. This has been tempered by the introduction of multiculturalism into the curriculum, enabling students to see how their nation is enriched by other nationalities and cultures. This can, however, sustain the view that people carry a home-nation—or is it just a culture and race?—on their backs like snails, as they have made their way in the world.

The curriculum has also grown more global in its perspective, and I am encouraged by reports that a greater sense of the world's interconnectedness can be found in some social studies classes, at least in America.[30] Yet Merry M. Merrifield, a curriculum professor at Ohio State, has also found that this globalism carries underlying assumptions of both capitalism's triumph and America's continuing dominance. Not surprisingly, she calls for "moving the center of global education from institutionalized divisions of people and ideas to the complexity of the interaction and syncrety of the global human experience" (in press). This move would help the school curriculum catch up to what the world has long been about.

But oh, the continuing force of those institutionalized divisions. The complexity that the students also need to understand, now as much as ever, is how this still-powerful idea of the nation can shape the very way we see and understand each other; the students need to appreciate how the idea of the nation has worked historically for and against its very promise of self-determination and self-definition, its promise of political deliberation and consent. They need to see how globalization may pose a threat to hard-won democratic forms of state governance, no less in areas of education than in trade or law.[31]

III

My educational goal, then, is to explore with students how the nation-state has long been about both the patriotic call to loyalty and an open commitment to protecting dissent and other democratic processes. I want to ask how we can begin to study the nation-state in ways that reduce our chauvinistic fixing of who-belongs-where and increase our chances of seeing how the nation can extend democratic and civil processes within our lives and work. The schools have long worked both the civil and nativist tendencies of the nation, teaching about the rights and liberties of democratic participation while celebrating allegiance to the nation, with their flags, anthems, and pledges, as well as their maps, histories, and stories. The schools have always sought to instill a spirit of patriotism in the young around a common cultural legacy, and as proponents of multiculturalism have made clear, this has meant the exclusion and alienation of too many students. I am proposing that all students need to understand how the idea of nation has been divided in ways that have worked against its own democratic promises, both in how we have learned about other nations and in how we have learned about the nation in which we live.

One means of rethinking who-belongs-where is by paying attention to those who already belong to many places. The emerging transnational ruling class might be one critical point of attention.[32] But then so might the new transnational migrant classes. For who can tell us more about the multiplicity of rootedness, of being variously local, than people who freely move among a number of nations. This jet set, however, flies with the rest of us in coach. These are working people who "develop networks, activities, patterns of living, and ideologies that span their home and host society," according to the anthropological work of Linda Basch, Nina Glick Schiller, and Cristina Szanton Blanc.[33] But distinctions between a "home" and "host" society doesn't really work for these "transmigrants." They circulate rather than immigrate. They are at home on the streets of New York and in a Trinidadian village. Their roots in both nations are not just social, but economic, political, and religious. Their coexistence defies traditional notions of nation and nationality, not least of all through their selfless efforts to redress national inequities their families suffer by sending money to those in need. Here, then, is how people live and work on a global level and among nations. Here they contribute to two nations' vitality while defying claims to a necessary, sustaining nationality. Here is a model of the nation as a place for people who are here and elsewhere, an idea of the nation not so wholly focused on itself, a collection of scattered communities, devoted to working together to share their mobile opportunities.

This transnational, transmigrant sense of connection and support, of responsibility and opportunity, could well temper our far more closed sense of nationality. This fixing of people to nations is what we need to give up in learning and teaching about what we are, about what cultures and nations are, and about what we owe each other in the circulation of goods and understandings. It is what we need to take up in thinking about the nation as defining a group's efforts to extend and refine democratic forms of justice and governance. The nation need not be thought of as that special place to which we are given. It needs to be more a place where we gather together equally, to imagine and to work together on imagining, what want to make of this world. It is but one of many units for organizing and improving the way we live, and we need to think about what, given its size, its administrative structures, its history, it can best do to ensure that it reduces the harm that we are capable of doing each other, and especially the harm that has, in the past and today, that it does in its own name of nationality and nationalism.

Yet in bringing this measure of reason to why and how this concept nation has operated, I do not want to deny the need for roots.[34] There is no giving up our sense of belonging, of having deep and abiding feelings for a place or more likely a series of places, demarcated by memory's streets, hills, a line of trees, the turn of a river, no less than a way of talking and cooking, than the color of the buses, than the music playing in the corner store. There are times, too, when this country has sent in troops. Within these places lie aspects of our identity and thus what we bring to the deliberations of the nation. This sense of place, infused with memories, may mean that I want to keep my streets as they were and seem always to have been. These sentiments are directed at times toward restricting immigration, and here, in Vancouver, they resulted in regulations, in an earlier era, that kept properties in certain neighborhoods from being sold to Jews and Asians. And this is why, I would argue, that we need to help students see that the nation is a place where our attachments to memory and identity cannot be allowed to override fundamental democratic principles of what we owe each other. It means looking critically with students at how this idea of the nation operates. It means explaining why at this time we are focusing on the nation as a means of realizing the rights and obligations of citizenship, while worrying that it can too often serve as a source of sentimental and occasionally hostile nativism and nationality.

We need to explore with our students how this concept of nation makes necessarily insecure claims to a people as well as to the land they live on. As long as some people within the nation are thought of as rooted elsewhere by their nationality or race, their full and equal participation in this democratic nation is undermined. That is, the basic premises of the democratic state have not been realized. How much less true is it today, we can ask them, than it was in 1903 when W. E. B. Du Bois spoke of African Americans as ever having to possess this "double-consciousness," ever having to feel this "two-ness—an American, a Negro; two souls, two thoughts, two unreconciled strivings."[35] How is it that the nation is so identified with one race that others must live divided lives? Is this not finally a time in which an American can be understood to identify no more than one who is living in America? That has always been true, at one level, but now it has taken on a moral political imperative if this democratic quality of the nation is going to continue to advance.

We need to track how prevailing ideas of *nationhood* are changing in the face of a wide range of forces that include globalization, but also the spread of democracy, feminism, and environmentalism. We need to press these new global communication technologies so that they advance public interests within this growing knowledge economy. We need to ask, at every turn, how our work in the study of education helps identify and clarify ways of extending the democratic basis of the state. We need to specify projects of educational intervention in the face of what can otherwise be a platitudinous approach of joining the chorus now given to denouncing the evils of globalization.

Take the critical question of language, from bilingual education programs to the official English movement in the United States. There is no question that access to English is now a global issue. But against the hegemony of this language, can we explore with students how democratic processes operate in multilingual communities? Can we consider with them the assumptions that often guide ESL programs (Norton, 2000)?[36] Can we explore the role of translation within these communities and how it can be better supported by the schools and students themselves? What are the sources of political information, the processes of local and public deliberation? How are rights exercised within multilingual communities? How can they be extended as a part of an educational process? Can a greater place for multilingual literature and arts in the schools and communities support the idea of the nation and its schools as a place of meeting, of inquiry and exchange?

Or consider the new information technologies. These machines may be the mainstay of a knowledge-based global economy, but they can also be used to deliver on the national promise of democratic access and action. The question is then one of how this technology can further expand the public sphere, providing opportunities for greater awareness, understanding, and participation, on a national and global level. How, then, are students being prepared to take advantage of greater public access to government documents, and related research and policy analysis? How ready are they to utilize these new information sources to foster greater public deliberation and participation? Are there ways for these new information systems to extend democratic processes into the workplace and other walks of life?

To turn to my own struggle with these new technologies, for a moment, I am working with a team dedicated to improving the public value of research, as means of advancing the democratic basis of the nation. The Public Knowledge Project, as we call it, is exploring how our scholarly activities could do more to support the deliberative qualities of the democratic state and to extend this spirit of deliberation to more of our lives.[37] It is work that draws inspiration from Dorothy Smith when she advocates a social science "that would extend people's own good knowledge of the local practices and terrains of their everyday/everynight living, enlarging the scope of what becomes visible from that site, mapping the relations that connect one local site to another. Like a map it would be through and through indexical to the local sites of people's experience, making visible how we are connected into the extended social ruling relations and the economy."[38] The Public Knowledge Project's challenge is to situate and support this large and unwieldy body of research so that people can readily connect local understandings and ruling relations. Smith offers a helpful guiding principle for this work when she allows that, "though some of the work of inquiry would be technical, as making a map is, its product could be ordinarily accessible and usable as a map is" (p. 95).

Yet we also realize that simply creating access to this body of knowledge will not be enough. As Smith insists, "knowledge must be differently written and differently designed if it is bear other social relations than those of ruling" (p. 94). Our belief is that we can actually facilitate a greater public engagement with research and researchers in the social sciences; it is bound to change how research is conducted and written, encouraging, for example, a greater concern with the coherence and connection with not only research studies but with work going on within that greater public realm, as researchers begin to see how the work they do can better serve those whom they would help. Bringing this social sciences research to bear on national debates over First Nations rights, immigration, education, and social welfare is, of course, only one potential playing field for this work. But my point is that the nation offers both opportunity and motive when it comes to a rethinking of how it has positioned who-belongs-where, in schools and out, in ways that work decidedly against its democratic aspirations.

One reason for this concern that we work more directly on exploring democratic processes is the notable loss of faith and confidence in the democratic governments of Europe, North America, and Japan over the last three decades.[39] We may be bowling alone now (which is totally understandable to me, at least, given those bowling-team shirts), but we are also far better informed and ready to act on that information, if only in the areas of health, finance, sports, and comparison shopping.[40] Surely, there are political lessons to be learned from this knowledge economy. Consider this declaration of independence from October 6, 2000: "A revolution . . . has occurred. You won. Never before have individual[s] . . . had the power and access they have today. Information and opportunities previously available only to large institutions and the very wealthy are now in the hands of the people—in your hands." It does sound like a renewed sense of the political state. But, of course, it's from a two-page spread for E*TRADE, guided by the fundamental democratic principle, "It's your money."

Let us at least imagine an education system that prepared students with "information and opportunities previously available only to large institutions and the very wealthy" that supported their participation in a nation largely concerned with democratic deliberation. As we think of democracy as an ongoing experiment, then here is, perhaps, a chance to work afresh with how it is served by the nation-state. Here is a chance to see if education within democratic nations, once it is far less absorbed in questions of nationality and national identity, can do more for the exercise of public reason. The historical and present lessons that we learn within this national forum, in defense of minority rights, on the art of political compromise, and in setting up checks and balances, can then be applied to full and very wide range of political demarcations that we now face, which might, in one instance, be focused on neighborhood efforts to extend green spaces or, in another, on global initiatives to counter sweatshops.

The modern nation-state has a history that we are by no means done with yet. It will take more than all of the cyber-hype of globalization to sweep away such history. But then I am not keen on having us rush into becoming citizens of the world—as easily distracted as we are by all that glitters—at least not before we have finished learning how to be citizens of this earlier democratic experiment of such promise. The nation is not, then, to be discarded. It is, however, ready to be moved along, if not into a higher state, then into being less of a state of being and more of a place where we gather to recognize what we owe each other and this land. It begins with challenging our own seemingly natural perceptions of who-belongs-where. It means calling ourselves on this need to constantly position others, to fix them as we ourselves would not be fixed, by such categories as nationality with all of its racial overtones. The nation is no small habit of mind, but one that is reinforced daily by school and media. But if the mind needs ready ways of organizing the world, by labeling the parts and people, then we need to study how those labels work with and against what we want of the world. We need to challenge and check those habits of mind, seeking to reduce their dour consequences.

This is why we, as educators, need to take hold of this idea of the nation, calling its current state into question in our research and with our students. We need to ask how our work can advance the idea of the state, against the nation, as far more of a political forum and civil space concerned with the making of local and larger worlds. We need to better understand how the nation-state can facilitate and structure a fair and cooperative agreement among people to work and live together, as well as how it can do a better job, as a democratic force, of mediating between local and global concerns. We have too often taken the nation as a given, as a singular force that shapes history and identity. The modern nation, as an enlightened and enlightening association of people who have agreed to work together on improving the quality and degree of self-governance, has all along been within our reach and responsibility. We readily recognize the need to ensure that the nation-state delivered a greater part of its promise, a greater part of our hopes for it. What follows, then, is a need to consider how our work will open the places in which we live, changing the very ideas of the nation in the process, to a greater concern with the free and democratic association among people.

Notes

* An earlier version of this essay appeared as "The Nation-State after Globalism," *Educational Studies* 15 (2001). This work has benefited from both the work of and helpful discussions with Kara Macdonald and Airini, and was supported, in part, by the Peter Wall Institute of Advanced Studies at the University of British Columbia.

1. B. Crossette, "Canada Tries To Define Line Between Human and National Rights," *New York Times* (September 14, 2000): A11.

2. John Tomlinson, *Cultural Imperialism* (Baltimore, MD: Johns Hopkins University Press, 1991), p. 175.

3. See Anthony D. Smith, *National Identity* (Reno, NE: University of Nevada Press, 1991) for a detailed discussion of the elements of national identity.

4. In acting on the nation out of a regard for something larger, Amy Gutman cites Martin Luther King Jr. speech opposing the Vietnam War, in which he speaks of "us who deem ourselves bound by allegiances and loyalties which are broader and deeper than nationalism and which go beyond the nation's defined goals and positions . . ."; *Democratic Education* (Princeton, NJ: Princeton University Press, 1999), p. 310.

5. Ernest Gellner, *Nations and Nationalism* (Oxford: Blackwell, 1983), p. 125.

6. Sunera Thobani, "Closing Ranks: Racism and Sexism in Canada's Immigrant Policy," *Race & Class* 42: 1 (2000): 34.

7. Gutman, *Democracy and Education*, p. 11.

8. The liberal principles of free association and informed consent among equals gathered together to protect the rights and liberties of all are secured in the Western tradition through Locke and Mill: "That which begins and actually constitutes any political society," John Locke held, as the very voice of reason in the seventeenth century, "is nothing but the consent of any number of freemen, capable of majority, to unite and incorporate into such a society," in *Of Civil Government: Two Treatises* (London: J. M. Dent, 1924, originally 1690), p. 166. Or as John Stuart Mills had it nearly two centuries later: "The ideally best form of government is that in which the sovereignty, or supreme controlling power in the last resort is vested in the entire aggregate of the community every citizen not only having a voice in the exercise of that ultimate sovereignty, but bring at least occasionally, called on to take an actual part in the government, by the personal discharge of some public function, local or general." Mills, John Stuart, "Of Representative Government," in *Utilitarianism, Liberty and Representative Government* (London: Dent, 1910, originally 1861), p. 207.

9. Ernest Renan, "What is a Nation?" in *Narration and Nation*, ed. H. K. Bhabha (New York: Routledge, 1990, originally 1882), p. 11.

10. Partha Chatterjee, *The Nation and Its Fragments* (Princeton, NJ: Princeton University Press, 1993), p. 6.

11. Partha Chatterjee, *Nationalist Thought and the Colonial World* (Delhi: Oxford University Press, 1986), p. 170.

12. Nearly three decades ago, Walker Connor estimated that only a very small portion of nation-states—he put it at 10%—come even close to lining up with a single ethnicity; "Nation-Building or Nation-Destroying?" *World Politics* 24 (1972): 319–355. This move toward the civil state is also been picked up by Jean-Marie Guéhenno, France's ambassador to the European Union, "The nation is no longer camouflage for the tribe, but a political space in which democracy can be constructed"; *The End of the Nation-State* (Trans. V. Elliott). (Minneapolis: University of Minnesota Press, 1995), p. 3.

13. For examples in history, geography, science, language, and literature, see my *Learning to Divide the World: Education at Empire's End* (Minneapolis: University of Minnesota Press, 1998).

14. Amartya Sen, "East and West: The Reach of Reason," *New York Review of Books* (2000, July 20): 36.

15. It would also be misleading to overlook the non-Western influences on what we take to be Western thought, as George Siuoi's (1992), for example, demonstrates Amerindian influences on the democratic thinking of Rousseau, Diderot and others; *For an Amerindian Autohistory: An Essay in the Foundations of a Social Ethic*, Trans. S. Fischman (Montreal: McGill-Queen's University Press, 1992). See also Tu Wei-Ming's

analysis of Confucian thought: "It seems reasonable that one can endorse an insight into the self as a basis for equality and liberty without accepting Locke's idea of private property, Adam Smith's and Hobbe's idea of private interest, John Stuart Mill's idea of privacy, Kierkegaard's idea of loneliness, or the early Sartre's idea of freedom"; *Confucian Thoughts: Selfhood as Creative Transformation* (Albany, NY: SUNY Press, 1985), p. 78.

16. Mohammed Bamyeh, *The Ends of Globalization* (Minneapolis: University of Minnesota Press, 2000), p. 2.

17. Ibid., *Ends of Globalization*, p. 24. Also see Arif Dirlik (1996) on the local organizations as a source of hope against global forces; "The Global in the Local," in *Global/Local: Cultural Production and the Transnational Imaginary*, ed. R. Wilson and W. Dissanayake (Durham, N.C.: Duke University Press, 1996).

18. 1998, p. 237.

19. Cohen, 2000, p. WK1.

20. Khan, 2000, p. A6.

21. 2000, p. 25.

22. I discuss these issues of the public sphere elsewhere, in *If Only We Knew: Increasing the Public Value of Social Science Research* (New York: Routledge, 2000), pp. 195–220; *Technologies of Knowing: A Proposal for the Human Sciences* (Boston: Beacon, 1999), pp. 126–152. See also Craig Calhoun (ed.), *Habermas and the Public Sphere* (Cambridge, MA: MIT Press, 1992).

23. Martha Nussbasum, "Patriotism and Cosmopolitanism," in *For Love of Country: Debating the Limits of Patriotism*, ed. J. Cohen (Boston: Beacon, 1996), p. 7.

24. Martha Nussbasum, *Women and Development: The Capabilities Approach* (Cambridge, UK: Cambridge University Press, 2000).

25. Nussbaum, "Patriotism and Cosmopolitanism."

26. Michael Walzer, "Spheres of Affection," in *For Love of Country: Debating the Limits of Patriotism*, ed. J. Cohen (Boston: Beacon, 1996); Hilary Putman, "Must We Choose between Patriotism and Universal Reason," in *For Love of Country: Debating the Limits of Patriotism*, ed. J. Cohen (Boston: Beacon, 1996).

27. Nussbaum, "Patriotism and Cosmopolitanism," p. 14. However, the recent evidence drawn from the Los Alamos National Laboratory indicates otherwise, at least for the FBI, U.S., Department of Justice and *New York Times*, in the case of Wen Ho Lee. On September 26, 2000, the *New York Times* published extraordinary critical appraisal of its own handling of the Wen Lo Hee case, in which Lee was charge with multiple counts of mishandling U.S. atomic secrets, allegedly betraying them to China (p. A2).

28. Although I am only examining the national aspect in this paper, I have considered the blend elsewhere "Curriculum after Culture, Race, Nation," *Discourse: Studies in the Cultural Politics of Education* 20: 1(1999): 89–112.

29. In this province, the study of the nation, as an idea, formally takes place in grade 9 social studies in which students, in the course of studying Europe and North America, 1500–1815, are expected to "define colonialism, imperialism, and nationalism; analyze factors that contribute to revolution and conflict; and analyze the contributions of the English, French, and American revolutions in the development of democratic concepts." Prescribed Learning Outcomes, Grade 9, B.C. Ministry of Education, available at http://www.bced.gov.bc.ca/irp/curric/sslo810/lo2.htm.

30. Merry M. Merryfield, "Moving the Center of Global Education: From Imperial World Views that Divide, The World to Double Consciousness, Contrapuntal Pedagogy, Hybridity, and Cross-Cultural Competence," in *Social Studies: Research, Priorities and Prospects*, ed. W. B. Stanley (Greenwich, CT: Information Age Publishing, in press).

31. In introducing a recent book on globalization and education, Nicholas Burbles and Carlos Torres warn that if public education ignores globalization, "it runs the risk of becoming increasingly superseded by educational influences that are no longer accountable to public governance and control," to which they add (open to the misreading that the current nation-state is what needs to be protected) that "in our view, nothing less is at stake than the survival of the democratic form of governance and the role of public education in that enterprise"; "Globalization and Education: An Introduction." In *Globalization and Education: Critical Perspectives*, ed. Nicholas Burbles and Carlos Torres (New York: Routledge, 2000), p. 23.

32. William I. Robinson and Jerry Harris, "Toward a Global Ruling Class: Globalization and the Transnational Capital Class," *Science and Society* 64: 1 (2000): 11–54.

33. Linda Basch, Nina Glick Schiller, and Cristina Szanton Blanc, *Nations Unbound: Transnational Projects, Postcolonial Predicaments and Deterritorialized Nation-States* (Basel: Gordon and Breach, 1994), p. 4.

34. This reference to the need for roots is borrowed from Simone Weil, whose work on this topic I deal with elsewhere; "The Educational Politics of Identity and Category," *Interchange* 29: 4 (1998b): 385–402.

35. W. E. B. Du Bois, *The Soul of Black Folk* (Harmondsworth, UK: Penguin, 1989, originally 1903).

36. Norton, 2000.

37. See Willinsky, *If Only We Knew*, and the Public Knowledge Project, available at http://pkp.ubc.ca.

38. Dorothy Smith, "The Ruling Relations," *Writing the Social: Critique, Theory, and Investigations* (Toronto, ON: University of Toronto Press, 1999), pp. 93–94.

39. S. J. Pharr, Robert D. Putman, and R. J. Dalton, "A Quarter Century of Declining Confidence," *Journal of Democracy* 11: 2 (2000): 5–21.

40. The bowling hypothesis, which addresses a more general decline in civic participation, is found in Robert D. Putman, *Bowling Alone: The Collapse and Revival of American Community* (New York: Simon and Schuster, 2000).

Chapter 4 ~

Culture, Postmodernity, and Education: oil_H$_2$O@no.com

Blane R. Després

> Nostalgia is . . . an important theme within the question of the limits of post-modernization; the quest for the local, the contextual and the everyday represents a quest for a point of security within a world characterized by an incomprehensible plethora of viewpoints, lifestyles, modes of discourse and opinions. (Turner, 1994, 207)

This chapter is about postmodernity as an artifact of culture and its arguable paradoxical relation to formal education, equally an artifact and deliberate endeavor of culture. My intent is to probe the possibility that postmodernism and formal education are incompatible. Culture, of course, plays an influential role in both. That incompatibility is located in a series of apparent paradoxes from within culture in general and in light of challenges from within the postmodernist mind-set. In the end, I comment on the ensuing challenges and considerations for educators, policy makers, and theorists.

In at least the majority of years that I taught before reading Maurice Gibbons's, *The Walkabout Papers* (1990), I was struck more and more by the process of formal education, or schooling, and its intensity (certainly not its *adventure*). In that time, I sought ways and means of enlivening the practice of teaching, particularly my practice of teaching, and of making the process more "learner friendly" without degrading the content of teaching or the purpose of learning. Altering evaluation techniques, teaching cooperatively, field trips, and personal projects are all important and satisfying, but only to a limited extent. For myself, I was caught between having to deliver course content within a managed time frame and wanting to be able to help students address more practical issues, like how philosophy or science or French as a second language might possibly be helpful or practical for life situations or even in a time of crisis. Adults are quick to ask such "practical" questions. Why should adolescents be deprived of the same consideration? Is it because of the Curriculum? Or is it really a question of dominant cultural pressure? And what of the postmodern influence on society and, eventually, education?

But there are problems working from the postmodern foundation that mitigate against hopeful synthesis. Rosenau (1992), in her work on postmodernism and its interplay in the social sciences, and sounding faintly like Sartre (and Hegel before him), states, "[w]ithout any standard or criteria of evaluation post-modern inquiry becomes a hopeless, perhaps even a worthless, enterprise" (p. 136). With that as a possible reality, education might be transformed by reform projects but plausibly in a direction that business or governments or even dominant culture might not willfully accept or anticipate. After all, alternative standards may develop as cultural shifts create new directions and vying hegemonies, postmodern or otherwise. The postmodern bent toward fluid norms—there are supposedly no absolutes—leaves sociocultural shifting as at least one norm.

In the first place, public education demands a practical cultural solidity, both epistemologically and morally. In a judicial case of 1980 between a school student and the district school board concerning freedom of speech, the judge concluded, "the community has a legitimate, even a vital and compelling interest in the choice of adherence to a suitable curriculum for the benefits of our young citizens" (Macmillan, 1998, 12). Macmillan claims that the result of this case was to provide "a license to indoctrinate" (p. 12). Such public demands are also necessary if one is to raise concerns or expectations for reform.[1] The paradox here is to be found in the dominant culture's demand for certain ends (e.g., quality, content, utility, marketability, reasonable return for tax-dollars spent on public education, or preparation for employment, "suitable curriculum") and that culture's presuppositional framework. In other words, how can education be expected to deliver when the foundations of the dominant culture's mandates shift like twilight shadows, when what is determined to be culturally right is challenged and even altered, whether through media or social revolutions? If the legacy of philosophical constructs within the secularist's closed system of thinking/responding is that all is temporal and in the process of "phase-shifting," then it would appear that Western society has wandered sufficiently afar to stumble into the Eastern mystical camp. Alas, perhaps *maya* is the problem: the illusion, the simulacra, and not so much the unraveling of paradoxes as their being subsumed into one; but the unnerving of educators who want—no, demand—a reality that is both knowable and immutable.

So long as discussions about education—a cultural event as much as it is a social one—continue to function from within the present closed system of thinking, the rhetoric of reform, from whatever ideological stance, will never break the bonds of solipsisms. The closed system of thinking I am referring to is one that begins from a merely human conception of what constitutes reality (Enlightenment, modernist, postmodernist, or whatever). Such a closed system is not relegated to any particular historio-cultural hegemony or its counter challenges. Whether patriarchal, Western, Eastern, Afrocentric, feminist, homosexual, or religious, such closed systems afford no foundational beginning point from which to draw sufficient or necessary conclusions.

That is, I believe, the essence of the postmodern challenge and, to make a value judgment, it is a good challenge. It foregrounds the hypocrisy of the Enlightenment ideology of *homo sapiens* as *homo mensura. Solo homo sapiens (scientia)* is not the maker of meaning (in any final sense), but simply the purveyor of myths, metaphors, and meanings. On these points it seems most readers could agree with postmodernism.

This preamble on the old debate about closed systems—versus systems open to being acted in and upon by an external, and imminent, source—is not just about debate or postmodern challenges. In fact, my purpose for this brief introduction of sorts is to position myself, to draw some points together and to set the parameters for the ensuing discussion about culture and education, particularly some ramifications. In the end, I hope to demonstrate that aspects of postmodernity are, paradoxically, compatible but incommensurable with much of education.[2]

Culture as Paradoxes

Any given culture is essentially a peculiar narrative, a mythos, that unites individuals by adopted assumptions and practices, and that is generally resistant to change.[3] In a sense that could be summed up as "culture narratives." That differs from the "social" which, in the context of this thesis at least, is the collective and contractual, or political, arrangements among people inhabiting a common area. Those "arrangements" can change very rapidly.[4] Culture operates as a predominantly chauvinistic attitude and includes a multiplicity of subcultures, or interest groups, that are socially tolerated, and encouraged or rejected by others. "Culture" functions as the theoretical framework for a national social group. For example, theoretically there is a dominant or overriding culture that is determinably Canadian, one that is American, Japanese, French, and so on.[5] There are also subcultures, or those subsets of dominant culture in any social sphere. Examples would include techno-babes, skinheads, rock-band groupies, political party affiliates, regional quirks, religious affiliations (secular humanist, atheist, Protestant, Catholic, cultic), clubs, blue-collar workers, academics, and professionals. Also, while there is a national culture that distinguishes one geographic social group from another, there is also a popular culture that animates a large segment of any national culture and that may even transcend national boundaries. Popular music is an example that, although there may be regional peculiarities, is able to move transnationally, whether classical, rock, or operatic.

Over the course of time and through collective experiences or challenges, culture narratives can become altered. Some of them even become unstable and collapse, such as the culture narratives of the Greeks and their gods, or the Nordic tribal culture narratives, or the culture narratives of the French Revolution or Russian communism. This organic nature of culture narratives runs into conflict with educational ideals from time to time. The 1960s are just one example of a culture narrative in turbulent flux.

The various threads, or issues, presented above are indicative of various dilemmas. Those dilemmas present a number of paradoxes. In terms of culture, various paradoxes clutter media, the judicial system, national issues, on into the personal. Paradoxes will include, for example, the desire for national identity but tolerance of conflicting heritages, or improved standards and accountability in education but reduction in funding, or public cry for increased medical benefits while the government reduces services, and so on. A specific example can be drawn from a fairly recent

Canadian judicial decision permitting Sikh's to wear turbans and a ceremonial knife while serving as Royal Canadian Mounted Police officers thereby challenging the traditional hat long accepted as a functional while cultural icon.

At the same time, the dominant culture claims relativity and private passion about existence while demanding allegiance to its own brand of absolutes, the hypocrisy of which feeds into a new brand of culture. Out of the narcissistic bent of some subcultures[6] rises a harder conscience toward moral obligation. For example, youths band together—called swarming—and, like frenzied hyenas on a kill, beat, kick, and head-stomp another youth. Adults express horror or exasperation at a generation gone mad, but what are the parents doing? Do they really know where their children are (physically, intellectually, spiritually)? And schools demand timeliness, completion of tasks, preparation for work, respect for authority, others and of property. In other words adolescents are expected to look good, be productive, and act civilly.

Meanwhile a series of messages bombards youth ever so succinctly but not so subtly: commitment, fidelity, and honor are relics of modernity; psychobabble and politspeak are of greater practical value because these achieve results that further personal and preferred social causes; truth is what you make it provided you follow the proper psychobabble and politspeak; violence is the message, so is adolescent indifference; extreme violence is normal, according to various media, after all they kill babies in the womb, so why not kill them when they're just a bit older; "school sucks," but so does home; parents don't care, why should anyone else?; "philosophy is useless, theology is worse";[7] there is no God, therefore anything goes, provided you're willing. Bryan Turner (1994), in his work on culture and postmodernity's influences, understands the message stating that:

> Critical theorists like Adorno and Marcuse saw the development of mass culture and the culture industry as a threat to the authenticity of cultural distinction. The consequence of their rejection of mass culture was paradoxical in that there was a convergence between conservative and critical responses to the mechanization of artistic production, growth of a culture industry and the global impact of mass popular culture. *Postmodernism can be seen as an extension of this mixing of high and low culture. Indeed, postmodernism is a celebration of these changes.* (p. 205, emphasis added)

Paradox Lost

It is unfortunate that the humanities have assimilated architecture's postmodern concepts for their own purposes. It is unfortunate because some critical features have been forsaken that would benefit the discussion. Take for example the fact that even though architecture has thrown down the challenge against the long-standing formats that dominated architecture, nevertheless skepticism was selectively applied to only certain aspects of the formalism in the profession. Although postmodern buildings have been built in the meantime, that architect would be a short-lived professional and fool to design a structure without following principles of load and design characteristics. Also, a building without a proper foundation would be hazardous to peoples' life, and although some designs might purposefully assault others' tastes, it would be asinine to suggest a building design be completely "inappropriate" for the setting. Adobe buildings with loose-fitting doors and windows and flat roofs, then, would be unsuitable for most northern climates where snow load and rainfall are major considerations regardless of how much the architect or builders might desire the "statement."

All that makes sense in the practical sciences. But within the humanities, features once considered foundational have become included in the debate. The debate, of course, is about certainty, whether about life or events in life. Actually that is not completely fair. The debate also includes, and very much in the forefront, *selective* certainty. Whereas Huston Smith (1982) suggests that the "Modern Mind is flat . . . [but] the Postmodern Mind . . . is blurred and amorphous" (p. 232), it would seem more relevant to liken the postmodern mind to the mysterious seas that transported the ships across the "flat earth" in the quest for new lands. The marked difference, however, is that there is no real quest in postmodernism in the sense of something being objectively there, as in the "New World." It should be obvious that the Vikings and Columbus did not set out on the high seas for a Sunday afternoon sail or just to see more sea. Similarly the Russian and U.S. inquisitiveness about outer space is directly linked to an overt acceptance of an objective reality that exceeds our personal biospheres.

Part of postmodernism's dilemma is its paradoxical rejection of some certainties in favor of others.[8] The most blatant preferential certainty is the one concerning totalizing systems or thought. In other words, postmodernism claims with some certainty that any totalizing system or thought must be suspect. Postmodernism, like any thought system, becomes psychosocially influential to the degree that members of a culture assimilate its tenets. The academic community of higher education has much to do with the dissemination of ideas, old or recycled. In the case of postmodernism, the key tenets include skepticism toward recorded history, toward philosophy, and the rejection of totalizing systems of thought—including postmodern. All expressions of human thought and wisdom, even from down through the ages, are recast as textual narratives with no single account supposedly worthy of particular privileging or foregrounding. Hence truth is merely a peculiar narrative account of no particular significance, and seen as valuable, but a temporary textual repose in the progression of humanity.

While postmodernism on the one hand haughtily proclaims criticism of *homo sapiens'* attempt to determine and justify meaning, it does so at the peril of its own foundational structure through its suspicion of virtually everything. The paradox is noted in Norris's (1993) comments on postmodernism where he states in his dissection of postmodernism,

if the texts of philosophy are indeed just that—an assortment of rhetorics, favoured vocabularies, subliminal metaphors and covert "allegories of reading"—then clearly this offers a welcome opportunity for people in departments of English or Comparative Literature to get up on their overweening colleagues down the corridor. And it also raises the more important question as to whether philosophers can go some way with the "linguistic turn", that is to say, the currently prevailing view that issues of language, meaning and representation are inseparable from questions of truth, reason and right understanding, while at the same time resisting the "textualist" drift toward

a standpoint of extreme cognitive skepticism or an allout [*sic*] deconstructive rhetoric of
tropes. (p. 183)

Cultural expression is played out as a kind of sophisticated understanding and
defense of the world. The impact of postmodern skepticism has to at least raise the
eyebrows of those outside academe. The influence on social structures may have
frightening results. Indeed, if the postmodern critic is correct—and of course who is
to say—then life, reality, true truth, ethics, theories of education, and the dominant
culture, teaching styles, class sizes, among a host of particulars, can ever and only be
a matter of personal preference whose support strength is associated with numbers in
authority. Thus educational reform in the form of Goodlad's (1986) structural suggestions, Giroux's (1995) or Freire's (1974) systemic revolution, or Sergiovanni's
(1987) or Bacharach and Shedd's (1989) administrative considerations become part
of Norris's "rhetoric of tropes": a smorgasbord of linguistic delights whose champions
are the like-minded and those willing to strike out. Strike and Soltis (1992) ask
whether this leads to total skepticism, whether, for example,

> the difference between the Hitlers of the world and decent people is merely that they
> have different preferences? . . . Interestingly, even skeptics and ethical relativists, when
> they are trying to decide what to do rather than being theoretical and philosophical,
> seem to be willing and able to consider ethical arguments. How do they do this? In our
> everyday thinking we and they do not simply treat ethical matters as arbitrary . . .
> Moreover, we often appear to succeed. Are we simply deluded? (p. 9)

Paradoxically, tolerance is touted in the postmodern world, especially in academic
circles, but the walk is clearly "louder." The selectively tolerable is the tolerated. The
dilemma is not that we cannot all be right, or that some, by the simple process of
noncontradiction, will be marginalized or bracketed out. The dilemma is what is
truly true and how we know. Postmodernism denies that anyone can know with certainty, or that there is objective truth (amongst a number of notions). But, as Terry
Eagleton and Norris have already noted, such posturing really amounts to alternative
dogmas, and ones that marginalize.[9] In the end, postmodern skepticism does more
than just leave us with a discussion about narratives; it effectively eradicates all meaningful communication for there is no foundation of certainty that what is being communicated, or attempting to be communicated, is anything more than the
nonsensical tropes of a mad man. The argument leads me to recall Nietzsche's mad
man and his nihilistic conclusion. Are we to simply conclude that everything is just a
matter of personal belief? Is all that remains just Nietzsche's mad man and his nihilistic conclusion? And is belief, or some leap of "faith," a matter of ultimate hedonistic
ends? Shall we plea-bargain certainties?

On the issue of belief, Roger Simon (1992) wonders:

> To suggest that education is a moral and political enterprise raises at least two central
> questions that must enter into deliberations as to how one should formulate one's
> responsibilities as a teacher. The first is what the moral basis of one's practice should
> be . . . What are the *desired versions* of a future human community implied in the ped-
> agogy in which one is implicated? The second is, given our own moral commitments,

how should we relate to other people who also have a stake and a claim in articulating future communal possibilities? (p. 15, emphasis added)

Simon's first question is a critical matter. What are the "desired versions," or version? What with the multiplicity of views, whether cultural, philosophical, or non-sensical espoused (selective) tolerance of *différence*, and postmodernists' skeptical stance toward history, authority, and truth claims, or metanarratives, how does one confidently make a move toward a legitimate "version"? Do we discard "legitimate"? And, concerning how we should "relate to other people," who is to say, and who determines to what end(s)?

Postmodernism threatens the theoretical framework of culture. The skeptical ends of postmodernism potentially undermine key functions of the dominant culture. Education is bound to be affected as the dominant culture gradually becomes subsumed by the (anti)philosophy of postmodernism via media and the humanities departments of academic institutions.[10] It is the absence of the postmodern, even the modern and positivistic, concerns in parts of the field—perhaps even the critical parts of the field—that should give alarm. What with Cuban's (1984) observance that little, really, has changed in schooling, what hope is there that postmodernists could herald a positive reform of anything? On what grounds, to what end, and what's the point?

Living in Paradox

The "adventure" of education remains largely defined by culture, and it is also confined by the cultural. And perhaps I should add education *could* be an adventure. As the setting for mere enculturation along the lines of the utilitarian thrust of governmental curricula, or the training ground for social transformation according to the likes of Freire (1974) or Giroux (1995), education *is* a function of the cultural: definitively, practically, and presumptively. Education is defined both by the cultural and by the dominant culture. Therein lies another paradox of sorts. The dominant culture—that dominant social, presupposed understanding that is accepted more or less as common by a controlling interest group—legislates the general curriculum and typically even the parameters for locally developed courses. Practically, schools tend to be built on primarily economic reasons housing large numbers of adolescents and not according to research findings. The underlying assumption that directs education is that it is structured wholly by government agency (dominant culture) and guarded by and large by a disinterested public.[11]

But education transcends culture, too. In its raw definition as personal learning, education is about individual intellectual, moral, and emotional development. In that sense it exists across the planet, across cultures, across economic spheres of influence, and regardless of the current epistemological thrust of the dominant culture. Nonetheless, because of education's umbilical connection with politics and economics—both in the larger dominant culture and in the culture of the school itself—education remains a hostage within the confines of the cultural (and cultural here is defined by a number of different variables, such as politics and economics, business, administration, community involvement, teachers, and students). I say "hostage" because it is not a reciprocal arrangement: culture is not influenced by education.[12] If education is to provide a basis for success (in a broad sense of the term) for graduates—whether utilitarian employability or for lifelong learning—then there has to be in place a means of understanding the difference between what is truly good and what is truly evil. Otherwise how are we to be assured about what is being taught, developed as curriculum, and perpetrated on society?

In another paradox of sorts, formal education or schooling remains a *non*-adventure. Least ways that is what one could draw from writings in education over the past twenty years (see, e.g., Becher, 1992; Cuban, 1984; Gibbons, 1976, 1990). An example is drawn from Cuban citing one teacher who observed, "traditional teaching approaches drive students into boredom. If we were ever to teach sex the way we teach other things . . . it would go out of style" (p. 176). The opportunity for the individual student to deal effectively or to learn to deal effectively with a personal issue or interest is generally left to the counseling department or administration. There is little room left in the already crowded timetable and particular curricula for teaching students other skills that will be, in many respects, more practical in day to day living now let alone in adulthood. And the opportunity to do so with the view in mind that education is fun, exciting, an adventure, is not the practice of schooling. In that context, then, education is little more than narrow training that revolves around—does not stray from—the Curriculum.

Formal education tends to be dominated by an emphasis on academics where the substance of learning is overshadowed by preparation for assessment. Gibbons (1990) argues that there are, among others, three "tendencies in schooling[:] . . . the tendency to cultivate failure, isolation and confusion. In the traditional paradigm [i.e., schooling] all learning leads to the test and its proven success in it. . . . While tests create pressure to learn, they primarily serve the needs of management and create serious downside risk for the learning of many students" (p. 147). He also suggests that:

> Education *designed* as a continuous lifelong process requires an approach to teaching and learning suitable for such a long-range perspective. If we acknowledge education as designing resources for development—a strategic array of experiences, activities, relationships, and training to supplement normally available resources for growth—then we must view learning as the desire and ability to use those resources. (p. 29, emphasis added)

Notice the paradoxes there. Education implies learning. I would even argue that it implies adventure, which one sees easily enough in the eagerness of young children. Yet, schooling so relegates adventure to the extracurricular that "education" is lost, replaced with preparations for tests, for university, and for institutional conformity. The dominant culture demands education, fosters *status quo*, sways with insatiable desires to be amused (see Collins and Skover, 1996), and demands reform.

Paradox is also found in teaching where, according to Andy Hargreaves (1993), teachers are isolationistic and individualistic due to the nature of schooling with its "chambers" and one teacher per *N* students, where there is little recourse to professional dialogue between fellow teachers, and where there is a system that does not foster ongoing professionalism.[13] What becomes of the problem can only hope to be compounded as public funding decreases, class sizes increase, the dominant culture places more demands on educators, and general material resources become scarcer. Added to that is the potential influence of postmodern thinking.

Another consideration of the teaching paradigmatic paradox is pronounced by Bacharach (1988) who challenges, "if schools are going to help disadvantaged students, teachers need "skills in responding to students' life experiences, purpose, and perspectives. To the degree that standardization inhibits these efforts, an argument can be made that standardization only provides an illusion of equality and an obstacle to equity" (p. 494). In a similar vein, Eisner (1983) comments:

> Attention to the sensibilities in schooling has always been a low priority. The senses are supposedly bodily functions, somehow unconnected to the mind. Feeling, or awareness of qualities, is supposed to rely upon soma, and educational experience is supposed to deal with psyche. The break between mind and body is further legitimated by the reification of cognition and affect. We tend to regard the former as linguistically mediated thought—kind of inner thought—and the latter as feelings that need no help from mind or intelligence. (p. 53)

Cuban (1984) notes that one explanation for teaching practice as it is/has been is the

> occupational ethos of teaching that breeds conservatism and resistance to change in institutional practice. This conservatism, i.e., preference for stability and caution toward change, is rooted in the people recruited into the profession, how they are informally socialized, and the school the dominant culture of which teaching itself is a primary ingredient. (p. 243)

One possible reason for these observed peculiarities is found in Bacharach and Shedd (1989) who capture the essence of Giroux's (1983) thesis and Hargreaves's (1993) later observations in their consideration of power and empowerment. They determine that:

> Time schedules, physical structures, one-teacher-per-class staffing patterns and high teacher/administrator ratios make day-to-day contact with other adults haphazard . . . Norms of "non-interference" discourage the asking and offering of advice . . . *Curriculum policies*, [including efforts to reform education] *if they do not square with a teacher's judgment of what his or her students need or are capable of learning, often go unobserved and unenforced.* (p. 146, emphasis added)

For all the conflict, or Marxist theories (Agger, 1992; Blackledege and Hunt, 1985), functionalist theories (Mifflen and Mifflen, 1982; Turner and Maryanski, 1979), or their neo-counterparts, and curriculum theories, students continue to be processed in institutions that, by and large, structurally exhibit the viewed worth of the individual (Agron, 1993; Toll, 1991), teachers continue to be both directed externally by bureaucracy and internally by experience and personal interests, and theorists continue to offer social, political, and philosophical explanations for the nature and functions of schooling and society. In the end, what is the effect of theories? And does postmodernism become an issue if there is no discernable effect? Does the dominant culture really want adolescents to know more or better, or be prepared for "productive maintenance" in society? Is lifelong learning really a desirable focus of education? Does not the postmodern stance of skepticism even challenge those seemingly worthwhile endeavors? That is where the paradox becomes lost. It becomes lost in the cacophony of voices or narratives that are all that arguably remain in a postmodern culture. Paradoxically, there is no more paradox in postmodernism, just a myriad of voices, a sea of curriculum, and a variety of practices.

The paradox—that the excitement of education is stifled by the weight and practice of schooling, and of the dominant culture—is the ongoing paradox. And for all the writings and findings of researchers and reformist challenges, there are no radical departures from the *status quo*, the norm. Schooling continues. Adolescents continue to leave school without a sense of accomplishment or readiness for what comes next (see, e.g., Bibby, 1990; Steele, 1992). Perhaps as postmodernism influences education, paradoxes will drift into fractal silences by which I mean without an objective reference point to undergird what is, then what is becomes silenced by the weight, and wait, of that cataclysmic final end. Does making meaning mean nothing more than meandering thoughts momentarily attracting attention here only to dissolve into another meaningless venture into the long drift of cosmic silence?

Paradox/ologies

Imagine if Nietzsche and Sartre are both right; it is only people living in denial, who refuse their conclusions, who want to have security even at the risk of living in an irrational universe. By this I mean simply that people in Western societies refuse to accept meaninglessness as the outcome of existence in the universe and as a conclusion of theorists arguing within the confines of a self-imposed closed system. Although the rhetoric exists about the sum total of existence as meaningless, my experience is that people still speak quite meaningfully and with varying degrees of emotional investment.

However, meaninglessness is a real function and acceptable outcome of some Eastern philosophies. Perhaps it is only a temporary discomfort intellectually as academe shifts from the dominant Western mind-set to the East, as it appears to be doing. In that case, education becomes supremely simplified: lifelong learning is but the pursuit of transcending the illusory; a kind of deliberate awakening to the divine within and the one with all; acquiescence to or transcendence of subliminal simulacra.

That perhaps raises this argument to a new level, to a kind of plain of transference, of discarding the old and donning the "new." It is critical here to raise the question of whether or not—given the upheaval, or the social dis-ease prevalent in Western societies—there is a movement afoot to restructure what we know to accommodate a more Eastern construct. Although that would demand more time to examine the ground of transition, that has serious repercussions for the whole argument and discussion about culture, postmodernism and culture, and particularly about education.

Given the flight of postmodernism, Turner's (1994) final statement is worthy of reflection. Although his thesis deals principally with limited theistic matters, his conclusion that, "In short, we are confronted by the postmodernization of polytheism" (p. 208) has some application for this essay. That is, the "postmodernization of polytheism" makes sense if it is acknowledged that the acceptance of the multiplicity of views that postmodernists imply really amounts to a tolerance of many points of allegiance. Because allegiance requires an object of preference, and because postmodernism un/wittingly extends particular preferences to the theoretical constructs and thought systems that are more inclusive than exclusive, it becomes apparent that those systems whose *pan*-inclusiveness are treated most favorably. This is certainly a case in some discussions when Christian theistic principles, for example, are applied in secular settings. Although general principles are acceptable (tolerated)—such as "be a good Samaritan"—as soon as the discussion moves to include absolutes, or true truth, the exclusive nature of the Christian message seems rejected as somehow evil or naive. Some Eastern teachings are tolerated, however, as representing (supposedly) greater inclusiveness. Because one can argue the practical necessity of all stances/beliefs having a reference point, that reference point effectively becomes a "god" or a focal point of allegiance upon which rests one's frame of identity and reference. With that in mind, the supposed inclusiveness of Eastern philosophy—of pantheism—would appear to slip easily into the postmodern coat of many colors. The "polytheism," then, is suitable in this discussion in so far as it is acknowledged that postmodernism has many gods, or reference points, with no one theoretically privileged more than the other.

A myriad of questions arise. For example, from an Eastern vantage point, there are questions about how a curriculum of illusion could be developed; there is the ethics of dealing with people bent on alternative views of the universe, or what a theory, or theories, of education might look like based on *maya*, and what a teacher education program would consist of in such a scenario. Such is the stuff of further debate and discussion. Although I am suspicious that there is the potential to slide into Eastern mysticism via postmodern skepticism, I am cautious at this point and merely raise a red flag.

In the meanwhile, academe, it would seem from some camps, would have history reviled, Christianity repudiated,[14] the overthrow of anything "white," embracing soft anarchy in the guise of feminisms, Afrocentricism, or homosexualism arguably as a social reprieve against "Western Eurocentricity." What does that leave for public education: select ethnocentricity, gynocentricity, animicentricity, *pan*centricity? Dominant culture wants and demands standards and accountability, but with a conflicting reciprocating effort on its social part, something is bound to give. For example, Postman (1996) believes that "the idea of a '*public* school' is irrelevant in the absence of the idea of a public; that is, Americans are now so different from each other, have so many diverse points of view, and such special group grievances that there can be no common vision or unifying principles" (p. 196).

Endpoints

Postmodernism does not offer culture an improved viewpoint or starting place to begin to discuss the implications for education. Postmodernism in fact betrays an internal incommensurability with education. To bring together the parts of this essay into a somewhat conclusive finale, postmodernism, with its instability as a mainstay mode of making meaning and its decidedly *a priori* naturalistic frame of reference, betrays its incommensurability with formal education in at least the following areas:

(1) As stated at the outset, formal education is a function of specific direction, showing its roots in, and influence from, the scientific method. That runs contrary to postmodernism's antistatic, antiscientific method.

(2) Formal education has changed practically imperceptibly in over a century despite cultural influences. Postmodernism eschews rigid formalism, both structurally and practically.

(3) Postmodernism rejects totalizing. Formal education presents on going totalization through curriculum, testing, and institutional entrance requirements.

(4) Postmodernism assumes no absolutes. Formal education likewise espouses a soft relativism, but practically demonstrates rigid guidelines that serve as absolutes (as in no. 3 above, e.g.).

(5) Postmodernism seeks multiple paths to understanding. Formal education accepts only one: the curriculum of the dominant culture.

(6) Postmodernism leans toward a more constructivist approach to knowledge and meaning making. Formal education leans toward a more hierarchical and imperialistic approach (see Willinsky, 1998).

But where does that leave the impact that postmodernism is bound to have on education? Contemplating Frederic Jameson (1995) in the following quote, it would appear to be another paradox of sorts. He states:

> As for the postmodern revolt . . . it must be stressed that its own offensive features— from obscurity and sexually explicit material to psychological squalor and overt expressions of social and political defiance, which transcend anything that might have been imagined at the most extreme moments of high modernism—no longer scandalize anyone and are not only received with the greatest complacency but have themselves become institutionalized and are at one with the official or public culture of Western society. (p. 4)

Apart from speculating, it seems reasonable enough to assume that as academic institutions become more and more impregnated with postmodern thinking—or variations of it, and as teacher education program instructors become more and more influenced by postmodernists, more and more new teachers will infiltrate education with postmodern attitudes. This in turn will have effects on the way education is "done." But, having said that, given the structure of schooling (institutionalized formal education) and its resistance to change, and given the cultural changes— influenced as they are by social forces, postmodernism is likely to be just another in a series of systems of social critique that further erodes public and personal confidence.

Postmodernism, then, is theoretically incompatible with education as much as it is with much or all of living. Jameson (1995) opines:

> But if Michael Speaks is right, and there is no pure postmodernism as such, then the residual traces of modernism must be seen in another light, less as anachronisms than as necessary failures that inscribe the particular postmodern project back into its context,

while at the same time reopening the question of the modern itself for reexamination. (p. xvi)

It is postmodernism strained, mixed, and altered that finds its way into education and cultural settings; it is, once again, the personal dimension that decides the utility, or extent applied, of postmodern thought. For educators, policy makers, and theorists, postmodernism stands as much of an intellectual challenge as previous philosophical systems have. Kantian ethics, Judeo-Christian relationship, Nietzschean nihilism, Eastern mysticisms, all cause us to think and to question. Rather paradoxically, postmodernism no less has some very useful questions that could challenge the practice of education such that it would be an adventure. Or the theorists could acknowledge that the rhetoric of postmodern thinking undercuts even itself, and that one cannot escape the bounds of reason any more than one can escape oneself. And policy makers could rework education from the ground up such that people who happen to be adolescents would begin to be treated with a new priority over and above economics and management.

Notes

1. The content could easily change, but the necessity of the society to preserve itself leads naturally to the inculcation of certain preferred values.
2. The clarity of what I want to say is, I hope, to come.
3. Ben Agger (1992) defines *culture* as anthropological and demonstrated as "any expressed activity contributing to social learning," versus "high culture, or a more academic understanding or fostering" (p. 2). Dick Hebdige (1993), on the other hand, states that, "Culture is notoriously ambiguous" (p. 359) echoed in Homi Bhabha's (1994) statement that, "it is the 'inter'—the cutting edge of translation and negotiation, the *in-between* space—that carries the burden of the meaning of culture" (p. 38; italics in original). Andrew Milner (1994), in apparent agreement with Hebdige, claims that culture "has become a theoretical problem . . . because it is already socially problematic" (p. 4), by which he means it is nigh impossible to accurately pinpoint a precise definition of *culture*. Additionally, Roslyn Arlin Mickelson, Sumie Okazaki, and Dunchun Zheng (1995) speak of society comprising "a cultural model or folk theory that serves as a framework for interpreting the world" (p. 88). For Frederic Jameson (1995), there is another dimension to consider: "American, postmodern culture is the internal and superstructural expression of a whole new wave of American military and economic domination throughout the world: in this sense, as throughout class history, the *underside of culture is blood, torture, death, and terror*" (p. 5, emphasis added).
4. The difficulty of culture and social understandings at this point is that the discussion wants to engage further clarifications and arguments; all important, but not the message that is key in this thesis. Of course any culture can be influenced or radically altered by social forces in a relatively brief time frame. Examples are evident throughout history (e.g., the French Revolution, Stalin's takeover of Russia, or the globalization of the Internet). Meanwhile the older adherents, or those with greater "investment," tend not to be so radically moved.
5. At the same time, however, culture lacks a unified theory, or as Andrew Milner claims, "Cultural theory is, in fact, one of the central discontents of our civilization" (1994: 4). In other words, and as has been noted, culture is a vague representation, or sign, of a peculiar group of persons.

6. See e.g., Collins and Skover (1996).
7. Mark Knophler (1982) *Industrial Disease*. Dire Straits, *Love Over Gold*, Phonogram, London.
8. I acknowledge here the writings of Christopher Norris, Terry Eagleton, and David Dockery, and many discussions in helping me to clarify my understanding of postmodernism.
9. Fairlamb (1994) likewise deals with the epistemological question, but from a liberal perspective and still from within a naturalist framework.
10. The fallout can be seen in considering just these examples: It is rather difficult to conduct practical science with an attitude of supreme skepticism or an antitotalizing spirit. As someone has asked, would you take your car to a deconstructionist mechanic? In a similar vein, who would risk a trip to the moon if the space vehicle, trajectory, and calculations had been done by a staunch believer in antihistory? Or who would be the first to get on an airplane piloted by an avowed nihilist?
11. The suggestion that the public is disinterested is predicated on the paradoxical demand by the (anonymous) public for quality and accountability in education and the reluctance of the public to become educated about alternative learning possibilities or about educators as other than blue-collar workers. "Public" here includes government, parents, and educators in particular.
12. See Marshall and Tucker (1992), for example, who claim that education in the United States—and I would offer in Canada as well—is "finishing" students ready for a workplace of 50 years ago. (See note 11.)
13. Some will obviously counter with Professional Development in-service days at teachers' disposal along with conferences. Listening to teachers in "Pro-D" days, at conferences and in the staff room over the course of 20 years has lead me to agree with and confirm Hargreaves's observation.
14. Interestingly enough, Buddhism, or the New Age's *Celestine prophecy*, or spiritual practices of First Nations people, and even pagan worship appear to be acceptable alternatives, even in academic circles of discussion. Perhaps "progressive postmodernism"—or the notion that postmodernism is advancing, improving, and maturing—is a better concept to employ in this discussion; that way, at least, there is a *sense* of hope (without admitting hope since that would be to admit at least one metanarrative, although Eagleton (1996) has already exposed the postmodernist myth of metanarrative neutrality, but that is another story).

References

Agger, Ben. (1992). *Cultural Studies as Critical Theory*. Bristol, PA: Falmer.

Bacharach, Samuel B. "Four Themes of Reform: An Editorial Essay." *Educational Administration Quarterly* 24:4 (1988): 484–496.

Bacharach, Samuel B. and Shedd, Joseph B. (1989). *Power and Empowerment: The Constraining Myths and Emerging Structures of Teacher Unionism in an Age of Reform*. In *The Politics of Reforming School Administration*, ed. J. Hannaway and R. Crowson. London: Falmer, pp. 139–160.

Becher, R. (1992). *The Aesthetic Classroom Environment and Student Attitude Toward Education*. Ed.D. Dissertation: University of Missouri.

Bhabha, Homi. (1994). *The Location of Culture*. London: Routledge.

Bibby, Reginald W. (1990). *Mosaic Madness*. Toronto: Stoddart.

Collins, Ronald K. L. and Skover, David M. (1996). *The Death of Discourse*. Boulder, Co: WestviewPress.

Cuban, Larry. (1984). *How Teachers Taught: Constancy and Change in American Classrooms, 1890–1980*. New York: Longman.

Eagleton, Terry. (1996). *The Illusions of Postmodernism*. Oxford: Blackwell.

Eisner, Elliot W. (1983). "The Kind of Schools We Need." *Educational Leadership*, October, 48–55.

Fairlamb, H. L. (1994). *Critical Conditions: Postmodernity and the Question of Foundations*. New York: Cambridge University Press.

Freire, Paulo. (1974). *Pedagogy of the Oppressed*. New York: The Seabury Press.

Gibbons, Maurice. (1976). *The New Secondary Education*. Bloomington, IN: Phi Delta Kappa.

Gibbons, Maurice. (1990). *The Walkabout Papers*. Vancouver: EduServ.

Giroux, Henry. "Ideology and Agency in the Process of Schooling." *Journal of Education* 165:1 (1983): 12–34.

Giroux, Henry A. (1995). "Teachers as Public Intellectuals." In *Teaching: Theory into Practice* ed. A. C. Ornstein. Mass: Allyn & Bacon, pp. 373–384.

Goodlad, John I. (1986). "A New Look at an Old Idea: Core Curriculum." *Educational Leadership*, December, 8–16.

Hargreaves, A. (1993). "Individualism and Individuality: Reinterpreting the Teacher Culture." In *Teachers' Work: Indivduals, Colleagues, and Contexts*, ed. J. W. Little and M. W. McLaughlin. New York: Teachers College Press, pp. 51–76.

Jameson, Frederic (1995). *Postmodernism or, the Cultural Logic of Late Capitalism*. Durham: Duke University Press.

Macmillan, C. J. B. "The Inevitability of Indoctrination." *Educational Foundations*, 12:1 (1998): 7–15.

Marshall, Ray and Tucker, Marc. (1994). *Thinking for a Living: Work, Skills, and the Future of the American Economy*. New York: BasicBooks.

Mickelson, Roslyn Arlin, Okazaki, Sumie, and Zheng, Dunchun. (1995). "Reading Reality More Carefully Than Books: A Structural Approach to Race and Class Differences in Adolescent Educational Performance." In *Transforming Schools*, ed. Peter W. Cookson, Jr. and Barbara Schneider. New York: Garland, pp. 81–105.

Mifflen, Frank J. and Mifflen, Sydney C. (1982). *The Sociology of Education: Canada and Beyond*. Calgary, Alberta: Detselig Enterprises.

Milner, Andrew. (1994). *Contemporary Cultural Theory: An Introduction*. London: University College London Press.

Norris, Christopher. (1993). *The Truth About Postmodernism*. Oxford: Blackwell.

Postman, Neil. (1996). *The End of Education: Redefining the Value of School*. New York: Alfred A. Knoph.

Rosenau, Pamela M. (1992). *Postmodernism and the Social Sciences*. Princeton, NJ: Princeton University Press.

Sergiovanni, T. J. (1987). The School as a Political Organization. In *Educational Governance and Administration* (2nd edition). Englewood Cliffs, NJ: Prentice Hall, pp. 180–203.

Simon, Roger (1992). *Teaching Against the Grain: Texts for a Pedagogy of Possibility*. New York: Bergin & Garvey.

Steele, Douglas Lee. (1992). *Profile of the School Dropout: Perceptions of the Early School Leaver*. Doctoral dissertation, Texas A. and M. University.

Turner, Bryan S. (1994). *Orientalism, Postmodernism & Globalism*. New York: Routledge.

Turner, Jonathan H. and Maryanski, Alexandra. (1979). *Functionalism*. California: The Benjamin/Cummings Publishing Company.

Willinsky, John. (1998). *Learning to Divide the World: Education at Empire's End*. Minneapolis: University of Minnesota Press.

Chapter 5

Critical Pedagogy in the Age of Neoliberal Globalization

Peter McLaren

The Crisis of the Educational Left in the United States

Part of the problem faced by the educational Left today is that even among the most progressive educators there appears to exist an ominous resignation produced by the seeming inevitability of capital, even as financial institutions expand capacity in inverse proportion to a decline in living standards and job security. It has become an article of faith in the critical educational tradition that there is no viable alternative to capitalism. When class relations are discussed, they are not talked about in the Marxist sense of foregrounding the labor/capital dialectic, surplus value extraction, or the structure of property ownership, but instead refers to consumption, lifestyle politics, theories of social stratification in terms of access to consumption, or job, income, and cultural prestige. The swan song for Marxist analysis apparently occurred during the intellectual collapse of Marxism in the 1980s after the Berlin Wall came crashing down and along with it a bipolar imperialist world. Capitalism was loudly proclaimed to be the victor over socialism. The globalization of capital was to be the savior of the world's poor and powerless. But as it is now known, its function, far from supplicatory or transitive, has been deadly alienating. Gobbling up the global lifeworld in the quest for an endless accumulation of surplus value, capital has produced some world-historical excretory excesses, turning the world into a global toilet of toxic waste while adding legions to Marx's reserve army of labor. The cutbacks in government expenditure on health, education and housing investment, the creation of shantytowns in urban industrial areas, the concentration of women in low-wage subcontracted work, the depletion of natural resources, the rampant de-unionization, the growth of labor discipline, the growth of temporary and part-time labor, the pushing down of wages and the steady decline of decent working conditions have proceeded apace but the rule of capital is not challenged, only its current "condition." In Russia today, the *prikhvatizatisiya* (grabitization) that has been bequeathed to the masses by a kleptocratic capitalism that dragged itself out of the carrion house of economic shock therapy has led to "blitzkrieg liquidations," the destruction of industry, the disappearance of health benefits and housing, the slashing of salaries, and the transfer of wealth to a dozen or so private owners who now commandeer one public property. As poverty shifts from 2 to 50 percent, Western free-market fundamentalists keep reminding the Russians how awful it must have been to live under communism. Western countries that had established their economic fiefdoms by protecting key industries and subsidizing some domestic producers continue to preach the gospel of free trade and deregulation to other countries. Even when the messianic monopoly fantasies of Enron, WorldCom, and Global Crossings CEOs end in bankruptcy disasters that shake the very pillars of the marketplace, the belief in the sanctity of the market remains undisturbed. Capital stealthily hides behind Nietzsche's veil, maintaining its secret of reversibility—that its economic assistance to the Third World reproduces underdevelopment and ensures the continuity of dependency.

The belief that there is no alternative to capitalism had pullulated across the global political landscape before the fall of the Soviet Union and the Eastern Bloc, attaching itself like a fungus to regional and national dreams alike. The winds of the Cold War had spread its spores to the farthest reaches of the globe. After laying dormant for a decade, these spores have been reactivated and have seemingly destroyed our capacity to dream otherwise. Today most nations celebrate capital as the key to the survival of democracy. Watered by the tears of the poor and cultivated by working-class labor, the dreams that sprout from the unmolested soil of capital are those engineered by the ruling class. Plowed and harrowed by international cartels of transnational corporations, free marketeers, and global carpetbaggers poised to take advantage of Third World nations in serious financial debt to the West, the seeds of capitalism have yielded a record-breaking harvest. The capitalist dream factories are not only corporate board rooms and production studios of media networks that together work to keep the capitalist dream alive, but a spirit of mass resignation that disables the majority of the population from realizing that capitalism and exploitation are functional equivalents, that globalization of capital is just another name for what Lenin (1951) termed imperialism. U.S. imperialism—what Tariq Ali (2002, p. 281) calls "the mother of all fundamentalisms"—has decamped from its Keynesian position of pseudo-liberalism to fully embrace a fanatical neoliberalism. The grand mullah of neoliberalism, Von Hayek, an avatar to both Thatcher and Reagan, favored military actions to defend U.S. interests abroad. On the domestic front he favored the invisible magic of a manipulated market. No state intervention against the interests of capital was to be tolerated. But the state was vital to undertake military operations in the sphere of international relations (Ali, 2002, p. 286).

Further, Von Hayek's neoliberal followers were staunch defenders of the Vietnam war. They supported the U.S. backed military *coup* in Chile. In 1979, Hayek favored bombing Tehran. In 1982, during the Malvinas conflict, he wanted raids on the Argentinian capital. This was the creed of neoliberal hegemony most favored by its founder (Ali, 2002, p. 286).

The fact that neoliberalism—the midwife to the return of a fanatical belief in non-state intervention into capital movements that was spawned by nineteenth-century libertarianism—has resoundingly defeated the bureaucratic state capitalism of the former Soviet "evil empire," has created a seismic shift in the geopolitical landscape. Michael Parenti grimly comments that the overthrow of the Soviet Union has abetted a reactionary "rollback" of democratic gains, public services, and common living standards around the world as the United States continues to oppose economic nationalism and autonomous development in Asia, Africa, and Latin America, primarily though debt payments and structural adjustment programs imposed by the World Bank and the International Monetary Fund. Particularly hard hit have been the so-called Third World countries. The Soviet Union's collapse has opened the political floodgates of U.S. imperialism, permitting the United States to pursue virtually uncontested an agenda of "arrogance and brutality." The United States is no longer faced with a competing superpower that imposed constraints on the dream of U.S. global dominance. He offers this disillusioned comment:

> The record of U.S. international violence just in the last decade is greater than anything that any socialist nation has ever perpetrated in its entire history. U.S. forces or proxy mercenary forces wreaked massive destruction upon Iraq, Mozambique, Angola, Nicaragua, El Salvador, Guatemala, East Timor, Libya, and other countries. In the span of a few months, President Clinton bombed four countries: Sudan, Afghanistan, Iraq repeatedly, and Yugoslavia massively. At the same time, the U.S. national security state was involved in proxy wars in Angola, Mexico (Chiapas), Colombia, East Timor, and various other places. And U.S. forces occupied Macedonia, Bosnia, Kosovo, and Afghanistan, and were deployed across the globe at some 300 major overseas bases—all in the name of peace, democracy, national security, counter-terrorism, and humanitarianism (2002, p. 44).

Today's international political economy is the toast of the global ruling class, and the bourgeoisie see it as their biggest opportunity in decades to join their ranks. Freemarketeers have been given the New World Order's *imprimatur* to loot and exploit the planet's resources and to invest in global markets without restriction with impunity. The menacing concomitant of capital's destructive juggernaut is the obliteration of any hope for civilisation, let alone democracy. While liberals are plumping for fairer distribution of economic resources, the working class are taught to feel grateful for the *maquiladoras* that are now sprouting up in countries designated to provide the cheap labor and dumping grounds for pollution for the Western democracies. They are taught that socialism and communism are congenitally evil and can only lead to a totalitarian dictatorship. In short, capitalism and the legitimacy of private monopoly ownership has been naturalized as common sense.

It is no longer just the capitalists who believe that they are the salvation for the world's poor, but the workers themselves have become conditioned to believe that without their exploiters, they would no longer exist. The entrails of the eviscerated poor now serve as divining mechanisms for the soothsayers of the investment corporations. Even many trade unions have been little more than adjuncts of the state, reimposing the discipline of capital's law of value. Those who wish to avoid both Communist-type centralized planning and the disequilibrium and instability of laissez-faire capitalism have turned to a type of market socialism through labor-managed firms, but doing little to challenge the deep grammar of capital itself.

Everywhere we look, social relations of oppression and contempt for human dignity abound. It is not that workers are being press-ganged to serve in the social factory; it is more like they are being made to feel grateful that they have some source of income, as meager as that may be. As the demagogues of capitalist neoliberal globalization spin their web of lies about the benefits of "global trade" behind erected "security" walls, protesters are gassed, beaten, and killed. As the media boast about the net worth of corporate moguls and celebrate the excesses of the rich and famous, approximately 2.8 billion people—almost half of the world's people struggle in desperation to live on less than US\$ 2 a day (McQuaig, 2001, p. 27).

The "free-market revolution," driven by continuous capitalist accumulation of a winner-take-all variety, has left the social infrastructure of the United States in tatters (not to mention other parts of the globe). Through policies of increasing its military–industrial–financial interests, it continues to purse its quivering bourgeois lips, bare its imperialist fangs, and suck the lifeblood from the open veins of South America and other regions of the globe. The sudden collapse of the Soviet Union in the 1990s and the shift to capitalism in Eastern Europe has brought nearly 5 billion people into the world market. The globalization of capitalism and its political bedfellow, neoliberalism, work together to democratize suffering, obliterate hope, and assassinate justice. The logic of privatization and free trade—where social labor is the means and measure of value and surplus social labor lies at the heart of profit—now odiously shapes archetypes of citizenship, manages our perceptions of what should constitute the "good society," and creates ideological formations that produce necessary functions for capital in relation to labor. Schools have been effectively transformed into holding pens where students exercise their everyday consciousness, assert their private interests, articulate their practical intentions, and dream their secret lives within given capitalist social relations and objective forms of thought that emerge from categories of bourgeois social economy, which themselves are bound up with the structural characteristics of stages of social development. The ideological formations intergenerationally reproduced within schools betray a pragmatic efficacy and validity of apologetic purpose as well as the fetishistic character of everyday thinking. Such formations help to orient students into an unreflexive acceptance of the capitalist social world. Of course, the accession into the social order has always been incomplete, always in process, in that there has always been a space between self-formation and its dismemberment. Critical pedagogy seizes upon this space as its major terrain of struggle.

As schools become increasingly financed more by corporations that function as service industries for transnational capitalism, and as bourgeois think-tank profiteerism and educational professionalism continues to guide educational policy and practice, the U.S. population faces a challenging educational reality. Liberals are calling for the need for capital controls, controls in foreign exchange, the stimulation of growth and wages, labor rights enforcement for nations borrowing from the United States, and the removal of financial aid from banking and capital until they concede to the centrality of the wage problem and insist on labor rights. However, very few are calling for the abolition of capital itself.

The commercialization of higher education, the bureaucratic cultivation of intellectual capital—what Marx referred to in the *Grundrisse* as the "general intellect" or "social brain"—and its tethering to the machinery of capital, the rise of industrial business partnerships, the movement of research into the commercial arena of profit and in the service of trade organizations and academic–corporate consortia, have garnered institutions of higher learning profound suspicion by those who view education as a vehicle for emancipation. In the hands of the technozealots, teachers are being re-proletarianized and labor is being disciplined, displaced, and deskilled. Teacher autonomy, independence, and control over work is being severely reduced, while workplace knowledge and control is given over more and more to the hands of the administration.

The educational Left is finding itself without a revolutionary agenda for challenging in the classrooms of the nation the effects and consequences of the new capitalism. Consequently, we are witnessing the progressive and unchecked merging of pedagogy to the productive processes within advanced capitalism. Education has been reduced to a subsector of the economy, designed to create cybercitizens within a teledemocracy of fast-moving images, representations, and lifestyle choices brought powered by the seemingly frictionlessness of finance capital. Capitalism has been naturalized as commonsense reality—even as a part of nature itself—while the term "social class" has been replaced by the less antagonistic term, "socioeconomic status." It is impossible to examine educational reform in the United States without taking into account continuing forces of globalization and the progressive diversion of capital into financial and speculative channels—what some have called "casino capitalism on a world scale."

Critical Education against Neoliberalism

William Robinson (2001) has made a convincing argument for the appearance of a transnationalist capitalist class. By employing a renewed historical materialist conception of the state in this current epoch of neoliberal globalization, Robinson is able to de-reify the state/nation-state in order to identify the social classes operating within formal state institutions and to analyze the constellation of social forces in cooperation and in conflict as they develop historically. Robinson argues for a conception of globalization that transcends the nation-state system. He has effectively reconceptualized the dominant Weberian conception of the state through a Marxist problematic as the institutionalization of class relations around a particular configuration of social production in which the economic and the political are conceived as distinct moments of the same totality. Here, the relation between the economy and states is an internal one. There is nothing in this view that necessarily ties the state to territory or to nation-states. While it is true that, seen in aggregate nation-state terms, there are still very poor countries and very rich ones, it is also true that poverty and marginalization are increasing in so-called First World countries, while the Third World has an expanding new strata of consumers. The labor aristocracy is expanding to other countries such that core and periphery no longer denote geography as much as social location. The material circumstances that gave rise to the nation-state, are, Robinson argues, being superceded by globalization such that the state—conceived in Marxist terms as a congealment of a particular and historically determined constellation of class forces and relations (i.e., a historically specific social relation inserted into larger social structures)—can no longer simply be conceived solely in nation-state-centric terms. Robinson's argument—that a transnational state apparatus is emerging under globalization from within the system of nation-states—rests on the notion that the production process itself has become increasingly transnationalized as national circuits of accumulation become functionally integrated into global circuits. Neoliberal globalization is unifying the world into a single mode of production and bringing about the organic integration of different countries and regions into a single global economy through the logic of capital accumulation on a world scale. Nonmarket structures are disappearing as they are fast becoming penetrated and commodified by capitalist relations. Global class formation has involved the accelerated division of the world into a global bourgeoisie and a global proletariat. The transnationalized fractions of dominant groups have become the hegemonic fraction globally. Social group and classes are central historical actors rather than "states" as power is produced within the transnational capitalist class by transnationally oriented state-managers and the cadre of supranational institutions such as the World Bank, the World Trade Organization, the Trilateral Commission, and the World Economic Forum. Of course, there is still a struggle between descendant national fractions of dominant groups and ascendant transnational fractions. The class practices of a new global ruling class are becoming condensed in an emergent transnational state in which the transnational capitalist class have an objective existence above any local territories and polities. The purpose of the transnational ruling class is the valorization and accumulation of capital and the defense and advance of the emergent hegemony of a global bourgeoisie and a new global capitalist historical bloc. This historical bloc is composed of the transnational corporations and financial institutions, the elites that manage the supranational economic planning agencies, major forces in the dominant political parties, media conglomerates, and technocratic elites. This does not mean that competition and conflict has come to an end or that there exists a real unity within the emergent transnational capitalist class. Competition among rivals is still fierce and the United States is playing a leadership role on behalf of the transnational elite, defending the interests of the emergent global capitalist historical bloc.

Marxists have long recognized the dangers of the rule of capital and the exponentiality of its expansion into all spheres of the lifeworld. Today capital is in command of the world order as never before, as new commodity circuits and the increased speed of capital circulation works to extend and globally secure capital's reign of terror. The site where the concrete determinations of industrialization, corporations, markets, greed, patriarchy, technology, all come together—the center where exploitation and dominated is fundamentally articulated is occupied by capital. The insinuation of the coherence and logic of capital into everyday life—and the elevation of the market to sacerdotal status, as the paragon of all social relationships—is something that has successfully occurred and the economic restructuring that we are witnessing today offers both new fears concerning capital's inevitability and some new possibilities for organizing against it. Critical pedagogy is, I maintain, a necessary (but not sufficient) possibility.

Particularly during the Reagan years, hegemonic practices and regulatory forces that had undergirded postwar capitalism were dramatically destabilized. And it is an ongoing process. The halcyon days before the arrival of the New Leviathan of globalization—when liberal Keynesian policy-making established at least a provisional social safety net—have been replaced by pan-national structures of production and distribution and communication technologies that enable a "warp speed capitalism" of instant worldwide financial transactions. According to Scott Davies and Neil Guppy (1997), one of the central tenets of the neoliberal argument is that schools must bring their policies and practices in line with the importance of knowledge as a form of production. According to the neoliberal educationalists, schools are largely to blame for economic decline and educational reform must therefore be responsive to the postindustrial labor market and restructured global economy.

Business has been given a green light to restructure schooling for their own purposes, as the image of *homo economicus* drives educational policy and practice, and as corporations and transnational business conglomerates and their political bedfellows become the leading rationalizing forces of educational reform. Davies and Guppy argue that globalization has also led schools to stress closer links between school and the workplace in order to develop skills training, and "lifelong learning." In a knowledge-intensive economy, schools can no longer provide the skills for a lifetime career. This means that schools are called upon by the market-oriented educational thinkers to focus more on adult learners through enterprise-based training. And further, schools are called upon to teach new types of skills and knowledge.

It is growing more common to hear the refrain: "education is increasingly too important to be left to the educators," as governments make strong efforts at intervention to ensure schools play their part in rectifying economic stagnation and ensuring global competitiveness. And standardized tests are touted as the means to ensure the educational system is aligned well with the global economy. There is also a movement to develop international standardized tests, creating pressures toward educational convergence and standardization among nations. Such an effort, note Davies and Guppy, provides a form of surveillance that allows nation-states to justify their extended influence and also serves to homogenize education across regions and nations. School choice initiatives have emerged in an increasing number of nations in North America and Europe, sapping the strength of the public school system and helping to spearhead educational privatization.

Because capital has itself invaded almost every sphere of life in the United States, the focus of the educational Left has been distracted for the most part from the great class struggles that have punctuated this century. The leftist agenda now rests almost entirely on an understanding of asymmetrical gender and ethnic relations. While this focus surely is important, class struggle is now perilously viewed as an outdated issue. When social class is discussed, it is usually viewed as relational, not as oppositional. In the context of discussions of "social status" rather than "class struggle," techno-elite curriculum innovation has secured a privileged position that is functionally advantageous to the socially reproductive logic of entrepreneurial capitalism, private ownership, and the personal appropriation of social production. This neoliberal dictatorship of the comprador elite has resecured a monopoly on resources held by the transnational ruling class and their allies in the culture industry. The very meaning of freedom has come to refer to the freedom to structure the distribution of wealth and to exploit workers more easily across national boundaries by driving down wages to their lowest common denominator and by eviscerating social programs designed to assist laboring humanity. Territories that were once linked to national interests have given way to networks inscribed within world markets largely independent of any national political constraints. History, the economy, and politics no longer are bound together in a secure fashion but operate as if they constituted independent spheres. Yet behind this chimera of separation is the transnationalization of the means of production.

What should today's global educators make of the structural power embodied within new forms of today's transnational capital, especially in terms of the shift in the relation between nation-states and formerly nation-based classes, the scope of economic restructuring and its ability to erode the power of organized labor, and the extent to which global mass migrations pit groups in fierce competition over very scarce resources. William Robinson notes that the transnational elite has now been able to put democracy in the place of dictatorship (what can be called the neoliberal state) in order to perform the following functions at the level of the nation-state: adopting fiscal and monetary policies that guarantee macroeconomic stability; providing the necessary infrastructure for global capitalist circuitry and flows; and securing financial control for the transnational comprador elite as the nation-state moves more solidly in the camp of neoliberalism, while maintaining the illusion of "national interests" and concerns with "foreign competition." In fact, the concept of "national interests" and the term "democracy" itself function as an ideological ruse to enable authoritarian regimes to move with a relative lack of contestation toward a transformation into elite polyarchies. So many of the literary practices in today's schools are functionally linked to this new global economy—such as "cooperative learning" and developing "communities of learners"—and promote a convenient alliance between the new fast capitalism and conventional cognitive science. While these new classroom measures are helping to design and analyze symbols, they are also being co-opted by and facilitating the new capitalism.

Farewell to All That

These days it is far from fashionable to be a radical educator. The political gambit of progressive educators these days appears to silence in the face of chaos, with the hope that the worst will soon pass. There are not many direct heirs to the Marxist tradition among left educational scholars. To identify your politics as Marxist—especially in the slipstream of the recent terrorist attacks on September 11 and the bombastic odes to the military machine and the unilateral quest of the United States to create a New World Order that are now suffusing U.S. politics—is to invite derision and ridicule from many quarters, including many on the Left. It is to open one's work to all species of dyspeptic criticism, from crude hectoring to sophisticated Philippics. Charges range from being a naive leftist, to being stuck in a time warp, to being hooked on an antediluvian patriarch, to giving in to cheap sentimentality or romantic utopianism. Marxists are accused with assuming an untenable political position that enables them to wear the mantle of the revolutionary without having to get their hands dirty in the day-to-day struggles of rank-and-file teachers who occupy the front lines in the schools of our major urban centers. Marxist analysis is also frequently derided as elitist in its supposed impenetrable esotericism, and if you happen to teach at a university your work can easily be dismissed as dysphoric ivory tower activism—even by other education scholars who also work in universities. Critics often make assumptions that you are guilty of being terminally removed from the lives of teachers and students until proven otherwise. Some of the criticism is productive and warranted but much of it is a desperate attempt to dismiss serious challenges to capitalism—to displace work that attempts to puncture the aura of inevitability surrounding global capitalism. While some of it is substantive—including a welcomed critique of the enciphered language of some academics and a challenge to radical educators to come up with concrete pedagogical possibilities—much of it is small-minded and petty. The beneficiaries of the current disunity among the educational Left are the business–education partnerships and the privatization of schooling initiatives that are currently following in the wake of larger neoliberal strategies.

Marxist educationalists maintain that neoliberal ideology as it applies to schooling is often given ballast by poststructuralist–postmodernist/deconstructive approaches to educational reform because many of these approaches refuse to challenge the rule of capital and the social relations of production at the basis of the capitalist state. Neoliberalism ("capitalism with the gloves off," or "socialism for the rich") refers to a corporate domination of society that supports state enforcement of the unregulated market, engages in the oppression of nonmarket forces and antimarket policies, guts free public services, eliminates social subsidies, offers limitless concessions to transnational corporations, enthrones a neomercantilist public policy agenda, establishes the market as the patron of educational reform, and permits private interests to control most of social life in the pursuit of profits for the few (i.e., through lowering taxes on the wealthy, scrapping environmental regulations, and dismantling public education and social welfare programs). It is undeniably one of the most dangerous politics that we face today.

Neoliberal free-market economics—the purpose of which is to avoid stasis and keep businesses in healthy flux—functions as a type of binding arbitration, legitimizing a host of questionable practices and outcomes: deregulation, unrestricted access to consumer markets, downsizing, outsourcing, flexible arrangements of labor, intensification of competition among transnational corporations, increasing centralization of economic and political power, and finally, widening class polarization. As Dave Hill and Mike Cole (2001) have noted, neoliberalism advocates a number of procapitalist positions: that the state privatize ownership of the means of production, including private sector involvement in welfare, social, educational, and other state services (such as the prison industry); sell labor-power for the purposes of creating a "flexible" and poorly regulated labor market; advance a corporate managerialist model for state services; allow the needs of the economy to dictate the principal aims of school education; suppress the teaching of oppositional and critical thought that would challenge the rule of capital; support a curriculum and pedagogy that produces compliant, pro-capitalist workers; and make sure that schooling and education ensure the ideological and economic reproduction that benefits the ruling class. Of course, the business agenda for schools can be seen in growing public–private partnerships, the burgeoning business sponsorships for schools, business "mentoring" and corporatization of the curriculum (McLaren and Farahmandpur, 2001a, b), and calls for national standards, regular national tests, voucher systems, accountability schemes, financial incentives for high-performance schools, and "quality control" of teaching. Schools are encouraged to provide better "value for money" and must seek to learn from the entrepreneurial world of business or risk going into receivership. In short, neoliberal educational policy operates from the premise that education is primarily a subsector of the economy.

In this interregnum, in particular, where the entire social universe of capital is locked up in the commodity form, where capital's internal contradictions have created a global division of labor that appears astonishingly insurmountable, and where the ecological stakes for human survival have shifted in such seismic proportions, creating a vortex in which reactionary terrorism has unleashed its unholy cry, we lament the paucity of critical/pedagogical approaches to interrogating the vagaries of everyday life within capital's social universe.

In retrospect, progressive educators are often wont to ask: Were the 1960s the last opportunity for popular revolutionary insurgency on a grand scale to be successful? Did the political disarray of prodigious dimensions that followed in the wake of the rebuff of the post-1968 leftist intelligentsia by the European proletariat condemn the revolutionary project and the "productionist" metanarrative of Marx to the dustbin of history? Have the postmodernist emendations of Marxist categories and the rejection—for the most part—of the Marxist project by the European and North American intelligentsia signaled the abandonment of hope in revolutionary social change? Can the schools of today build a new social order?

A nagging question has sprung to the surface of the debate over schooling and the new capitalist order: Can a renewed and revivified critical pedagogy distinctly wrought by an historical materialist approach to educational reform serve as a point of departure for a politics of resistance and counter-hegemonic struggle in the twenty-first century? And if we attempt to uncoil this question and take seriously its full implications, what can we learn from the legacy and struggle of revolutionary social movements? The fact that Marxist analysis has been discredited within the educational precincts of capitalism America does not defray the substance of these questions. On the surface, there are certain reasons to be optimistic. Critical pedagogy has, after all, joined antiracist and feminist struggles in order to articulate a democratic social order built around the imperatives of diversity, tolerance, and equal access to material resources. But surely such a role, while commendable as far as it goes, has seen critical pedagogy severely compromise an earlier, more radical commitment to antiimperialist struggle that we often associate with the antiwar movement of the 1960s and earlier revolutionary movements in Latin America.

What does the historical materialist approach often associated with an earlier generation of social critics offer educators who work in critical education? I raise this question at a time in which it is painfully evident that critical pedagogy and its political partner and rough congener, multicultural education, no longer serve as an adequate social or pedagogical platform from which to mount a vigorous challenge to the current social division of labor and its effects on the socially reproductive function of schooling in late capitalist society. In fact, critical pedagogy no longer enjoys its status as a herald for democracy, as a clarion call for revolutionary praxis, as a language of critique and possibility in the service of a radical democratic imaginary, which was its promise in the late 1970s and early 1980s. Part of this has to do with the lack of class analysis evinced in its work, but it also is related to the general retreat of the educational Left in the United States over the last several decades.

Postmodernist Theory and the Disappearance of Class

It is impossible to disclose all the operative principles of critical pedagogy. Suffice it here to underscore several of its salient features. Critical pedagogy's basic project over the last several decades has been to adumbrate the problems and opportunities of political struggle through educational means. In is incoherent to conceptualize critical pedagogy, as do many of its current exponents, without an enmeshment with the political and anti-capitalist struggle. Once considered by the faint-hearted guardians of the American dream as a term of opprobrium for its powerful challenge to the bedrock assumptions characterizing the so-called U.S. "meritocracy," critical pedagogy has become so completely psychologized, so liberally humanized, so technologized, and so conceptually postmodernized, that its current relationship to broader liberation struggles seems severely attenuated if not fatally terminated. While its urgency was once unignorable, and its hard-bitten message had the pressure of absolute *fiat* behind it, critical pedagogy seemingly has collapsed into an ethical licentiousness and a complacent relativism that has displaced the struggle against capitalist exploitation with its emphasis on the multiplicity of interpersonal forms of oppression. The conceptual net known as critical pedagogy has been cast so wide and at times so cavalierly that it has come to be associated with anything dragged up out of the troubled and infested waters of educational practice, from classroom furniture organized in a "dialogue friendly" circle to "feel-good" curricula designed to increase students' self-image. Its multicultural education equivalent can be linked to a politics of diversity that includes "respecting difference" through the celebration of "ethnic" holidays and themes such as "black history month" and "Cinco de Mayo." I am scarcely the first to observe that critical pedagogy has been badly undercut by practitioners who would mischaracterize its fundamental project. In fact, if the term "critical pedagogy" is refracted onto the stage of current educational debates, we have to judge it as having been largely domesticated in a manner that many of its early exponents, such as Brasil's Paulo Freire, so strongly feared.

Arguably the vast majority of educationalists who are committed to critical pedagogy and multicultural education propagate versions of it that identify with own their bourgeois class interests. One doesn't have to question the integrity or competence of these educators or dismiss their work as disingenuous—for the most part it is not—to conclude that their articulations of critical pedagogy and multicultural education have been accommodated to mainstream versions of liberal humanism and progressivism. While early exponents of critical pedagogy were denounced for their polemical excesses and radical political trajectories, a new generation of critical educators have since that time emerged who have largely adopted what could be described as a pluralist approach to social antagonisms. Their work celebrates the "end of history" and the critique of global capitalism is rarely, if ever, brought into the debate. These pedagogues primarily see capital as sometimes maleficent, sometimes beneficent, as something that, like a wild stallion, can eventually be tamed and made to serve humanity. Marxism is seen from this perspective as a failed experiment and that the teaching of Marx should be put to rest since the persistence of capital appears to have rendered the old bearded devil obsolete. Apparently no one noticed—or cared to notice—that Marx had outwitted its Cyclopian capitalist foe by clinging to the underbelly of lost revolutionary dreams that have been herded out of the caves of the Eastern Bloc. After biding time for the last decade—a period that witnessed a particularly virulent example of capital's slash and burn policy—his ghost is reappearing in reinvigorated form in the West (at least among some members of the academic Left) where Marx is now seen to have anticipated much about the manner in which the current world-historical crisis of capitalism would manifest itself.

Authoritative as the term may sound, "critical pedagogy" has been extraordinarily misunderstood and misrepresented. To penetrate the glimmering veil of rhetoric surrounding it would require an essay of its own. Suffice it to say that it is an approach to curriculum production, educational policy-making, and teaching practices that challenges the received "hard sciences" conception of knowledge as "neutral" or "objective" and that is directed toward understanding the political nature of education in all of its manifestations in everyday life as these are played out in the agonistic terrain of conflicting and competing discourses, oppositional and hegemonic cultural formations, and social relations linked to the larger capitalist social totality. The critical pedagogy we are envisioning here operates from the premise that capital in its current organizational structure provides the context for working-class struggle. Specifically in the context of school life, capital produces new human productive and intellectual capacities in alienated form. In its U.S. variants, the genesis of critical pedagogy can be traced to the work of Paulo Freire in Brazil, and John Dewey and the social reconstructionists writing in the post-depression years. Its leading exponents have cross-fertilized critical pedagogy with just about every transdisciplinary tradition imaginable, including theoretical forays into the Frankfurt School of critical theory, and the work of Richard Rorty, Jacques Lacan, Jacques Derrida, and Michel Foucault. Here the focus has mainly been on a critique of instrumental reason and the nature of governmentality in educational sites. An emphasis has been placed on the nonconceptual in which thinking is constructed as a performance of ethics, or as a post-truth pragmatics, or as an open-ended, nondeterminate process that resists totalizing tropological systems (hence the frequent condemnation of Marxism as an oppressive totalizing metanarrative). Critical pedagogy's reach now extends to multicultural education, bilingual education, and fields associated with language-learning and literacy (including media literacy). My concern over the last five years has been to introduce Marxist scholarship into the field of critical pedagogy, since it has been taken over by postmodernists who have been attempting to suture together in recent decades the ontological tear in the universe of ideas that was first created when history was split in two by the dialectical wave of Marx's pen in the *Communist Manifesto* and the subsequent development of the communist movement in the mid-1800s. My own Marxism is informed by the philosophy of Marxist-Humanism, which posits, after Hegel, that forward movement emerges from the negation of obstacles. It is the negation of "what is" and a critique of the given that spurs development and creates the path to liberation. Absolute negativity occurs when negativity becomes self-directed and self-related to become the seedbed of the positive. According to *News and Letters*, a Marxist-Humanist publication, the key is the difference between the first and second negation—the two moments of the dialectic. The first negation is the negation of the given; it takes what appears positive, the immediate, and imbues it with negativity. The second negation, "the negation of the negation," turns the power of negativity upon the act of negation; it takes what appears negative and shows that it is the source of the truly positive (2002).

It is not my purpose here to develop an exegesis of Marxist-Humanism (one of dozens of identifiable schools of Marxist thought) but merely to draw attention to the ways in which the Marxist tradition has been woefully absent from critical pedagogy as it is engaged in the U.S. academy (i.e., in Colleges of Education or University Departments of Education)—an absence that has brought with it irreparable damage to the tradition of critical education. Unscrolling the present state of critical pedagogy and examining its depotentiated contents, processes, and formations puts progressive educators on notice in that few contemporary critical educators are either willing or able to ground their pedagogical imperatives in the concept of labor in general, and in Marx's labor theory of value in particular. This is certainly more the case in North American educational settings than it is in the United Kingdom, the latter context having had a much more serious and salutary engagement with the Marxist tradition in the social sciences, and in one of its professional offshoots: adult education.

In the United States, critical pedagogy has collapsed into Left liberal attempts by progressive educators to remediate the educational enterprise. This has resulted in a long list of reform initiatives that include creating "communities of learners" in classrooms; bridging the gap between student culture and the culture of the school; engaging in cross-cultural understandings; integrating multicultural content and teaching across the curriculum; developing techniques for reducing racial prejudice and conflict resolution strategies; challenging Eurocentric teaching and learning as well as the "ideological formations" of European immigration history by which many white teachers judge African American, Latino/a, and Asian students; challenging the meritocratic foundation of public policy that purportedly is politically neutral and racially color-blind; creating teacher-generated narratives as a way of analyzing teaching from a "transformative" perspective; improving academic achievement in culturally diverse schools; affirming and utilizing multiple perspectives and ways of teaching and learning; and de-reifying the curriculum and exposing "metanarratives of exclusion." Most of these pedagogical initiatives are acting upon the recommendations of the National Commission on Teaching and America's Future—a commission bent upon challenging social class and ethnicity as primary determinants of student success. And for all the sincere attempts to create a social justice agenda by attacking asymmetries of power and privilege and dominant power arrangements in U.S. society, progressive teachers have, unwittingly operated under the assumption that these changes can be accomplished within the existing social universe of capital. Critical pedagogy has been taken out of the business of class analysis and focused instead on a postmodernist concern with a politics of difference and inclusion that effectively substitutes truth for singular, subjective judgment and silences historical materialism as the unfolding of class struggle (Ebert, 2002).

The above is unavoidably a sweeping synthesis of the limitations of critical pedagogy in the North American context. The main bone of contention that I have with the direction of increasingly postmodernized critical pedagogy over the last several decades is its studied attempt to leave the issue of sexism and racism—that is, the politics of difference—unconnected to class struggle. Of course, this conveniently draws attention away from the crucially important ways in which women and people of color provide capitalism with its superexploited labor pools—a phenomenon that is on the upswing all over the world. E. San Juan (2002) sees the continuing racialization of the American national identity occurring in novel ways as long as citizenship is based on citizenship and individual rights are needed to legitimate private property and to further capital accumulation. Capitalism *is* an overarching totality that is, unfortunately, becoming increasingly invisible in postmodernist narratives that eschew and reject such categories *tout court*. Postmodernist educators tend to ignore that capitalism is a ruthless "totalizing process which shapes our lives in every conceivable aspect" and that "even leaving aside the direct power wielded by capitalist wealth in the economy and in the political state" capitalism also subjects all "social life to the abstract requirements of the market, through the commodification of life in all its aspects." This makes a "mockery" out of all aspirations to "autonomy, freedom of choice, and democratic self-government" (Wood, 1995, pp. 262–263).

In this fundamental regard, the voguish academic brigandism of educational postmodernists that gives primacy to incommensurability as the touchstone of analysis and explanation has diverted critical analysis from the global sweep of advanced capitalism and the imperialist exploitation of the world's laboring class. Their pedagogically distilled animosity toward Marxism is no secret. This is not the time to evaluate the jousts between Marxists and postmodernists for the spoils of the critical edition (see Hill et al., 2004). Suffice it to say that in the years that "difference politics" have taken hold of the Left, the rich are getting richer and the poor even poorer in every part of the globe.

Critical Pedagogy: Contemporary Challenges

Critical pedagogy has had a tumultuous relationship with the dominant education community both in North America (McLaren, 1997) and the United Kingdom (Allman, 1999, 2001a) for the past twenty-five years. Clearly, on both sides of the Atlantic, the educational community has been aprioristically antagonistic to Marxist critique, effectively undercutting the development of Marxist criticism in education. Much of the current attempts to muster a progressive educational agenda among education scholars in suffused with an anticommunist bias. Only occasionally is the excessive rejectionism of Marxism by postmodern educationalists accompanied by analysis; rarely is it ever accomplished beyond the level of fiat. To borrow a commentary that Barbara Foley (1998) directs at the post-Marxism of Laclau and Mouffe, "it conflates politics with epistemology in an irrevocably linked chain of signifiers: the authoritarian party equals class reductionism equals logocentricity; totality equals totalitarianism."

I do not wish to rehearse this decidedly potted history here in any great detail, and as such will forgo a prolegomenon about critical pedagogy, since a polycondensation of its attributes will serve little purpose other than adding cumbersomely to its growing theoretical weight or rehashing what I assume most progressive educators already know or about which they at least have some working idea. Suffice it to say that in the mid-1970s to mid-1980s the role of critical pedagogy was much more contestatory than in the decade of the 1990s with respect to dominant social and economic arrangements. Critical pedagogy has always had an underground rapport with the working class, a rapport that virtually disappeared post-1989. In contrast to its current incarnation, the veins of critical pedagogy were not in need of defrosting in the early 1980s but were pumped up with Marxist-inspired work coming from the Birmingham School of Contemporary Cultural Studies, as well as a reengagement with the work of John Dewey, Paulo Freire, and the Frankfurt School. During that time, critique flowed generally unimpeded and were directed not just at isolated relations of domination but at the totality of social relations. That it was often conflated with liberation theology in Latin America and with anti-imperialist struggle worldwide accounts for its failure to be preconised in the cultural chambers of the ruling elite. My major point here is that the debates over educational reform are far richer today when seen through the palimpsest of Marxist critique. Marxist critique serves as a counterpoint to the subversive acts of the proto-Foucauldians-and- Derrideans, who, garbed in theoretical attire of Ninja academics, relish in foot-sweeping the metaphysics propping up the "totalitarian certainties" of the Marxist problematic, dismembering "totalities" by inworming them and opening them up to multiple destinies other than those circumscribed by Marx. The point is not that the gallery-hoping titans and fierce deconstructors from the postmodern salons have not made some important contributions to a fiene-de-siecle politics, or that they have not exerted some influence (albeit proleptically) in the arena of radical politics, but that, in the main, their efforts have helped to protect the bulwark of ruling-class power by limiting the options of educational policy in order to perpetuate the hegemony of ruling-class academics. Their herniated ideas have made for good theater, but their words have often turned to ashes before leaving their mouths. They have not left educators much with which to advance a political line of march within a theoretical framework capable of developing an international strategy to oppose imperialism.

Our own practices—what Paula Allman (2001a) has christened "revolutionary critical pedagogy"—ups the radical ante for progressive education which, for the most part over the last decade, has been left rudderless amidst an undertow of domesticating currents. It ups this ante by pivoting around the work of Karl Marx, Paulo Freire, and Antonio Gramsci and in doing so brings some desperately needed theoretical ballast to the teetering critical educational tradition. Such theoretical infrastructure is necessary, we argue, for the construction of concrete pedagogical spaces—in schools, university seminar rooms, cultural centers, unions, social movements, popular forums for political activism, and the like—for the fostering and fomenting of revolutionary praxis.

While it certainly remains the case that too many teachers take refuge in a sanctuary of assertions devoid of critical reflection, it would be wrong to admonish the educational activism of today as a form of pedagogical potvaliancy. Courageous attempts are being made in the struggle for educational reform on both sides of the Atlantic. In this case, we need to be reminded that the lack of success of the educational Left is not so much the result of the conflicted sensibilities of critical educators, as it is a testament to the preening success of Western Cold War efforts in indigenizing the cultural logic of capitalism, the fall of the Eastern Bloc nonprofit police states, and the degradation and disappearance of Marxist metanarratives in the national-popular agendas of decolonizing countries. It can also be traced to the effects of the labor movement tradition, which keeps labor-Left educators struggling inside the labor/capital antagonism by supporting labor over capital, rather than attempting to transcend this divide entirely through efforts to implode the social universe of capital out of which the labor/capital antagonism is constituted.

Clearly, critical pedagogy is checkered with tensions and conflicts and mired in contradictions and should in no way be seen as a unified discipline. My purpose in this essay is not to develop a comprehensive perspective on or programmatic architectonic of critical pedagogy, something that has already been accomplished in the works of Paula Allman and others. My more modest purpose therefore is to uncoil some of the conceptual tensions that exist in linking up the concept of critical pedagogy to that of class struggle. In doing so I wish to rehearse a number of provision points: (1) a sense of what constitutes critical agency and revolutionary praxis, and (2) a nuanced notion of what liberation means at this particular historical juncture.

My approach to understanding the relationship between capitalism and schooling and the struggle for socialism is premised upon Marx's value theory of labor as developed by British Marxist educationalist, Glenn Rikowski, and others (see Cole et al., 2001). In developing further the concept of revolutionary critical pedagogy and its specific relationship to class struggle, it is necessary to repeat, with a slightly different emphasis, some of the positions we have discussed earlier on in the essay. We follow the premise that value is the substance of capital. Value is not a thing. It is the dominant form that capitalism as a determinate social relation takes. Following Dinerstein and Neary (2001), capital can be conceived as "value-in-motion." Marx linked the production of value to the dual aspect of labor. Workers do not consume what they produce but work in order to consume what others have produced. Labor is thus riveted in both use-value and exchange-value (see also Allman, 2000, 2001; Rikowski, 2000b, 2001a, 2001d). Domination in this view is not so much by other people as by essentially abstract social structures that people constitute in their everyday social intercourse and sociopolitical relations. In the *Grundrisse*, Marx emphasized that "society does not consist of individuals; it expresses the sum of connections and relationships in which individuals find themselves . . . [Thus,] to be a slave or to be a citizen are social determinations" (cited in San Juan, 1999, p. 248). Labor, therefore, has a historically specific function as a social mediating activity.

Labor materializes both as commodified forms of human existence (labor-power) and structures that constitute and enforce this process of generalized social mediation (such as money and the state) against the workers who indirectly constituted them. These determinate abstractions (abstract labor) also constitute both human capital and the class struggle against the exploitation of living labor and the "capitalization" of human subjectivity.

This split within capital-labor itself is founded on the issue of whether labor produces value directly or labor-power. Following Dinerstein and Neary (2001), we adopt the premise that abstract labor is underwritten by value-in-motion, or the expansive logic of capital (referring to the increases in productivity required to maintain capitalist expansion). Abstract labor is a unique form of social totality that serves as the ground for its own social relation. It is socially average labor-power that is the foundation of the abstract labor that forms value (Rikowski, 2001d). In the case of abstract labor, labor materializes itself twice—first as labor and the second time as "the apparently quasi-objective and independent structures that constitute and enforce this process of generalised social mediation: money (economics) and the state (politics) against the workers who constituted them" (Neary, 2001, p. 7; see also Postone, 1996). This value relation—captured in the image of the capitalist juggernaut driving across the globe for the purpose of extracting surplus-value (profit)—reflects how the abstract social dimension of labor formally arranges (through the imposition of socially necessary labor-time) the concrete organization of work so that the maximum amount of human energy can be extracted as surplus-value. Here, concrete labor (use-value) is overwhelmed by abstract labor (value-in-motion) so that we have an apparently noncontradictory unity. That is to say, capital's abstract-social dimension dominates and subsumes the concrete material character of labor and so becomes the organizing principle of society—the social factory where labor serves as the constituent form of its own domination. This is the process of "real subsumption" where humanity's "vital powers" are mightily deformed. This helps to explain how workers become dominated by their own labor. Labor becomes the source of its own domination.

Following Marx, Rikowski notes that labor-power—our capacity to labor—takes the form of "human capital" in capitalist society. It has reality only within the individual agent. Thus, labor-power is a distinctly *human force*. The worker is the active subject of production. He or she is necessary for the creation of surplus-value. He or she provides through living labor the skills, innovation, and cooperation upon which capital relies to enhance surplus-value and to ensure its reproduction. Thus, by its very nature, labor-power cannot exist apart from the laborer.

Labor power is what Rikowski (2000, 2001a, 2001b) describes as the primordial form of social energy within capital's social universe. Labor-power is a special kind of commodity whose use-value possesses the possibility of being transformed into a source of value. It constitutes value in a unique manner as the special living commodity that possesses the capacity to generate more value—that is, surplus-value—than is required to maintain its social existence as labor-power. In other words, surplus-value is possible because labor-power expends more labor-time than is necessary for its maintenance. It rests upon the socially necessary labor-time required to produce any use-value under conditions normal for a given society. This presupposes labor-power as the socially average. The value of labor-power is represented by the wage. The key point here is that while the labor-power that the worker expends beyond the labor necessary for her maintenance creates no value for her, it does create value for the capitalist: *surplus-value*. Education and training are what Rikowski refers to as processes of labor-power production. They are, in Rikowski's view, a sub species of relative surplus-value production (the raising of worker productivity so that necessary labor is reduced) that leads to a relative increase in surplus labor-time and hence surplus-value. Human capital development is necessary for capitalist societies to reproduce themselves and to create more surplus-value. The core of capitalism can thus be undressed by exploring the contradictory nature of the use-value and exchange-value of labor-power.

Rikowski's adaptation of Marx's value theory of labor, which reveals how education is implicated in the social production of labor-power in capitalism, becomes crucial here. Rikowski's premise, which is provocative yet compelling (and perhaps deceptively simple), can be summarized as follows: Education is involved in the direct production of the one commodity that generates the entire social universe of capital in all of its dynamic and multiform existence: labor-power. Within the capital's social universe, individuals sell their capacity to labor—their labor-power—for a wage. In fact, the only thing that workers can sell in order to obtain their own necessities is their labor-power; thus, they have only one life-sustaining commodity to sell as long as they are trying to survive within capitalist social relations. Within this process labor provides an important use-value for capital. Furthermore, as human will or agency is partially incorporated within labor-power (though never totally, as the will is also an aspect of ourselves constituted as *labor against capital*), and because it is impossible for capital to exist without labor-power, this strange living commodity is therefore *capital's weakest link*. The unique, living commodity that capital's social universe depends upon for its existence and expansion, labor-power, is subject to an aspect of the human will that is antagonistic to capital's depredations and demands: ourselves *constituted as labor against capital*. This aspect of our social existence as laborers drives us on to maximize the quality of our existence within capitalist life; better wages, better working conditions, and fewer working hours and so on. As labor against capital workers yield labor-power conditionally, at times grudgingly and in extreme circumstances (e.g., strikes) not at all. This creates massive insecurities for human representatives of capital. Such insecurity is expressed in management and business studies through attention to the perennial problem of workers' attitudes, and studies on the "motivation" problem regarding workers' willingness to expend their precious commodity by transforming their capacity to labor into *actual* labor in the labor process.

In so far as schooling is premised upon generating the living commodity of labor-power, upon which the entire social universe of capital depends, it can become a foundation for human resistance. In other words, labor-power can be incorporated only so far. Workers, as the sources of labor-power, can engage in acts of refusing alienating work and delinking labor from capital's value form. As Dyer-Witheford argues: "Capital, a relation of general commodification predicated on the wage relation, needs labor. But labor does not need capital. Labor can dispense with the wage, and with capitalism, and find different ways to organize its own creative energies: it is potentially *autonomous*" (1999, p. 68, italics original).

In the face of such a contemporary intensification of global capitalist relations and permanent structural crisis (rather than a shift in the nature of capital itself), we need to develop a critical pedagogy capable of engaging everyday life as lived in its midst. We need, in other words, to face capital down. This means acknowledging global capital's structurally determined inability to share power with the oppressed, its implication in racist, sexist, and homophobic relations, its functional relationship to xenophobic nationalism, and its tendency toward empire. It means acknowledging the educational Left's dependency on the very object of its negation: capital. It means struggling to develop a lateral, polycentric concept of anticapitalist alliances-in-diversity to slow down capitalism's metabolic movement—with the eventual aim of shutting it down completely. It means looking for an educational philosophy that is designed to resist the "capitalization" of subjectivity, a pedagogy that we have called revolutionary critical pedagogy.

Marxist humanists believe that the best way to transcend the brutal and barbaric limits to human liberation set by capital is through practical movements centered around class struggle. But today the clarion cry of class struggle is spurned by the bourgeois Left as politically fanciful and reads to many as an advertisement for a B-movie. The liberal Left is less interested in class struggle than in making capitalism more "compassionate" to the needs of the poor. This only leads to the renaturalization of scarcity. What this approach exquisitely obfuscates is the way in which new capitalist efforts to divide and conquer the working class and to recompose class relations have employed xenophobic nationalism, racism, sexism, ableism, and homophobia. The key here is not for critical pedagogues to privilege class oppression over other forms of oppression but to see how capitalist relations of exploitation provide the ground from which other forms of oppression are produced and how postmodern educational theory often serves as a means of distracting attention from capital's global project of accumulation.

Unhesitatingly embraced by most liberal educationalists is, of course, a concern to bring about social justice. This is certainly to be applauded. However, too often such a struggle is antiseptically cleaved from the project of transforming capitalist social relations. When somebody tries to make the case for class struggle among liberals who fervently believe that capitalism is preferable to socialism or—god forbid—communism, people react as if a bad odor has just entered the room. I am not arguing that people should not have concerns about socialism or communism. After all, much horror has occurred under regimes that called themselves communist. We are arguing that capitalism is not inevitable and that the struggle for socialism is not finished. Perhaps today this struggle is more urgent than at any other time in human history. Socialism is no longer a homogeneous struggle but, as Dunayevaskaya (2002) elaborates, must involve coalition-building and international working-class collaboration of struggle against global capitalism. Such a politics is one of difference and inclusion, but a politics whose center of gravity is the struggle for alternatives to capital.

In so far as education and training socially produce labor-power, this process can be resisted. As Dyer-Witheford notes: "In academia, as elsewhere, labor power is never completely controllable. To the degree that capital uses the university to harness general intellect, insisting its work force engage in lifelong learning as the price of employability, it runs the risk that people will teach and learn something other than what it intends" (1999, p. 236). Critical educators push this "something other" to the extreme in their pedagogical praxis centered around a social justice, anticapitalist agenda. The key to resistance, in our view, is to develop a critical pedagogy that will enable the working class to discover how the use-value of their labor-power is being exploited by capital but also how working-class initiative and power can destroy this type of determination and force a recomposition of class relations by directly confronting capital in all of its hydra-headed dimensions. Efforts can be made to break down capital's control of the creation of new labor-power and to resist the endless subordination of life to work in the social factory of everyday life (Cleaver, 2000; see also Rikowski, 2001). Students and education workers can ask themselves: What is the maximum damage they can do to the rule of capital, to the dominance of capital's value form? Ultimately, the question we have to ask is: Do we, as radical educators, help capital find its way out of crisis, or do we help students find their way out of capital? The success of the former challenge will only buy further time for the capitalists to adapt both its victims and its critics, the success of the later will determine the future of civilization, or whether or not we will have one.

For those of us fashioning a distinctive socialist philosophy of praxis within North American context, it is clear that a transition to socialism will not be an easy struggle, given the global entrenchment of these aforementioned challenges. The overall task ahead is what Petras and Veltmeyer refer to, after Marx and Engels, as the creation of a dictatorship *of* the proletariat, not a dictatorship *over* the proletariat. It consists of managing the inherent contradiction between the internal socialist relations and the external participation in the capitalist marketplace. Meeting this challenge will require, among other things, a long list of initiatives such as those put forward by Petras and Veltmeyer. These follow from an effort to move from a globalized imperial export strategy to an integrated domestic economy, which entails reorienting the economy away from the reproduction of financial elites and replacing privatization with a socialization of the means of production. These initiatives include but are not limited to the following: increasing local capacity to advance the forces of production and democratizing its relations; increasing the internal capacity to deepen the domestic market and serve popular needs; subordinating external and internal market relations (economic exchanges) to a democratic regime (as in an assembly-style democracy); moving away from an "enclave" type of export strategy that serves the interests of overseas and domestic investor elites; building linkages between the domestic economy sectors; adapting the economy to local needs and developing autonomous, innovative capacities; creating democratic control over economic processes; forging socioeconomic linkages between domestic needs and the reorganization of the productive system; dismantling the current export strategy where the labor force is perceived as a cost rather than as consumers; shifting from hyperspecialization in single commodities and limited industrial production to diversified production; establishing a better balance between local consumption and export production; creating a domestic market based on equalized property, income, education, and health; refusing to allow external economic exchanges to substitute for local production and local centers of technical knowledge creation; the redistribution of land and the transfer of property ownership to facilitate food production for mass consumption at affordable prices; replacing luxury-producing and importing enterprises with quality goods for mass domestic consumption; avoiding the disarticulation of the rural economy and thus avoiding the bankrupting of provincial industries; the creation of a livable income for rural producers; and expanding agro-industrial complexes but on a decentralized plan where direct producers make the basic decisions on exchanges between regions, sectors, and classes. It is important that the state and the nation become the central units for reconstructing a new internationalist socialist order. Petras and Veltmeyer suggest that socialists use neoliberal shock therapy in reverse by reducing profits, freezing bank accounts and financial holdings, suspending overseas payments and creating a moratorium on debt payments in order to prevent hyperinflation and capital flight. In opening the economy for domestic production, credit and investment could be offered for expending production and exchanges at the national, regional, and local level. Petras and Veltmeyer also suggest implementing a "structural adjustment program from below"—redistributing land, income, and credits; breaking up private monopolies; reforming the tax system; protecting emerging industries; opening the trade of commodities that don't compete with local producers; eliminating speculative activity by means of financial controls; redirecting investments toward human capital formation and employment; decentralizing the administration of state allocations and redistributing them to local recipients in civil society to local recipients able to vote on their own priorities; generating public works and interregional production; imposing a tight monetary policy (monetarism from below) by refusing state bailouts of corrupt companies; eliminating cheap credit to exporters and tax abatements for multinational corporations in "free"-trade zones; and creating local and regional assemblies to debate and resolve budget allocations (much along the lines of the participatory budget created by Brazil's Workers Party). Kovel argues that the transition to socialism will require the creation of a "usufructuary of the earth." Essentially this means restoring ecosystemic integrity across all of human participation—the family, the community, the nation, the international community. Kovel argues that use-value must no longer be subordinated to exchange-value but both must be harmonized with "intrinsic value." The means of production (and it must be an ecocentric mode of production) must be made accessible to all as assets are transferred to the direct producers (i.e., worker ownership and control). Clearly, eliminating the accumulation of surplus-value as the motor of "civilization" and challenging the rule of capital by directing money toward the free enhancement of use-values goes against the grain of the transnational ruling class.

The struggle among what Marx called our "vital powers," our dispositions, our inner selves and our objective outside, our human capacities and competencies and the social formations within which they are produced, *ensures* the production of a form of human agency that reflects the contradictions within capitalist social life. Yet these contradictions also provide openness regarding social being. They point toward the possibility of collectively resolving contradictions of "everyday life" through revolutionary/transformative praxis (Allman, 1999). Critical subjectivity operates out of practical, sensuous engagement within social formations that enable rather than constrain human capacities. Here critical pedagogy reflects the multiplicity and creativity of human engagement itself: the identification of shared experiences and common interests; the unraveling of the threads that connect social process to individual experience; rendering transparent the concealed obviousness of daily life; the recognition of a shared social positionality; unhinging the door that separates practical engagement from theoretical reflection; the changing of the world by changing one's nature.

In his "Fragment on Machines" in the *Grundrisse* ([1857], 1978), Karl Marx argues that the production of wealth will not always be the result of the direct expenditure of labor-power in production but the result of a general "social knowledge" or "social intellect" or the "general powers of the human head." Marx believed that the development of the general intellect that accompanies the increasing importance of fixed capital (machine technology, and the like) will lead to capital undermining itself in the sense that technological advances reduce the requirements of direct labor in production and as a result the need for people to sell their labor-power (the basis of capital's social order) is diminished. That is, the increased importance of fixed capital and the accompanying process of deindustrialization has expelled living labor from the production process. In addition, as science is directly appropriated into the production process, information thus becomes a source of labor in its own right. However, instead of the development of the general intellect leading to the transition toward socialism, capital, instead, is reorganizing itself (and in the process reproducing the social intellect) in order to increase its global domination (Dyer-Witheford, 1999). As Dyer-Witheford notes, the push to socialize the "social brain" of workers in the days of the Taylorist economy (i.e., educating for certain forms of intersubjectivity among workers developed for the accumulation of industrial capital) has been superseded by a new makeover of the general intellect driven by the needs of post-Taylorist or post-Fordist capital (what some have called the information economy). Attempts at involving workers more in the production process, and capturing the souls of the workers through the establishment worker-teams of participatory management and "total quality management" have reflected novel attempts to dragoon worker subjectivity into the service of capital accumulation by intensifying automation, speeding up work, and increasing layoffs. Automation has created surplus labor-time and workers are struggling to prevent this labor-time from being harnessed to the advantage and the advance of capital. Capital continues to segment post-Fordist labor-power by containing the information revolution in vertically integrated empires of capital, forcing the general intellect of workers into the world of commodity production. Yet, at the same time, attempts to domesticate emancipatory forms of mass intellectuality among workers have at times backfired, and have resulted in the potential development for an oppositional general intellect led by global bands of grassroots organizers and workers who are making alliances with wider communities. While the European and North American "intellectual proletariats" engaged in technoscientific labor pose one type of challenge to capital through their "immaterial labour," the real toilers who engage in "material labor" struggle under different conditions throughout Latin America and the so-called Third World. Yet even in developing economies, there have occurred successful revolts of the world's global subjects, such as in the case of the Zapatistas in Mexico (Dyer-Witheford, 1999). Critical educators must play a role in preventing the domestication of the general intellect, and directly challenge capital in its role of preventing the production of emancipatory knowledge, of a critical social brain. But will our attempts be as domesticating as those of capital, only in a different register, and under the banner of social justice? This is perhaps the greatest future challenge of critical pedagogy.

My work in critical pedagogy—which I prefer to call (after Allman, 2001) critical revolutionary pedagogy—constitutes, in one sense, the performative register for class struggle. While it sets as its goal the decolonization of subjectivity, it also targets the material basis of capitalist social relations. Critical educators seek to realize in their classrooms social values and to believe in their possibilities—consequently I argue that they need to go outside of the protected precincts of their classrooms and analyze and explore the workings of capital there. Critical revolutionary pedagogy sets as its goal the reclamation of public life under the relentless assault of the corporatization, privatization, and businessification of the lifeworld (which includes the corporate–academic complex). It seeks to make the division of labor coincident with the free vocation of each individual and the association of free producers. At first blush this may seem a paradisiac notion in that it posits a radically eschatological and incomparably "other" endpoint for society as we know it. Yet this is not a blueprint but a contingent utopian vision that offers direction not only in unpicking the apparatus of bourgeois illusion but also in diversifying the theoretical itinerary of the critical educator so that new questions can be generated along with new perspectives in which to raise them. Here the emphasis not only is on denouncing the manifest injustices of neoliberal capitalism and serving as a counterforce to neoliberal ideological hegemony, but also on establishing the conditions for new social arrangements that transcend the false opposition between the market and the state.

In capturing the "commanding heights" of Left educational criticism, postmodernist educators have focused their analysis on the subject as consumer in contrast to the Marxian emphasis of the subject as producer and in doing so have emphasized the importance of a textual subversion of fixed identity, and a decentering of subjectivity. Too often this work collapses politics into poetics. Insofar as postmodern educationalists do not address the labor/capital dialectic or the social relations of production, postmodern educational criticism and neoliberalism can be considered to be two species of the same genus: capitalist schooling. They can be considered as two forms of one and the same social type. Both postmodern critique and neoliberalism serve as a justification for the value form of labor within capitalist society. Here postmodernists and neoliberals adopt the role of the sorcerer's apprentice who has been summoned to serve his master: capital. In contrast, revolutionary pedagogy emphasizes the material dimensions of its own constitutive possibility and recognizes knowledge as implicated within the social relations of production (i.e., the relations between labor and capital). I am using the term materialism here not in its postmodernist sense as a resistance to conceptuality, a refusal of the closure of meaning, or whatever "excess" cannot be subsumed within the symbol or cannot be absorbed by tropes; rather, materialism is being used in the context of material social relations, a structure of class conflict, and an effect of the social division of labor (Ebert, 2002). Historical changes in the forces of production have reached the point where the fundamental needs of people can be met—but the existing social relations of production prevent this because the logic of access to "need" is "profit" based on the value of people's labor for capital. Consequently, critical revolutionary pedagogy argues that without a class analysis, critical pedagogy is impeded from effecting praxiological changes (changes in social relations). Critical revolutionary pedagogy begins with a three-pronged approach: First, students engage in a pedagogy of demystification centering around a semiotics of recognition, where dominant sign systems are recognized and denaturalized, where common sense is historicized, and where signification is understood as a political practice that refracts rather than reflects reality, where cultural formations are understood in relation to the larger social factory of the school and the global universe of capital. This is followed by a pedagogy of opposition, where students engage in analyzing various political systems, ideologies, and histories, and eventually students begin to develop their own political positions. Inspired by a sense of ever-imminent hope, students take up a pedagogy of revolution, where deliberative practices for transforming the social universe of capital are developed and put into practice. Revolutionary critical pedagogy supports a totalizing reflection upon the historical-practical constitution of the world, our ideological formation within it, and the reproduction of everyday life practices. It is a pedagogy with an emancipatory intent.

Within the expansive scope of revolutionary critical pedagogy, the concept of labor is axiomatic for theorizing the school/society relationship and thus for developing radical pedagogical imperatives, strategies, and practices for overcoming the constitutive contradictions that such a coupling generates. The larger goal revolutionary critical pedagogy stipulates for radical educationalists involves direct participation with the masses in the discovery and charting of a socialist reconstruction and alternative to capitalism. However, without a critical lexicon and interpretative framework that can unpack the labor/capital relationship in all of its capillary detail, critical pedagogy is doomed to remain trapped in domesticated currents and vulgarized formations. The process whereby labor-power is transformed into human capital and concrete living labor is subsumed by abstract labor is one that eludes the interpretative capacity of rational communicative action and requires a dialectical understanding that only historical materialist critique can best provide. Historical materialism provides critical pedagogy with a theory of the material basis of social life rooted in historical social relations and assumes paramount importance in uncovering the structure of class conflict as well as unraveling the effects produced by the social division of labor. Today, labor-power is capitalized and commodified and education plays a tragic role in these processes. According to Rikowski, education "links the chains that bind our souls to capital. It is one of the ropes comprising the ring for combat between labour and capital, a clash that powers contemporary history: 'the class struggle' " (2001d, p. 2). Schools therefore act as vital supports for, and developers of, the class relation, "the violent capital-labour relation that is at the core of capitalist society and development" (2001d, p. 19).

Practising revolutionary critical pedagogy is not the same as preaching it. Revolutionary critical educators are not an apocalyptic group; they do not belong to a predicant order bent on premonizing the capitalist crisis to come. Revolutionary critical pedagogy is not in the business of presaging as much as it is preparatory; it is in the business of prerevolutionizing: preparing students to consider life outside the social universe of capital—to "glimpse humanity's possible future beyond the horizon of capitalism" (Allman, 2001a, p. 219). What would such a world be like? What type of labor would be—should be—carried out? Thus, critical revolutionary pedagogy is committed to a certain form of futurity, one that will see wage labor disappear along with class society itself.

But revolutionary critical pedagogy is not born in the crucible of the imagination as much as it is given birth in its own practice. That is, revolutionary critical education is decidedly more praxiological than prescored. The path is made by walking, as it were. Revolutionary educators need to challenge the notion implicit in mainstream education, that ideas related to citizenship have to travel through predestined contours of the mind, falling into step with the cadences of common sense. There is nothing common about common sense. Educational educators need to be more than the voice of autobiography, they need to create the context for dialogue with the Other so that the other may assume the right to be heard.

The principles that help to shape and guide the development of our "vital powers" in the struggle for social justice via critical/revolutionary praxis have been discussed at length by Allman (2001a, pp. 177–186). These include: principles of mutual respect, humility, openness, trust, and cooperation; a commitment to learn to "read the world" critically and expending the effort necessary to bring about social transformation; vigilance with regard to one's own process of self-transformation and adherence to the principles and aims of the group; adopting an "ethics of authenticity" as a guiding principle; internalizing social justice as passion; acquiring critical, creative, and hopeful thinking; transforming the self through transforming the social relations of learning and teaching; establishing democracy as a fundamental way of life; developing a critical curiosity; and deepening one's solidarity and commitment to self and social transformation and the project of humanization.

If every new society carries its own negation within itself, then it makes sense for critical educators to develop a language of analysis that can assist to identify the habits, ideas, and notions that help to shape and condition—either in a forward-or backward-looking way—the material and discursive forces of production. These habits, ideas, and notions—which stir as contradictions in the womb of subjectivity—are never static but always are in motion as possibilities given birth by history, that is, by class struggle. We need to develop a critical pedagogy, therefore, that can help students reconstruct the objective and subjective contexts of class struggle by examining the capitalist mode of production as a totality in relation to the aggregate of social relations that make the human—an examination that is centered upon Marx's labor theory of value. This mandates teaching students to think dialectically, to think in terms of "internal relations," such as creating an internal relation between diversity and unity, and between our individuality and our collectivity (Allman, 2001a). The idea here is not simply to play mediatively with ideas but to interrogate the social grammar of capitalist society inhibiting its refractory relations while struggling for a political recomposition of social subjects that want a different world; indeed, who seek a socialist alternative.

The myriad obstacles facing the progressive educational tradition in the United States—such as whether or not critical pedagogy can be revivified in this current historical juncture of neoliberal globalization—can be overcome—albeit haltingly rather than resoundingly. The recent advance of contemporary Marxist educational scholarship (Rikowski, 2001a, b; Hill, 2001; Hill and Cole, 2001; Hill et al., 2004; McLaren and Farahmandpur, 2001), critical theory (Giroux, 1981, 1983; Kincheloe, 1998), and a rematerialized critical pedagogy (McLaren, 2000; McLaren and Farahmandpur, 2001a, b; Fischman and McLaren, 2000)—although the offerings are still only modest glimmerings—in my view is sufficient enough to pose a necessary counterweight not only to neoliberal free-market imperatives but also to post-Marxist solutions that most often advocate the creation of social movements grounded in identity politics or, as evident in recent anti-Marxist pedagogical polemics, a pedagogy grounded in uncertainty.

The Politics of Organization

This brings us to the question of organization. Max Elbaum (2002) notes that organizations are crucial in the struggle for social justice. He writes that "[w]ithout collective forms it is impossible to train cadre, debate theory and strategy, spread information and analysis, or engage fully with the urgent struggles of the day. Only through organisations can revolutionaries maximise their contribution to ongoing battles and position themselves to maximally influence events when new mass upheavals and opportunities arise" (2002, p. 335). Yet at the same time, Elbaum warns that we must avoid what he calls "sectarian dead-ends" in our struggle for social justice. Reflecting on his experiences with the New Communist Movement of the 1970s, he explains that when a movement becomes a "self-contained world" that insists upon group solidarity and discipline, this can often lead to the suppression of internal democracy. The rigid top-down party model is obviously a problem for Elbaum. On the one hand social activists need to engage with and be accountable to a large, active, anticapitalist social base; on the other hand, there are pressures to put one's revolutionary politics aside in order to make an immediate impact on public policy. There is the impulse to "retreat into a small but secure niche on the margins of politics and/or confine oneself to revolutionary propaganda" (2002, p. 334). Elbaum cites Marx's dictum that periods of socialist sectarianism obtain when "the time is not yet ripe for an independent historical movement" (2002, p. 334). Problems inevitably arise when "purer-than-thou fidelity to old orthodoxies" are employed to maintain membership morale necessary for group cohesion and to compete with other groups. He reports that the healthiest periods of social movements appear to be when tightly knit cadre groups and other forms are able to coexist and interact while at the same time considering themselves part of a common political trend. He writes that "diversity of organisational forms (publishing collectives, research centers, cultural collectives, and broad organising networks, in addition to local and national cadre formations) along with a dynamic interaction between them supplied (at least to a degree) some of the pressures for democracy and realism that in other situations flowed from a socialist-oriented working-class" (2002, p. 335). It is important to avoid a uniform approach in all sectors, especially when disparities in consciousness and activity are manifold. Elbaum notes that Leninist centralized leadership worked in the short run but "lacked any substantial social base and were almost by definition hostile to all others on the left; they could never break out of the limits of a sect" (2002, p. 335). The size of membership has a profound qualitative impact on strategies employed and organizational models adopted. Elbaum warns that attempts to build a small revolutionary party (a party in embryo) "blinded movement activists to Lenin's view that a revolutionary party must not only be an 'advanced' detachment but must also actually represent and be rooted in a substantial, socialist-leaning wing of the working class" (2002, p. 335). Realistic and complex paths will need to be taken, which will clearly be dependent on the state of the working-class movement itself.

It is axiomatic for the ongoing development of critical pedagogy that it be based upon an alternative vision of human sociality, one that operates outside the social universe of capital, a vision that goes beyond the market, but also one that goes beyond the state. It must reject the false opposition between the market and the state. Massimo De Angelis writes that "the historical challenge before us is that the question of alternatives . . . not be separated from the organisational forms that this movement gives itself" (2002, p. 5). Given that we are faced globally with the emergent transnational capitalist class and the incursion of capital into the far reaches of the planet, critical educators need a philosophy of organization that sufficiently addresses the dilemma and the challenge of the global proletariat. In discussing alternative manifestations of antiglobalization struggles, De Angelis itemizes some promising characteristics as follows: the production of various counter-summits; Zapatista Encuentros; social practices that produce use-values beyond economic calculation and the competitive relation with the other and inspired by practices of social and mutual solidarity; horizontally linked clusters outside vertical networks in which the market is protected and enforced; social cooperation through grassroots democracy, consensus, dialogue, and the recognition of the other; authority and social cooperation developed in fluid relations and self-constituted through interaction; and a new engagement with the other that transcends locality, job, social condition, gender, age, race, culture, sexual orientation, language, religion, and beliefs. All of these characteristics are to be secondary to the constitution of communal relations. He writes:

> The global scene for us is the discovery of the "other," while the local scene is the discovery of the "us," and by discovering the "us," we change our relation to the "other." In a community, commonality is a creative process of discovery, not a presupposition. So we do both, but we do it having the community in mind, the community as a mode of engagement with the other. (2002, p. 14)

But what about the national state? According to Ellen Meiksins Wood, "the state is the point at which global capital is most vulnerable, both as a target of opposition in the dominant economies and as a lever of resistance elsewhere. It also means that now more than ever, much depends on the particular class forces embodied in the state, and that now more than ever, there is scope, as well as need, for class struggle" (2001, p. 291). Sam Gindin (2002) argues that the state is no longer a relevant site of struggle if by struggle we mean taking over the state and pushing it in another direction. But the state is still a relevant arena for contestation if our purpose is one of transforming the state. He writes:

> Conventional wisdom has it that the national state, whether we like it or not, is no longer a relevant site of struggle. At one level, this is true. If our notion of the state is that of an institution which left governments can "capture" and push in a different direction, experience suggests this will contribute little to social justice. But if our goal is to transform the state into an instrument for popular mobilisation and the development of democratic capacities, to bring our economy under popular control and restructure our relationships to the world economy, then winning state power would manifest the worst nightmares of the corporate world. When we reject strategies based on winning through undercutting others and maintain our fight for dignity and justice nationally, we can inspire others abroad and create new spaces for their own struggles. (2002, p. 11)

John Holloway's premise is similar to that of Gindin. He argues that we must theorize the world negatively as a "moment" of practice as part of the struggle to change the world. But this change cannot come about through transforming the state through the taking of power but rather must occur through the dissolution of power as a means of transforming the state. This is because the state reproduces within itself the separation of people from their own "doing." In our work as critical educators, Holloway's distinction between power-to do (potentia) and power-over (potestas) is instructive. Power-over is the negation of the social flow of doing. Power-to is a part of the "social flow of doing," the construction of a "we" and the practice of the mutual recognition of dignity. We need to create the conditions for the future "doing," of others through a power-to do. In the process, we must not transform power-to into power-over, since power-over only separates the "means of doing" from the actual "doing," which has reached its highest point in capitalism. In fact, those who exercise power-over separate the done from the doing of others and declare it to be theirs. The appropriation of the "done" of others is equivalent to the appropriation of "the means of doing," and allows the powerful to control the doing of others, which reaches its highest point in capitalism. The separation of doing from the doers reduces people to mere owners and nonowners, flattening out relations between people to relations between things. It converts doing into being. Whereas doing refers to both "we are" (the present) and "we are not" (the possibility of being something else) being refers only to "we are." To take away the "we are not" tears away possibility from social agency. In this case, possibility becomes mere utopian dreaming while time itself becomes irrefrangibley homogenized. Being locates the future as an extension of the present and makes the past into a preparation for the present. All doing becomes an extension of the way things are. The rule of power-over is the rule of "this is the way things are" which is the rule of identity. When we are separated from our own doing we create our own subordination. Power-to is not counterpower (which presupposes a symmetry with power) but anti-power. We need to avoid falling into identification, to an acceptance of what is.

Holloway reminds us that the separation of doing and done is not an accomplished fact but a process. Separation and alienation is a movement against its own negation, against antialienation. That which exists in the form of its negation—or antialienation (the mode of being denied)—really does exist, in spite of its negation. It is the negation of the process of denial. Capitalism, according to Holloway, is based on the denial of "power-to," of dignity, of humanity, but that does not mean power-to (counter-capitalism) does not exist. Asserting our power-to is simultaneously to assert our resistance against being dominated by others. This may take the form of open rebellion, of struggles to defend control over the labour process, or efforts to control the processes of health and education. Power-over depends upon that which it negates. The history of domination is not only the struggle of the oppressed against their oppressors but also the struggle of the powerful to liberate themselves from their dependence on the powerless. But there is no way in which power-over can escape from being transformed into power-to because capital's flight from labor depends upon labor (upon its capacity to convert power-to into abstract value-producing labor) in the form of falling rates of profit.

We are beginning to witness new forms of social organization as a part of revolutionary praxis. In addition to the Zapatistas, we have the important example of the participatory budget of the Workers Party in Brazil. And in Argentina we are seeing new forms of organized struggle as a result of the recent economic collapse of that country. We are referring here to the examples of the street protests of the *piqueteros* (the unemployed) currently underway and which first emerged about five years ago in the impoverished communities in the provinces. More recently, new neighborhood *asambleas* (assemblies) have arisen out of local streetcorner protests. Numbering around 300 throughout the country, these assemblies meet once a week to organize *cacerolas* (protests) and to defend those who are being evicted from their homes, or who are having their utilities shut off, and so on. The *asambleistas* (assembly members) are also coordinating soup kitchens to feed themselves and others. This anti-hierarchical, decentralized, and grassroots movement consisting of both employed and unemployed workers, mostly women, has taken on a new urgency since December 2002, when four governments collapsed in quick succession following Argentina's default on its foreign debt. According to a report in *News & Letters*,

> What is remarkable is how ferociously opposed the *asambleas* are to being controlled, and to any hint of a vertical, top down hierarchy. They insist on independence, autonomy self-determination, encouraging all to learn how to voice their opinions and rotating responsibilities. They are explicitly for individual, personal self-development at the same time as they are for fighting the powers that be with everything they've got at their disposal. (2002, p. 6)

The larger *asambleas interbarriales* (mass meetings of the various *asambleas*) elect rotating delegates from the *asambleas* to speak and vote on issues that have been generated in their local communities. In addition, workers have occupied a number of factories and work sites such as Brukman, Zanon, and Panificadora Cinco. Workers have also occupied a mine in Rio Turbio. Clearly, new revolutionary forms of organization are appearing. As Ernesto Herrera notes:

> The experiences of the piquetero movement and neighborhood assemblies allow the possibility of the construction of a revolutionary movement, a democratic popular power with a socialist perspective. The "great revolt" has put on the agenda the question of a strategy that links resistance and the struggle for power, representative democracy and/or the principle of revocability, the "saqueos" as acts of self-subsistence in food. (2002, p. 10)

Of course, there are many problems with the assemblies in that they are composed of members of different class fractions, with their many different political agendas. Yet all of the asambleas hold the re-statification of recently privatized industries as a top priority (even as they reject vanguardist parties). At the same time, in this new rise of popular mobilization, as subjectivities are becoming revolutionized under the assault of capitalism, there needs to occur a programmatic proposal for political regroupment of the radical and anticapitalist forces. There must be more options available for organizers of the revolutionary Left. Herrera writes:

> In Mexico, the Zapatista movement could not translate its capacity of mobilization in the Consultas and Marches into a political alternative of the left. There was no

modification of the relationship of forces. The theory of the "indefinite anti-power" or "changing the world without taking power" has produced neither a process of radical reforms, nor a revolutionary process. (2002, p. 13)

From a Marxist humanist perspective, what needs to be emphasized and struggled for is not only the abolition of private property but also a struggle against alienated labor. The key point here is not to get lost in the state (nationalized capital) versus neoliberalism (privatized capital) debate. As the resident editorial board of *News & Letters* have made clear, the real issue that must not be obscured is the need to abolish the domination of labor by capital. Capital needs to be uprooted through the creation of new human relations that dispense with value production altogether. This does not mean that we stop opposing neoliberalism or privatization. What is does mean is that we should not stop there.

One of the major tasks ahead is the breaking down of the separation between manual and mental labor. This struggle is clearly focused on dismantling the current capitalist mode of production and setting in motion conditions for the creation of freely associated individuals. This means working toward a concept of socialism that will meet the needs of those who are struggling within the present crisis of global capitalism. We need here to project a second negativity that moves beyond opposition (opposition to the form of property, i.e., private property)—a second or "absolute" negativity that moves toward the creation of the new. This stipulates not simply embracing new forms of social organization, new social movements, and the like, but addressing new theoretical and philosophical questions that are being raised by these new spontaneous movements. We need a new philosophy of revolution, as well as a new pedagogy, that emerges out of the dialectic of absolute negation.

The call for a new anticapitalist pedagogy is undertaken here in the spirit of Zizek's (2002) recent call to "repeat Lenin." Arguing that any acceptance of the liberal-parliamentary consensus "precludes any serious questioning of how this liberal-democratic order is complicitous in the phenomena it officially condemns" Zizek invokes Lenin not in a nostalgic sense of returning to the old Lenin, of reenacting former revolutionary moments or in a desire for dogmatic certainty. To call for repeating Lenin is to retrieve "the Lenin-in-becoming, the Lenin whose fundamental experience was that of being thrown into a catastrophic new constellation in which old coordinates proved useless, and who was thus compelled to *reinvent* Marxism" (2002, p. 195). Lenin is not being invoked for the purpose of an "opportunistic-pragmatic adjustment of the old program to 'new conditions' " but rather in the sense "of repeating, in the present, worldwide conditions, the Leninist gesture of reinventing the revolutionary project in the conditions of imperialism and colonialism" (2002, p. 195). This is certainly a call that is compatible with individual and social autonomy. But it is also a warning that if we appropriate Marx, we must appropriate a Marx that still has the power challenge the democratic consensus. Plumping for a fairer distribution of social resources within the social universe of capital is not enough. Zizek asserts that "actual freedom of thought means the freedom to question the predominant, liberal-democratic, 'postideological' consensus—or it means nothing" (2001, p. 194). The point I wish to make here is that despite the radical stance some postmodern educators may take toward the ills of capitalism, it is still a stance that does not directly contest capitalism's political form. As Zizek argues

> . . . anticapitalism without problematizing capitalism's *political* form (liberal parliamentary democracy) is not sufficient, no mater how "radical" it is. Perhaps *the* lure today is the belief that can undermine capitalism without effectively problematizing the liberal democratic legacy which (as some leftists claim), although engendered by capitalism, acquired autonomy and can serve to criticize capitalism. (2002, p. 196)

Keening the death of Marxism will do little more than momentarily stir the ghost of the old bearded devil. Clearly, present-day Left educationalists need to "suspend the stale, existing (post)ideological coordinates" (Zizek, 2002, p. 195) in order to rethink the state as a terrain of contestation while at the same time reinventing class struggle as we have been doing in the streets of Seattle, Porto Alegre, Prague, and Genoa. We have to keep our belief that another world is possible. We need to do more than to break with capital or abscond from it; clearly, we need to challenge its rule of value. The key to resistance, in our view, is to develop a revolutionary critical pedagogy that will enable working-class groups to discover how the use-value of their labor-power is being exploited by capital but also how working-class initiative and power can destroy this type of determination and force a recomposition of class relations by directly confronting capital in all of its multifaceted dimensions. This will require critical pedagogy not only to plot the oscillations of the labor/capital dialectic, but also to reconstruct the object context of class struggle to include school sites. Efforts also must be made to break down capital's creation of a new species of labor-power through current attempts to corporatize and businessify the process of schooling and to resist the endless subordination of life in the social factory so many students call home (Cleaver, 2000; see also Rikowski, 2001c). Novel ingressions toward rebuilding the educational Left will not be easy, but neither will living under an increasingly militarized capitalist state where labor-power is constantly put to the rack to carry out the will of capital. Whilst critical pedagogy may seem driven by lofty, high-rise aspirations that spike an otherwise desolate landscape of despair, where pock-marked dreams bob through the sewers of contemporary cosmopolitan life, they anchor our hope in the dreams of the present. Here the social revolution is not reborn in the foam of avant-garde anti-foundationalism, which only stokes the forces of despair, but emerges from the everyday struggle to release us from the burdens of political détente and democratic disengagement. It is anchored, in other words, in class struggle.*

Note

* Some sections of this essay have been based on Peter McLaren, "Marxist Revolutionary Praxis," *Journal of Critical Inquiry Into Curriculum and Instruction* 3: 3, 36–41.

Bibliography

Ainley, P. (1993). *Class and Skill: Changing Divisions of Knowledge and Labor.* London: Cassell.
Ali, Tariq. (2002). *The Clash of Fundamentalisms: Crusades, Jihads and Modernity.* London: Verso.

Allman, P. (1999). *Revolutionary Social Transformation: Democratic Hopes, Political Possibilities and Critical Education*. Westport, Ct: Bergin & Garvey.

———. (2001a). *Critical Education Against Global Capitalism: Karl Marx and Revolutionary Critical Education*. Westport, Connecticut: Bergin & Garvey.

———. (2001b). "Education on Fire!" In *Red Chalk: On Schooling, Capitalism and Politics*, ed. M. Cole, D. Hill, P. McLaren, and G. Rikowski. Brighton: Institute for Education Policy Studies.

Amin, S. "Imperialism and Globalization." *Monthly Review* 53:2 (2001): 6–24.

Cleaver, Harry. (2000). *Reading Capital Politically*. Leeds: Antitheses and Edinburgh: AK Press.

Cole, M. and Hill, D. (1999). *Promoting Equality in Secondary Schools*. London: Cassell.

Cole, M., Hill, D., McLaren, P., and Rikowski, G. (2001). *Red Chalk: On Schooling, Capitalism & Politics*. London: Tufnell Press.

———. (2001). *Red Chalk: On Schooling, Capitalism and Politics*. Brighton: Institute for Education Policy Studies.

Davies, Scott and Guppy, Neil. "Globalization and Educational Reforms in Anglo-American Democracies." *Comparative Education Review* 41: 4 (November 1997): 435–459.

De Angelis, Massimo. (2002). "From Movement to Society." *The Commoner* no. 4 (May). http://www.commoner.org.uk/01–3groundzero.htm.

Dinerstein, A. and Neary, M. (1998). *Class Struggle and the Communist Manifesto*, a paper presented in Paris: http://www.espaces-marx.eu.org/Archives/Marx_98/Contributions/Autre . . . /Dinerstein.htm.

———. (2001). *Marx, Labour and Real Subsumption, or How No Logo becomes No To Capitalist Everything*. Unpublished paper.

Dunayevskaya, R. (in press). *The Power of Negativity*. Boulder, CO: Lexington Press.

Dyer-Witheford (1999). *Cyber-Marx: Cycles and Circuits of Struggle in High-Technology Capitalism*. Urbana and Chicago: University of Illinois Press.

Ebert, Teresa. (2002). *University, Class, and Citizenship*. Unpublished manuscript.

Elbaum, Max. (2002). *Revolution in the Air: Sixties Radicals Turn to Lenin, Mao and Che*. London and New York: Verso.

Fischman, G. and McLaren, P. "Schooling for Democracy: Towards a Critical Utopianism." *Contemporary Society* 29:1 (2000): 168–179.

Foley, Barbara. "Roads Taken and Not Taken: Post-Marxism, Antiracism, and Anticommunism." *Cultural Logic* 1:2 (Spring 1998).

Forrester, V. (1999). *The Economic Horror*. Malden, MA: Blackwell Publishers.

Freire, P. (1998). *Pedagogy of the Heart*. New York: Continuum.

Gindin, Sam. "Social Justice and Globalization: Are They Compatible?" *Monthly Review* 54:2 (June 2002): 1–11.

Giroux, H. A. (1981). *Ideology, Culture & the Process of Schooling*. Philadelphia, PA: Temple University Press.

Giroux, H. (1983). *Theory and Resistance in Education: A Pedagogy for the Opposition*. South Hadley, MA: Bergin & Garvey.

———. (1988). *Teachers as Intellectuals: Towards a Critical Pedagogy of Learning*. South Hadley, MA: Bergin & Garvey.

Giroux, H. and McLaren, P. (1997). "Paulo Freire, Postmodernism and the Utopian Imagination: A Blochian Reading." In *Not Yet: Reconsidering Ernst Bloch*, ed. J. O. Daniel and T. Moylan. London and New York: Verso Press, pp. 138–168.

Hardt, M. and Negri, A. (2000). *Empire*. Cambridge and London: Harvard University Press.

Herrera, Ernesto. (2002). "Latin America: The Current Situation and the Task of Revolutionaries." *Fourth International Press*, pp. 1–16. Wednesday, July 17. FI-press—I@mail.comlink.apc.org.

Hill, D. (2001). "State Theory and the Neo-Liberal Reconstruction of Schooling and Teacher Education: A Structuralist neo-Marxist Critique of Postmodernist, Quasi-Postmodernist, and Culturalist neo-Marxist Theory." *British Journal of Sociology of Education* (forthcoming).

Hill, D. and Cole, M. (2001). "Social Class." In *Schooling and Equality: Fact, Concept and Policy*, ed. D. Hill and M. Cole. London: Kogan Page.

Hill, D., Sanders, M., and Hankin, T. (2001). "Marxism, Social Class and Postmodernism." In *Marxism Against Postmodernism in Educational Theory*, (forthcoming) ed. D. Hill, P. McLaren, and G. Rikowski (Lanham, ML: Lexington Books).

Holloway, John. (2002). Twelve Theses On Changing the World Without Taking Power. The Commoner, no. 4 (May). http://www.commoner.org.uk/04holloway2.pdf.

Kincheloe, J. (1998). *How do we Tell the Workers? The Socioeconomic Foundations of Work and Vocational Education*. Boulder, CO: Westview Press.

Lenin, V. (1951). *Imperialism: The Highest Stage of Capitalism*. Moscow: Foreign Language Publishing House.

Luxemburg, R. (1919). *The Crisis in German Social Democracy: The Junius Pamphlet*. New York: The Socialist Publication Society.

Marx, K. (1863) [1972]. *Theories of Surplus Value—Part Three*. London: Lawrence & Wishart.

———. (1973). *Critique of the Gotha Program*. New York: International Publishers.

———. (1866) [1976]. *Results of the Immediate Process of Production*, Addendum to "Capital," Vol. 1. Harmondsworth: Penguin.

———. (1844) [1977]. *Economic and Philosophical Manuscripts of 1844*. Moscow: Progress Publishers.

———. (1865) [1977]. *Capital: A Critique of Political Economy—Volume 3*. London: Lawrence & Wishart.

Marx, K. and Engels, F. (1850, March). Address of the Central Committee to the Communist League, London.

McChesney, R. W. (1999). "Introduction". In *Profit over People: Neoliberalism and Global Order*, ed. N. Chomsky. New York: Seven Stories Press, pp. 7–16.

McLaren, P. (1995). *Critical Pedagogy and Predatory Culture: Oppositional Politics in a postmodern Era*. London and New York: Routledge.

———. (1997). *Revolutionary Multiculturalism: Pedagogies of Dissent for the New Millennium*. Boulder, CO: Westview Press.

———. (1998a). *Life in Schools: An Introduction to Critical Pedagogy in the Foundations of Education* (3rd ed.). New York: Longman.

———. "Revolutionary Pedagogy in Post-Revolutionary Times: Rethinking the Political Economy of Critical Education." *Educational Theory* 48:4 (1998b): 431–462.

———. "Critical Pedagogy, Postmodernism, and the Retreat from Class: Towards a Contraband Pedagogy." *Theoria* 93 (1999a): 83–115.

———. (1999b). "Critical Multiculturalism and Globalization. Some Implications for a Politics of Resistance." *Journal of Curriculum Theorizing* 15:3 (1999b): 27–46.

———. (2000). "Reconsidering Marx in Post-Marxist Times: A Requiem for Postmodernism?" *Educational Researcher* 29:3 (2000): 25–33.

———. (2000). *Che Guevara, Paulo Freire, and the Pedagogy of Revolution*. Boulder, CO: Rowman & Littlefield.

———. (2001a). "Educational Policy and the Socialist Imagination: Revolutionary Citizenship as a Pedagogy of Resistance." *Educational Policy* 13:3 (July 2001a): 343–378.

McLaren, P. and Farahmandpur, R. "Teaching Against Globalization and the New Imperialism: Toward a Revolutionary Pedagogy." *Journal of Teacher Education* 52:2 (March/April 2001b): 136–150.

McMurtry, J. (1998). *Unequal Freedoms: The Global Market as an Ethical System*. West Hartford, CT: Kumarian Press.

McMurtry, J. (1999). *The Cancer Stage of Capitalism*. London, UK: Pluto Press.

————. "A Failed Global Experiment: The Truth about the US Economic Model." *Comer*, 12:7 (2000): 10–11.

McQuaig, Linda. (2001). *All You Can Eat: Greed, Lust and the New Capitalism*. Toronto, Penguin Books.

Mészáros, I. (1995). *Beyond Capital*. New York: Monthly Review Press.

————. "Marxism, the Capital System, and Social Revolution: An Interview with István Mészáros." *Science and Society* 63:3 (1999): 338–361.

————. (2001) *Socialism or Barbarism: From the "American Century" to the Crossroads*. New York: Monthly Review Press.

Neary, M. (2001). "Travels in Moishe Postone's Social Universe: A Contribution to a Critique of Political Cosmology." Unpublished paper, forthcoming in *Historical Materialism: Research in Critical Marxist Theory*.

Neary, M. and Rikowski, G. (2000). *The Speed of Life: the Significance of Karl Marx's Concept of Socially Necessary Labour-Time*. A paper presented at the British Sociological Association Annual Conference 2000, University of York, 17–20 April.

Ollman, B. (1976). *Alienation: Marx's Conception of Man in Capitalist Society* (2nd ed.) Cambridge: Cambridge University Press.

————. (2001). *How to Take an Exam and Remake the World*. Montreal: Black Rose Books.

Panitch, L. and Gindin, S. (2001). "Transcending Pessimism: Rekindling Socialist Imagination." In *After the Fall: 1989 and the Future of Freedom*, ed. G. Katsiaficas. New York and London: Routledge, pp. 175–199.

Parenti, M. (2001). "Rollback: Aftermath of the Overthrow of Communism." In *After the Fall: 1989 and the Future if Freedom*, ed. G. Katsiaficas. New York and London: Routledge, pp. 153–158.

————. "Global Rollback After Communism." *CovertAction Quarterly* 72 (Spring 2002). pp. 41–44.

Petras, J. (2000). "Globalization and Citizenship: Social and Political Dimensions." *Working Papers in Cultural Studies*, 22. Pullman, WA: Department of Comparative American Cultures, Washington State University, pp. 1–20.

Post, Charlie. (2002). *Review: Empire and Revolution*. Fourth International Press List.

Postone, M. (1996). *Time, Labour, and Social Domination: A Reinterpretation of Marx's Critical Theory*. Cambridge: Cambridge University Press.

Rikowski, G. (1999). "Education, Capital and the Transhuman." In *Postmodernism in Educational Theory: Education and the Politics of Human Resistance*, ed. D. Hill, P. McLaren, M. Cole, and G. Rikowski. London: Tufnell Press.

————. (2000a). *That Other Great Class of Commodities: Repositioning Marxist Educational Theory*. A paper presented at the British Educational Research Association Conference 2000, Cardiff University, session 10.21, September 9.

————. (2000b). *Messing with the Explosive Commodity: School Improvement, Educational Research and Labour-Power in the Era of Global Capitalism*. A paper prepared for the Symposium on "If We Aren't Pursuing Improvement, What Are We Doing?" British Educational Research Association Conference 2000, Cardiff University, Wales, 7 September.

————. (2001a). *The Importance of Being a Radical Educator in Capitalism Today*. A Guest Lecture in the Sociology of Education, The Gillian Rose Room, Department of Sociology, University of Warwick, Coventry, May 24.

————. (2001b). "Fuel for the Living Fire: Labour-Power!" In *The Labour Debate: An Investigation into the Theory and Reality of Capitalist Work* (forthcoming), ed. A. Dinerstein and M. Neary. Aldershot: Ashgate.

————. (2001c). *The Battle in Seattle: Its Significance for Education*. London: Tufnell Press.

————. (2001d). *After the Manuscript Broke Off: Thoughts on Marx, Social Class and Education*. A paper presented at the British Sociological Association Education Study Group, King's College, London, June 23.

Rikowski, R. and Rikowski, G. (2002). "Against What We Are Worth." A paper to be submitted to *Gender and Education*.

Robinson, W. and Harris, J. "Towards a Global Ruling Class? Globalization and the Transnational Capitalist Class." *Science & Society* 64:1 (2000): 11–54.

San Juan, Jr., E. "Raymond Williams and the Idea of Cultural Revolution." *College Literature* 26:2 (1999): 118–136.

Teeple, G. (1995). *Globalization and the Decline of Social Reform*. New Jersey: Humanities Press.

The Resident Editorial Board. *New & Letters*, 47:6 (July 2002): 5–8.

Wood, Ellen Meiksins. (2001). "Contradictions: Only in Capitalism." In *A World of Contradictions, Socialist Register, 2002*, ed. L. Panitch and C. Leys. London: Merlin.

————. (1994, June 13). "Identity Crisis." *In These Times*, pp. 28–29.

————. (1995). *Democracy Against Capitalism: Renewing Historical Materialism*. Cambridge, Cambridge University Press.

Zizek, S. (2002). *Repeating Lenin*. Unpublished manuscript.

————. "Have Michael Hardt and Antonio Negri Rewritten the Communist Manifesto for the Twenty-First Century?" *Rethinking Marxism* 13:3/4 (Fall/Winter 2001): 190–198.

Part 2

Language, Difference, Community

The Letter of the Law/The Silence of Letters: Poetic Ruminations on Love and School

Carl Leggo

When eros is present in the classroom setting, then love is bound to flourish. Well-learned distinctions between public and private make us believe that love has no place in the classroom. (hooks, *Teaching*, p. 198)

Our aim should be to encourage the growth of competent, caring, loving, and lovable people. (Noddings, p. xiv)

We've all got a mystic inside, yearning to play in the universe. And that play is eros, it's erotic. Once we get that energy going, we'll have the political imagination and the moral imagination to change our ways. (Fox, p. 77)

To open our hearts more fully to love's power and grace we must dare to acknowledge how little we know of love in both theory and practice. (hooks, *All*, p. xxix)

The administration of an elementary school in eastern Canada recently announced a rule banning all physical contact in the school. In order to prevent some students behaving in violent ways, such as hitting and pushing, all physical contact has been prohibited. The daily scene in that school probably looks like an episode of "The Twilight Zone"—600 children in a building designed for 400, creeping gingerly through the crowded hallways, timidly intent on not touching another person. In an effort to resolve the problem of pushing and shoving among a few students, the administrators of the school have legislated new problems. Above all, they have failed to acknowledge, to know, that school is a messy, tangled story that cannot be written with the letter of the law. And they have failed to acknowledge, to know, that the messy, tangled story of school is written in the silence of letters, the silent letters, always both present and absent.

Last winter I visited regularly a grade ten Language Arts class to observe the teacher and students as they engaged in the writing process. During my last visit I noticed that two students were missing. These two young women had generally been very vocal in class, but both had also complained that they had difficulty writing. When I asked the teacher where the students were, I was informed that one of the women was now two months pregnant, and that the two of them, always good friends, had argued about a boyfriend, and one of the women hit and broke the nose of the other. One student was suspended, and the other dropped out. During my visits to the class I was keenly interested in why these two students, impressively articulate in the whole class discussions, expressed ongoing frustration with their writing. Now I think I was asking the wrong questions. My ears are not well attuned to silence.

In this chapter I ruminate, anecdotally and poetically, on issues of relationship, identity, community, school climate, growing human(e), and silence. I focus on the word "love" as four silent letters that need to be heard in schools. My ruminations on love are autobiographical, and I confess, even before I begin, that my ruminations are riddled with silences. There are many more stories I want to tell, and some I do not think I can tell. Above all, I am convinced that the way I teach, and live among my students and colleagues, in schools and universities, is shaped and formed by my experiences with love, my joys and fears and wounds and hopes. And so I ruminate autobiographically in language in the hope that I can learn how to live with the persistent sense of lack and desire in the labyrinthine and ludicrous experience of love—fired always by a pedagogical commitment to writing the world a more caring space and time in which to linger.

All my life I have been a student or a teacher, and all my life I have been filled with both frustration and hope: on the one hand, schools are often unhappy places, and on the other hand, schools are always lively spaces for learning to live well in the world. I am concerned that schools are planned and organized and managed according to the letter of the law—in Greek, letter is "gramma," which is derivatively connected to our word "grammar." Octavio Paz in *The Monkey Grammarian* provides an intriguing perspective on grammar: "the difference between human writing and divine consists in the fact that the number of signs of the former is limited, whereas that of the latter is infinite; hence the universe is a meaningless text, one which even the gods find illegible. The critique of the universe (and that of the gods) is called grammar" (pp. 47–48). In school I learned that a sentence expresses a complete and unified thought, even though I knew constantly a keen sense of incompleteness in word-making, a keen sense of multiplicity in word-making. Paz suggests we need a "return to the original plurality" (p. 94). Instead of a grammar that defines a sentence as a complete thought, perhaps we need Paz's notion that "we are neither a one together, nor is each all. There is no one and no all: there are ones and there are alls. Always in the plural, always an incomplete completeness, the *we* in search of its each one: its rhyme, its metaphor, its different complement" (p. 95). The letter of the law, the gramma of the law, the law of grammar constitutes a pretense of order, constrains the imagination, and closes down possibilities, especially the interrogation of impossibilities.

But an exegetical reading of the New Testament presents a fertile connection between the letter of the law and the spirit of the law, between *gramma* and *pneuma*.

Gramma can be written, spoken, a presence that denies absence, an external code, while *pneuma* is unwritten, unspoken, an absence that constitutes presence, an internal dynamic. Teachers, literate, literal, want the letter, the gramma, when the spirit, the pneuma, is what we need to seek. According to Christian theology the God-given commandments or laws, sometimes even inscribed in tablets of stone, always indefatigably communicated and painstakingly interpreted, are a pedagogical device, an interim measure, a literal expression of a figurative experience, a kind of road map for people who are reluctant to journey without a map: "The law is only a shadow of the good things that are coming—not the realities themselves" (Hebrews 10:1). The apostle Paul suggests: "The commandments, 'Do not commit adultery,' 'Do not murder,' 'Do not steal,' 'Do not covet,' and whatever other commandment there may be, are summed up in this one rule: 'Love your neighbour as yourself.' Love does no harm to its neighbour. Therefore love is the fulfillment of the law" (Romans 13:9–10). The law then is a pedagogical device, an instructional strategy, a curricular design for leading teachers and students to the lived and living experience of love. But in schools we have reified and deified the law (gramma) and vilified and ostracized the spirit (the pneuma); we have constructed schools in the image of the law while ignoring the spirit without image.

I am concerned that love is a word used in so many different ways that we do not know what it means. Is the word devalued by overuse, or does the word "love" derive its value from lots of use? The effort to define love is motivated by a desire to inscribe, legalize, contain, control love, an attempt to write the grammar for a universe that defies grammar, an effort to write the grammar for a story—the story of school—that transcends all efforts to control it. Perhaps love is inexplicable. Consider a familiar effort to define love. Alan Soble in *Eros, Agape, and Philia: Readings in the Philosophy of Love* defines eros as "x loves y because y has attractive or valuable qualities" (p. xxiv), and agape as "x loves y independently of y's merit, and any merit of y's that plays a role in x's love is value that x attributes to or creates in y as a result of x's love" (p. xxiv), while philia "gets caught in the cracks between or among them" [eros and agape] (p. xxiv). In popular thinking eros is physical and sexual, connected with the body, falling in and out of love, while agape is spiritual, divine, godly, Dostoyevsky's "harsh and dreadful love," which insists on loving even the unloveable, while philia is the distant cousin of friendship, asexual, lacking fire or adoration or passion.

My trouble with Soble's distinctions is that he has set up contrasts that fail to do justice to the multiplicity and mystery of lived experiences of love. Human love is eros, agape, and philia. Our efforts to separate them lead to dangerous situations of silence, fear, guilt, and oppression. Soble claims that only erotic love "corresponds to our picture of a comprehensible, rational, unmysterious love" (p. xxiv). I think eros, agape, and philia are all intricately connected to mystery. Human love is always eros, agape, and philia, inseparably tangled. Instead of trying to separate love into several kinds or categories that can be labeled and defined, we need to acknowledge this complexity. There are not three kinds of love, only one kind. Love cannot be defined, argued, classified. Instead love can be professed, described, and interrogated from multiple perspectives, lived and narrated. As I grow older, I grow more convinced that love is the Holy Grail I am always searching for, not money, fame, health, promotion, but love, the singular love riddled with multiplicity and mystery.

As a teacher I choose to love, I choose to believe in love, I choose to teach in love. To accept the vocation of teacher/teaching is to enter into relationships of love where I will seek the value, the merit, the significance in my students, filled with hope (even in the face of hopelessness) that they, too, will seek the value, the merit, the significance in themselves, and one another, and me. This is love—eros, agape, philia love. It is no wonder that educators fear love in the classroom, fear its energy for creating havoc, fear its unpredictability. As we fear the body. And the heart. And the spirit. Instead we write more laws, stipulations, regulations, commandments, statutes, rules, edicts, and decrees, all in a fruitless, even counterproductive, effort to control what cannot be controlled.

In order to promote schools where love flourishes, schools where the spirit, not the letter of the law, is fostered, educators need to rethink conceptions of community, especially the commonplace notion that a community is characterized by commonality. I have been silenced in schools where unity was emphasized as the foundation of community. William Corlett "attempts to celebrate both community and difference" (p. 6). Corlett observes that "bringing unity seems always to require silencing the so-called parts that do not fit the holistic vision" (p. 6). Instead Corlett celebrates "the infinite differences of fellow beings" in community without unity (p. 22). For Corlett, "to live extravagantly is to give gifts freely, to cultivate one's gifts in all directions" (p. 211). Schools are typically focused on competition, power, domination, regimentation, and homogenization, which all preclude the promotion of love. Therefore, I support a conception of community that celebrates not unity but diversity, a notion of community which celebrates differences and individual perspectives and heterogeneity and individual desires. I advocate a vision of community where differences of gender, class, race, ethnicity, sexual orientation, personality, economic status, belief, talent, ability, age, and physical appearance are celebrated for their plurality, not construed as sources of potential conflict demanding destructive measures of stigmatizing and suppression and silencing in pursuit of some fundamentalist chimera of unity. Like Romand Coles I promote "a belonging in difference" (p. ix). The word "community" is derived from the Latin "communis," which means "common," as are the words "communicate," "commune," and "communion." Com-munity is about communicating, about revealing and imparting and sharing gifts of language, about participating in the formation of identity in our story-making. Corlett notes that "every life is fully implicated in discourse" (p. 211). We tell one another our stories; we listen to one another's stories.

Next, I will share six autobiographical poems. Each poem is a part of my efforts without end to understand the experience of love in my life. For the purposes of this writing, I preface each poem with a statement about love, not in an attempt to define love, but out of my eagerness to defend the notion that love can be discussed without efforts of categorical definition. I appreciate the efforts of philosophers like Soble to define love. I read recently in a delightful book titled *Holes and Other Superficialities* by the philosophers Casati and Varzi (1994) that "a philosophical theory originates from astonishment" (p. 7). On first reading that observation I was excited, but the second part of the statement asserts that a philosophical theory "is judged from its ability to silence astonishment" (p. 7). My objection is that astonishment is a good place to begin and a good place to linger. In sharing the following poems and thoughts about love, I am not seeking to silence astonishment. I hope instead to astonish silence.

The poems I include are mostly about family, about six women who have helped shape the person I am, the identities and positions I embody in the spatialized landscape of each day's geography. In *Hannah Arendt: Life Is a Narrative*, Julia Kristeva spells out Arendt's perspective on "the active life" that "can be represented by a *narrative*" (p. 7). According to Kristeva, Arendt "links the destinies of *life, narrative,* and *politics*" (p. 8). Arendt conceives of "human life as a political action revealed in the language of a narration" (p. 13). Narrative is "the invented story that accompanies history" and answers the question "Who are you?" (p. 15). In my writing I am writing "who I am," and in the writing I am engaged in a political endeavor to acknowledge that the personal and the public are not only never separate, but are in fact ecologically and organically connected like the two chambers of the heart. I am convinced that only by attending to personal locations, and the stories composed there, can I ever learn how to live well in the public and political spaces where I work and live as a poet and teacher. My poems are locations for poiesis and praxis, a way of narrating experience, and experiencing narratively, a journey of learning. As Susan Griffin notes, identity is "less an assertion of independence than an experience of interdependence" (p. 91).

Because writing is always both a personal and a social act, then autobiographical writing is especially connected to lively relationships of family and kin and community and culture. Language is the spirit that animates conversation so that competing and contested beliefs and perspectives and values can be negotiated in an ongoing process of making meaning of experience. Because we are constituted in language, because we know ourselves in language, because we constantly write ourselves, and rewrite ourselves, and write our relations to others, and seek to understand the loneliness, alienation, and separateness we know always, we need frequent opportunities to engage in discursive practices, and an environment that nurtures desire, insatiable desire, to know, to quest/ion, to seek. And so I write in poetry autobiographically, philosophically, narratively, interrogatively, ruminatively, lyrically, pedagogically, performatively. In my poetry I seek to dispel silence by disclosing possibilities for presence.

In *Pedagogy of the Heart*, published posthumously in 1997, Paulo Freire acknowledges from the perspective of a long life nearing its end that his childhood backyard was a space connected to many spaces. Freire encourages me that "the more rooted I am in my location, the more I extend myself to other places so as to become a citizen of the world. No one becomes local from a universal location" (p. 39). For more than a decade, I have been writing autobiographical poetry about growing up on Lynch's Lane in Corner Brook, Newfoundland. So far, I have published two books of poems, and I now acknowledge that the stories of my backyard are inexhaustible. I began the first autobiographical poems about growing up when I was 34 years old. I write about people and experiences that I never wrote about in school where I tried to imitate the writing I read in textbooks. For many years I heard a persistent voice of caution that it is not adequate to write about ordinary people with ordinary experiences and emotions in ordinary situations. Needed is an extraordinary subject or an extraordinary perspective on the ordinary. Why could I not write about the everyday experiences of my life? Finally, I am learning to breathe with the heart's rhythms as I seek to disclose and know again my location situated in specific local spaces that represent a location for locution in the expansively imagined world. And in these locations, remembered and constructed in poems, I ruminate on love, full of hope that I am learning how to write the world beyond the letter of the law so that I can hear the silence of letters.

Love is Language

Love is experienced and known and communicated and nurtured in talking, listening, writing, reading, thinking, dreaming, ruminating, viewing, and representing. I emphasize the performative and creative activity of language because human beings are really human be(com)ings constituted in the play of language. So often we use language to declare, assert, prove, argue, convince, and proclaim notions of "truth," but what happens when we emphasize the use of language to question and play with and savor and ruminate on notions of "truth"? Language as performance invites collaboration and conversation, and a keen sense of confidence that we are engaging together in creating intellectual, emotional, experiential, spiritual, and aesthetic possibilities. We all need to be committed to writing and rewriting our stories together, and we need to be committed to hearing one another's stories, too.

NAN'S BROOCH

My grandmother could never understand how
young women could kiss old men on *Another World.*

Oh, that old thing. She loved Bob Barker
like she loved salt, ordered from Carter's Store

pickled pig's knuckles, herring and turbot,
sneaked salt meat into the pot when Carrie wasn't looking,

laughed over salt cabbage, craved salt
like winter-starved deer on *The Forest Rangers*

where Gordon Pinsent, the only Newfoundland actor
we knew after Joey Smallwood, took care of the world,

while my brother and I resurrected Camelot in blankets,
our grandmother trapped in a kitchen corner

with a cup of tea, nowhere else to go,
till the crash of knights in battle left her

a damsel in distress. I'm going to tell your mother,
as soon as she gets home. She never did.

One Christmas I gave my grandmother a sterling
silver brooch from Silver's and Sons on Water Street.

I asked Mr. Silver to engrave the back,
        I love you, Nan,

words I'd never said to my grandmother, though
at sixteen, home just left behind, I wanted

to say the words. I gave my grandmother the brooch.
Read the back, Nan. She rubbed her eyes.

She couldn't see the words. Carrie read the words.
We all smiled. Always so many silent letters

in our story, but in the back of the brooch, concave,
I saw my grandmother and me upside down,

as I ride vertiginous each day a playground ride
spinning on an axis while I cling to the edge of a circle

and remember my grandmother who lived in the margins,
never in the world, never out of the world,

brought to her by neighbours, TV, and *The Western Star*,
and our final New Year's Eve, long ago, not so long ago,

when I stayed with my grandmother while Skipper
and Carrie went to a party. I slept in my old bed.

When the year ended with gunshots and pots,
I found my grandmother scratching the floor.

I picked her up. I put her back in bed.
I tucked the blankets in tight under the mattress,

the way my brother and I once built Camelot.
After decades when she seldom left the house,

my grandmother in her last year was bent on escape.
I didn't tell Carrie. My grandmother never told on me.

I am afraid of love, loving, saying "I love you," have known the words spoken with unfaithfulness and pretence and greed and a violent desire to consume. It is puzzling that a library search with the descriptors "love" and "school" turns up almost no sources. Obviously educators fear love, loving, saying "I love you," too, perhaps for the same reasons that I fear love. Why aren't we writing more about love? Why is love the stuff of Sandra Bullock films and country music videos. There is an abiding silence at the heart of my love, represented in the letter "o" which is like a lifesaver candy. When you eat a lifesaver candy, do you suck it so that the hole is prolonged or do you crush it? Most of us enjoy the lifesaver, at least in part, for the pleasure of sustaining the hole. A hole is not emptiness; a hole creates fullness. So, I know the silence at the heart of my love for my grandmother had its own poetry. She and I embodied and professed our love in action and silence and a long, loud laughter. Together we lived love. But, still, I wish I had, at least once, said to my grandmother, I love you, Nan.

Love is Lack

As one of my significant teachers, Barry Cameron, observes insightfully, "We . . . speak/write because we suffer from desire, seeking plenitude and presence" (p. 139). Like Cameron, I find a convincing explanation or metaphor or narrative for my human experience in the writing of Jacques Lacan. My story as a human be/com/ing is a story about the nagging recognition of lack and absence and separateness, a story about the unending desire for wholeness and fulfilment and completeness. According to Lacan when a child is born she or he does not recognize that she or he is separate from the mother. Instead there is the conviction of being one with the mother. Then around the age of 6–18 months, the child recognizes her or his separateness from the mother. Lacan observes that around this age children are also fascinated with their reflections in mirrors. The image that is seen is the image of an autonomous, whole self. But at the same time this image is perceived as separate and other, as well as desired and aspired to. Catherine Belsey clarifies this tension: "The mirror-phase, in which the infant perceives itself as other, an image, exterior to its own perceiving self, necessitates a splitting between the 'I' which is perceived and the 'I' which does the perceiving" (pp. 64–65). With the child's recognition that she or he is not one with the mother, and that she or he is separate from the image, the Other, in the mirror as well, comes her or his initiation into language use where the sense of separateness is enacted with every word spoken and written. The child can never say what she or he really wants to say in words, what she or he really intends to say. Following the mirror phase children are inaugurated into the symbolic order of language involving the same tension between the image as Other and the desire for that image. Always there is a separation between the "I" who speaks and writes and the "I" who is spoken and written in the discourse.

As Kaja Silverman explains, a critical Lacanian assumption is that "the human subject derives from an original whole which was divided in half" and whose "existence is dominated by the desire to recover its missing complement" (p. 152). The human subject desires the Other and desires the Other's desire. We spend our lives seeking the Other that will complement us and make us whole again as we believe we were once whole. Of course the wholeness never existed, and hence our desire for the complementary Other will never be satisfied. Desire is always frustrating and frustrated, always fruitful and freewheeling, frequently foolish, but fullsome, too.

And I know my desire in my word-making. In my writing, speaking, listening, thinking, and reading, I am compelled by a sense of lack and a desire for completion. In my word-making I experience myself as an unstable subject, caught up in an ongoing process of constitution in the symbolic order of language and social function. In my word-making I seek to give a face to "I," but the "I" in my writing is constantly effacing itself, slipping away, revealing only its multiplicity, its unconsummated relationships while seeking the Other.

The goal of my writing is often to use words to pin down truth, conviction, assurance. I interact with the words dialogically, intimately, passionately. Alone at a desk I converse with the words and the conversation is animated and exhausting. It leaves me both exhilarated and attenuated. The experience is overwhelming with desire, my desire to shape and control my words, my desire to disclose my world in words, my desire to be shaped and controlled by the words, my desire to be disclosed in words. But for all the expectation and desire involved in writing, the consummation is never total.

As a speaker and writer I use words to speak myself into existence, but I am always aware that I cannot get it right. Even now as I write, I ask, Who will understand these words? Who will desire these words enough to spend the time to respond to them? Who will care? Who will nod their heads with affirmation? Some? None? As a poet

I know constantly the slipping and sliding nature of language, which tantalizes me with promises of clarity, understanding, and communication, but provides me with mixed metaphors and flashy neckties for funerals and rejection slips and infrequent invitations to parties and blank stares and guests who sleep while I speak. Always I am aware of my difference, my separateness from all other human be/com/ings. And yet always there is the overwhelming desire to be connected with others, to bask in community, to know completion in interdependence with others, to word my wholeness in conjunction with the Other, even in the knowledge that the desire will never be satisfied because there is no wholeness, no oneness. I know intimately the eloquent words of Freire who understands how love is lack:

I feel my incompleteness inside me, at the biological, affective, critical, and intellectual levels, an incompleteness that pushes me constantly, curiously, and lovingly toward other people and the world, searching for solidarity and transcendence of solitude. All of this implies wanting to love, a capacity for love that people must create in themselves. This capacity increases to the degree that one loves; it diminishes when one is afraid to love. (*Politics*, pp. 197–198)

A(N) M(OTHER)

for almost two decades
I lived with you
but never knew you
    why?
you laughed much
at everybody's jokes
seldom told one yourself
    was the laughing happy?
    should I be asking?

you cried a few times only:
1. a mill strike, no money
    I asked for a dime
2. the new double bed
    the end board split
    in a dozen splinters
    no trampoline
3. your mother dead, finally
    years of illness
    a reversal of roles, you,
    your mother's mother, even
    diapers in the last days

mostly I remember:
1. your peeling potatoes
    for french fries
2. making tea for Skipper
3. hanging laundry, red hands
    in the frosted February air

4. posing for a Polaroid snap
    a new dress, eyes already
    at the New Year's Eve Dance
5. walking through the city
    and the seasons, fast
    like you had somewhere to go
    always returning with salt
    and pepper shakers shaped
    like pigs, porpoises, penguins

I can't remember
    kissing you
    hugging you
I remember
    wanting to
    but not knowing how
I know now you too
    didn't know how

a few stories only, scraps
from a vast store
most of it no longer
reclaimable, lost
as if it never happened

separate, an/other
like icebergs broken
from an Arctic glacier
riding the Labrador current
unlikely we will ever
cross the equatorial line
and become one again
in an Antarctic glacier

"A(n) M(other)" is a lamentation (a song of grief and wailing), but even in the lamenting, the love is known, and the lamenting becomes a link to a more vocal expression of hopeful love. Always there is a tension. Desire is the need to be completed, shaped whole, even as we burn with a need to know ourselves as separate, unique, alone (at one). Always there is a "tension between togetherness and separateness" (Soble, p. 2). I am writing love, and like all my writing, I am physically and emotionally and spiritually caught up, translated, in the words, the activity, the energy of the writing, the loving. I have never been able to share this poem with my mother. I wish I could write truthfully with my mother concerning experiences of love.

Love is Learned

Teachers need to love the people they aspire to teach. Therefore, they need to know their pupils. They need to enter imaginatively into the lived experiences of others. They need to listen to others. They need to learn from others. They need to listen to the stories of others. It is not enough to know how to manage the dynamics of a classroom or prepare effective report cards or organize a busy timetable. Teachers need to hear the stories of others so that they know the others they are serving. They need to be gentle and hopeful and tender and intimate. The teacher fills people with courage and hope and resolve to live in the now, to live each day with purpose.

I have lived for almost half a century, and all my life I have been a teacher or student, and the one consistent theme, the one thread that winds through all my living is hope, the anticipation that we can learn to live together well in the world. Last summer I visited St. John's, Newfoundland, and on Water Street I met Sandra, a former high school student who I taught in 1980. She is now a pediatric psychologist. She said, "I am where I am now because of you. I was in big trouble in school, but you cared about me, and I turned my life around." I still wonder what I really did. Recently I read Jean Vanier's *Becoming Human*, and I was impressed with his wise and optimistic vision of the world. Vanier asks: "Is this not the life undertaking of us all . . . to become human? It can be a long and sometimes painful process. It involves a growth to freedom, an opening up of our hearts to others, no longer hiding behind masks or behind the walls of fear and prejudice. It means discovering our common humanity" (p. 1). According to Vanier, "We human beings are all fundamentally the same. We all belong to a common, broken humanity. We all have wounded, vulnerable hearts. Each one of us needs to feel appreciated and understood; we all need help" (p. 37). Each of us needs "an accompanier . . . someone who can stand beside us on the road to freedom, someone who loves us and understands our life. An accompanier can be a parent, a teacher, or a friend—anyone who can put a name to our inner pain and feelings" (p. 128). Vanier concludes: "We do not have to be saviours of the world! We are simply human beings, enfolded in weakness and in hope, called together to change our world one heart at a time" (p. 163).

I began my first teaching job in 1976 at a high school in Robert's Arm in the northwest corner of Newfoundland. At 22 years old, I was young and enthusiastic and committed to being the best teacher I could be. My first teaching assignment was as a classroom teacher for grade seven with 48 students. Though the school was located in a small town with a thousand people, the school also served as the high school for several elementary schools in several towns around the bay, and students were bussed to R. C. Parsons Collegiate. Many of them were bussed to grade seven. On the first day of school when the 48 students squeezed into the grade seven classroom, located on the second floor of the school building, separated by a stairwell and the lobby and a hallway from the rest of the high school, I was full of fear. Some of the young men were bigger than I was. Some of the young women had a brazen bravado that belied their 14 years. Designed for about 30 students, the room soon looked like a crowded subway train. I felt claustrophobic. The month of September was four weeks of sore throats and red faces from shouting, a panic-stricken confrontation with chaos, long nights of talking with my wife about the horror. Near the end of September, one of the boys brought me a big stick. He had carved it out of oak from an old bed frame with a hand hold. He said, "I think you need this." That day I grew so angry and frustrated I banged the stick on the desk with a crack of fury. The violence left a vacuum of silence. I stared at the shard of oak in my hand, looked at the frightened faces of my students, and in that awful, awful moment knew my strategies for classroom management would never work. I spoke quietly to my students. I said, I'm sorry. From now on, we will have just one rule in this classroom. When a person is speaking, everyone else will be quiet and pay attention to the speaker. With that one rule of respect everything changed. I spent a mostly joyful year with those 48 students, and I have continued to live the one rule in my classes ever since. In the first month of my teaching life, I learned what bell hooks expresses in her book *All About Love: New Visions*: "It had become hard for me to continue to believe in love's promise when everywhere I turned the enchantment of power or the terror of fear overshadowed the will to love" (p. xvi). What I learned in my first month of teaching, and what I have been learning in more than two decades of teaching is to respect, care for, and love my students.

As Ursula A. Kelly writes, "Seizing the importance of re-presenting and re-writing our selves as we reconstruct our visions of world communities entails deconstructing the stories we tell (of) ourselves and the desires that inform them" (p. 49). I began dating my wife when we were both 16 and just graduated from grade eleven. We married at 20, and with her I have explored the experience of a long love. It is good to know long love, but long love must be written creatively, lovingly, with new beginnings rooted in the soil of old beginnings.

LESSONS ABOUT LOVE
(NOT) LEARNED IN SCHOOL
(for Lana)

In the beginning
of the decade
before the one
before this one,
a long time ago,
like yesterday,
you and I skated
all summer, a bonfire
of blue days.

I wore vertical stripes of lime
and horizontal stripes of lemon,
a clown with no balance,
while you wore the sun
tight with a low neck
and a scooter skirt with no horizon,
the most beautiful woman
I had ever seen even though I had seen
you every day of high school.

You had just lost Jimmy.
No one loves dogs like you.
You called Jimmy
and you called
and you called,
but Jimmy didn't come.
I came instead,

Jimmy's substitute,
a poor substitute perhaps.

In high school geography
we learned about faraway
places, bright colours
on a map, even the many
places we have lived,
but no textbook records
the places you and I have
seen together, places
beyond the lines of a map.

In high school history
we learned dates and facts,
but we did not learn the line
that unites the past and present.
Now we remember also to forget.
Our present to one another
is to live in the present.
Together we have learned
to taste the moment's savory.

In high school grammar
we learned the parts of a sentence,
separate, isolate,
but together we learned
how to write the parts
so the sentence
is whole. Together
we can be all parts of the sentence,
both subject and predicate.

In high school literature
we learned the poems of dead poets.
We did not learn to write
poems. We knew no poets.
You ask me why I do not
write you more poems,
but you and I live a poem,
a long lyrical poem
without end.

In high school geometry
we learned to divide the world
into points lines planes.
We did not learn
to take the measure of the world,
to listen for the rhythm of the world.
You and I are two angles,
acute, complementary,
composing a right angle.

Through many years
we have stood side by side,
writing a right angle,
a poem without end,
the sentence whole,
our story grounded in now,
knowing the place
where our feet stand firm
with the promise of beginning.

Love is Lived

I have been profoundly influenced by Ted Aoki who understands that "living in the spaces is what teaching is" ("Interview," 10). For Aoki "the important thing is to understand that if in my class I have 20 students, then there are 21 interspaces between me and students. These interspaces are spaces of possibilities. So what we allow to happen, what can be constituted and reconstituted in those interspaces is what we mean by life in the classroom" ("Interview," 10). Of course there are also interspaces between each student and all the others, contributing to an intricate network of lines and spaces of connection and communication, perhaps without end. Love is lived in relationship, in (mutual) dependence, not independence.

DRIVING LESSONS
(for Anna)

We have driven miles together, you and I,
but soon you will have your own license,
and you will not need me beside you:

check your blind spots
don't speed
watch out for other drivers
look down the road
watch the crosswalks
look both ways
turn off the signal light

This evening in early September
you cut a curb too close,
braked hard before an amber light
you hadn't seen, made an unsafe turn.

I barked. I didn't mean to.
Finally I looked at you, not the road.
You were driving blind, the wipers
useless in a torrent of tears.

I said, I'm an ogre of a father.
You said, No, you're a good daddy.

Once for Necktie Day at school,
you borrowed all my neckties,

and your mother explained,
She is taking neckties for her friends
who don't have fathers.
I was glad I had neckties,
even if I don't wear them anymore.

We parked on the side of St. Alban's Road
and ate Nuffy's donuts,
then under a full moon
wound our way through Richmond.

I am teaching you
how to drive,
but you are teaching me
how to be a father.

I learn from my daughter because I am willing to be vulnerable. She and I write one another in love. As Vanier wisely notes, "I have learned that the process of teaching and learning, of communication, involves movement, back and forth: the one who is healed and the one who is healing constantly change places" (p. 25).

Love is Labyrinthine

The universe is charged with love, afire with love's energy. Everywhere, every day, everything and everybody courses with love, seeking the course that twists and turns without end. Educators and students live in the space of the ecotone. Ecologists describe the place where two ecological habitats such as a meadow and a forest meet as an ecotone, a place of tension (from *oikos* or habitation, and *tonos* or tension). The ecotone is the place where two habitats meet and overlap, where they extend into one another and create a place of richness and fruitfulness that is only possible because of the overlapping. In other words, the ecotone is a space of productive tension where life can be more complex and intense than in either of the distinct habitats. To imagine school as an ecotone, a place of tension, a place of possibility, a place of fecund margins and edges, is to imagine a place where people dwell together in all their differences in a community without unity, seeking no oppressive and repressive homogeneity but inviting the celebration of heterogeneity.

VIEW FROM MY PATIO
(for Julia)

In the late August afternoon
I sit alone on my patio:
drunk with Spring Pale Ale,
biking on the dike,
chopping wood for December fires.

I can see the whole world through
the sun and half moon and star
that hang from my patio,
cut in iron, lined shapes
of light and lunacy and love,

but I cannot see you, faraway.
A spider's web anchors
the sun, moon, and star
to a sliver of earth where
oregano, rosemary, lemon balm grow.

Their fragrance pierces
my skin with exact jabs.
If I were a spider,
I'd cast my lines into the air
and hold the sun, moon, star,

and you, I first saw more than five years
ago, reading Shelley: dressed in black,
alone, leaning against a hallway locker
like a rock in a riverbank, as
students and teachers wended their ways.

I stopped. I had never seen anyone
read Shelley before, especially not
in the school I left long ago, a student,
and returned, a teacher, a hot, noisy
place like a pulp and paper mill.

You did not know my love affair
with Shelley, how I once told my students
about him, his life, his poetry,
and Calvin smiled, You're like Shelley, sir.
He knew the spirit of Shelley in me.

But I was not your teacher;
you were not my student.
With a few words I passed;
I didn't return for more words.
Perhaps I was scared.

To read Shelley is to be filled
with the spirit of trouble-making:
when the daughter of a tavern owner
complained about the tavern and her father,
Shelley eloped with Harriet,

but soon fell in love with the words
of Godwin and then with his daughter,
too, and ran across Europe
with Mary while Harriet drowned
herself in a lake in a London park,

as Shelley, not even thirty, died
a few years later in a storm.
Shelley's moonshone spirit
leaps off cliff edges without
looking for a river to fall into.

I carried the memory of your
reading Shelley to the steps of
241 Alfred Street where you waited,
holding in your hands
Shelley's sun, moon, and star.

Now you read mathematics,
and Anais Nin and Henry Miller,
Shelley's cousins, still wear black,
and you read me, too.
And since I'm still alive,

you invited me to a picnic
beside Lake Ontario
in the shadow of a tree, regaled me
with stories, more picnic food
than I can eat, more words, too.

I saw you enter Lake Ontario
giving yourself as the sun
pours out in the lake.
I watched, left behind,
when spelling light, you sang,

Are you coming in? I felt shy,
not dressed for walking in lakes,
but I took off my leather sandals,
and everywhere I stepped,
your black hair swept in waves.

From my Vancouver patio I cannot
see you, three time zones away,
while I spin out my lines,
seeking the sun, moon, and star,
the light lunacy of love in your eyes.

In the title of her influential book, bell hooks calls for *Teaching to Transgress*, but how about loving to transgress? Is there room for loving to transgress in schools? The universe is charged with love, afire with love's energy. There is so much danger in love. Yet there can be no teaching, no learning, no pedagogical relationship without love. With her characteristic insight, hooks suggests, "As a classroom community, our capacity to generate excitement is deeply affected by our interest in one another, in hearing one another's voices, in recognizing one another's presence" (p. 8). hooks knows "the transformative power of love" (p. 26): "To teach in a manner that respects and cares for the souls of our students is essential if we are to provide the necessary conditions where learning can most deeply and intimately begin" (p. 13).

Paradoxically love is and is not infatuated, blind, naive, foolish, ludic, and lunatic. Love acknowledges the real, the truth, the lived experience, the not beautiful, the stark. Love doesn't conceal or cover up or pretend. Love writes true, and love aspires to revision, change, forgiveness, not blind acceptance (you're okay, I'm okay), but hope. Love is foolish in hope. Love invites differences, passionate tensions and conflicts, questioning, the constitution of identities, the dizzying race of transformations—always becoming somebody else. Love is like Robin Blaser's claim that "the sacred returns with all its faces,/fiery-footed" (p. 39). While I agree with Jane Gallop that "teaching itself has been associated, since the common school movement of the early nineteenth century, with traditional 'good' femininity, that is, with selfless, sexless nurturance" (p. 83), love in the classroom cannot be contained by maternal metaphors alone. Gallop's view of "the teaching relation as enacted between persons" (p. 79) reminds me that teaching is always riddled with love in all its multiplicity. There is no barring love from the classroom.

In reading and writing and thinking for this essay I have learned how much I fear love, and loving, and love relationships, and the unpredictability of love, and the random acts of danger that are love. I continue to be struck by how much I am not willing to disclose and discuss—always so much silence. I conclude this rumination with a final proposition about love, a final poem, knowing full well that I am still seeking to astonish silence, to hear the meaning in the silent letters, to grow attuned to silence where love's energy can be trapped and untapped, but never stopped, never standing still.

Love is Ludicrous

In a recent issue of *Maclean's*, Diane Francis wrote: "Education is . . . one of society's most fossilized, rigid and change-averse institutions" (p. 50). That is a strong indictment, but whenever I grow pessimistic or cynical, I return to Paulo Freire in whom I hear a voice full of passion and hope, compassion and concern: "Each day be open to the world, be ready to think; each day be ready not to accept what is said just because it is said, be predisposed to reread what is read; each day investigate, question, and doubt" (*Politics*, p. 181). Madonna Kolbenschlag observes, "we know that social institutions like the Church, the corporation, the local schools, exist to enable human flourishing, but we experience deprivation within them" (p. 8). She proposes that "the refusal to relate is the sin of our times: the refusal to recognize and respect another's existence; the refusal to speak, to negotiate; the refusal to confront; the refusal to touch one another and cherish the flesh of the 'other' " (p. 41). As Kolbenschlag declares, "the challenge to both men and women is to invent new myths. People are changed, not by intellectual convictions or ethical urgings, but by transformed imaginations. We must begin to live out of new myths" (p. 179).

Frederick Franck in a delightfully wise book titled *A Little Compendium on That Which Matters* writes about "The New Order," which he describes as "the anonymous, unorganized, organic network of awareness beyond all ideological labels" (p. 23). I recognize my own connection to Franck's "New Order": "It is a network of loners, encompassing those who reflect on the meaning of being Human in our technotronic rat trap, who dare to fathom the depths of life, of death, in order to attain a life-praxis, an ethos suitable for this end-time: a religious orientation to existence. Without badge, without watchword, they recognize, hearten one another" (pp. 23–24). I am part of "a network of loners." I am a loner, but I am not alone. I do not speak as part of a collective voice. As a researcher and educator and poet, my voice echoes other voices, but it does not seek to mimic or impersonate other voices, or to silence other voices, or to harmonize with other voices. Instead, I seek to cry out like trumpet calls an urgent invitation to listen to the light, to wake up, to know the world differently, outside the typical parameters and predictions. I am part of a network of loners who seek to give heart to one another, speaking to the heart of the other, hearing the heart of the other in our hearts.

LOVE IS LUDICROUS

> love makes no sense
> Cupid shooting errant arrows
> random like randy rabbits
> will not go away
> laughs at the limits of law
> lives with steel in the heart
> and a wanton disregard for propriety or property
> revels in the chase
> litters with reckless abandon
> fires the body
> till the heart breaks
> reminds us
> that grammar
> the letter the law
> is chimeric
> love loves to laugh
> with rhythms and metaphors
> pneumatic and numinous
> in the language of lack
> learned and lived
> in the labyrinth of the ludic

Bibliography

Belsey, Catherine. (1980) *Critical Practice*. London: Methuen.

The Bible. (1978) *New International Version*. Grand Rapids: Zondervan Bible Publishers.

Blaser, Robin. (1983) "Image-Nation 17: opercula." *Syntax*. Vancouver: Talonbooks, pp. 37–39.

Cameron, Barry. (1987) "Lacan: Implications of Psychoanalysis and Canadian Discourse." In *Future Indicative: Literary Theory and Canadian Literature*, ed. John Moss. Ottawa: University of Ottawa Press, pp. 137–151.

Casati, Roberto and Varzi, Achille C. (1994) *Holes and Other Superficialities*. Cambridge: MIT Press.

Coles, Romand. (1992) *Self/Power/Other: Political Theory and Dialogical Ethics*. Ithaca: Cornell University Press.

Corlett, William. (1989) *Community Without Unity: A Politics of Derridian Extravagance*. Durham: Duke University Press.

Fox, Matthew. (1995) *Listening to the Land: Conversations about Nature, Culture, and Eros*. Ed. D. Jensen. San Francisco: Sierra Club Books, pp. 67–77.

Francis, Diane. (2001) "A Learning Revolution." *Maclean's*. March 5, 2001, p. 50.

Franck, Frederick. (1993) *A Little Compendium on That Which Matters*. New York: St. Martin's Press.

Freire, Paulo. (1997) *Pedagogy of the Heart*. Trans. Donaldo Macedo and Alexandre Oliveira. New York: Continuum.

Freire, Paulo. (1985) *The Politics of Education: Culture, Power, and Liberation*. Trans. Donaldo Macedo. South Hadley: Bergin and Garvey.

Gallop, Jane. (1995) *Pedagogy: The Question of Impersonation*. Bloomington: Indiana University Press.

Griffin, Susan. (1995) *The Eros of Everyday Life: Essays on Ecology, Gender and Society*. New York: Doubleday.

hooks, bell. (1994) *Teaching to Transgress: Education as the Practice of Freedom*. New York: Routledge.

hooks, bell. (2000) *All About Love: New Visions*. New York: William Morrow.

Interview with Ted Aoki. *Teacher*. 6.7 (1994): 10.

Kelly, Ursula A. (1997) *Schooling Desire: Literacy, Cultural Politics, and Pedagogy*. New York: Routledge.

Kolbenschlag, Madonna. (1988) *Lost in the Land of Oz: The Search for Identity and Community in American Life*. San Francisco: Harper Row.

Kristeva, Julia. (2001) *Hannah Arendt: Life Is a Narrative*. Trans. Frank Collins. Toronto: University of Toronto Press.

Leggo, Carl. (1994) *Growing Up Perpendicular on the Side of a Hill*. St. John's: Killick Press.

Leggo, Carl. (1999) *View from My Mother's House*. St. John's: Killick Press.

Noddings, Nel. (1992) *The Challenge to Care in Schools: An Alternative Approach to Education*. New York: Teachers College Press.

Paz, Octavio. (1974) *The Monkey Grammarian*. Trans. H. Lane. New York: Arcade Publishing.

Silverman, Kaja. (1983) *The Subject of Semiotics*. New York: Oxford University Press.

Soble, Alan, ed. (1989) *Eros, Agape, and Philia: Readings in the Philosophy of Love*. New York: Paragon House.

Vanier, Jean. (1998) *Becoming Human*. Toronto: House of Anansi Press.

Chapter 7 ~

A Metanarrative of Emancipation

Trevor Norris

Jurgen Habermas holds a unique place among contemporary philosophers as an original voice compelling us to reassess the accomplishments of modernity. Various critiques of the Enlightenment can be found in French postmodern and poststructural thinkers such as Derrida and Lyotard, while most Frankfurt school thinkers such as Horkheimer and Adorno share many of these criticisms. In contrast to other Frankfurt school thinkers, Habermas considers modernity to be an "unfinished project," whose resources have not yet been exhausted, and calls us to rethink the dehumanizing elements of modernity without abandoning the Enlightenment. In his own words, "the project of modernity has not yet been fulfilled."[1] Much of Habermas's work is a critique of both the turn against modernity and the progressivist excesses of positivism and scientism.

This essay begins with a brief review of reflections on the relationship between the *psyche* and the *polis*, followed by an explication of Habermas's analysis of the inner realm of subjectivity, as found in Freudian psychoanalysis. I will then go on to provide an exegesis of Habermas's analysis of sociology in a consideration of the objective realm of worldviews. At that point I will posit my own hypothesis regarding the latent correspondence between these two analyses, and will consider how the notion of development within the inner realm of subjectivity, as found in Freudian psychoanalysis, corresponds to modernization as a process of demythologization within the objective realm of worldviews. This will suggest that because demythologization allows for the very occurrence of the subjective realm, sociology holds greater critical possibility than psychoanalysis. In conclusion, I propose several possible avenues for future exploration that have been opened by these considerations.

The Subjective and Objective Realms

The correspondence between the inner realm of the subject and the objective realm of society has been a philosophical concern since the time of Socrates. The Platonic dialogues frequently consider this theme, phrased in terms of the correspondence between the *polis* and *psyche*, or the "regime of the soul." This theme appears in Books VIII–IX of the *Republic*, in which Socrates outlines the five types of human souls as they correspond to the five types of political regimes, stating that "it is necessary that there also be as many forms of human characters as there are forms of regimes . . . if there are five arrangements of cities, there would also be five for the soul of private men."[2] An entire dialogue, the *Charmides*, is dedicated to the political character of *sophrosyne*.[3] Furthermore, this correspondence is present within the Greek language itself, grounded in the root *syne*[4]: *dikaiosyne* refers to political justice, while *sophrosyne* refers to "sound-mindedness."[5] However, in our age the *querrelle des anciens et des moderns* has become a quarrel between the Enlightenment and counter-enlightenment, modernism and postmodernism. What emerges as a result is the question of progress or development: a "metanarrative of emancipation," or post-modern "incredulity towards metanarratives" and the "decline of narrative."[6] To examine this question we will turn to Habermas's response to modernity.

Few liberals discuss the subjective realm; most, such as Anglo-American liberal philosopher John Rawls, consider the "private" realm to be protected yet left unex-amined as the realm of autonomous rational moral agents. In contrast, several Frankfurt school thinkers have considered Freud and the theme of the correspon-dence between individual and social development, as for example the writings of Herbert Marcuse.[7] What is unique about Habermas is that he considers this corre-spondence yet incorporates it into a defense of modernity grounded in a metanarra-tive of emancipation. Although acknowledging this fact, David Held states that the "similarities between the development of the individual and development of the species"[8] is "a point Habermas makes a good deal of in his most recent writing."[9] He goes on to state that Habermas's aim is to "elaborate both a general model of indi-vidual development and a model of the development of forms of social integra-tion . . . the analysis of the conditions and possibilities of individual and social development."[10] While it may be true that his later work considers this similarity, this is often done in his shorter works, with respect to historical materialism[11] and to Jean Piaget and Lawrence Kohlberg's ideas of moral development.[12] However, we will find considerations of the notion of individual and social development in his two earlier texts, "Knowledge and Human Interests,"[13] and "The Theory of Communicative Action," volume I, "Reason and the Rationalization of Society."[14] In the former text these discussions occur in his chapters on Freud, who examined the inner dynamics of deviant self-formative processes and communicative practices within the subjective realm. The later text considers the emergence of the field of sociology, which origi-nated from a sense of crisis and social anomie entailed by the advent of capitalism and the process of societal rationalization. In fact, Habermas himself describes his own intention as "a comparison of the world-historical process of social organization with the socialization process of the individual."[15]

Subjectivity: Freudian Psychoanalysis

I now explicate Habermas's analysis of the inner realm of subjectivity, as found in Freudian psychoanalysis, beginning with one of Habermas's earliest texts, "Knowledge and Human Interests." Much of this text is concerned with a critique of the positivist equation of scientific knowledge with knowledge as such, and the ensuing eclipse of philosophy by scientism. Habermas states that as a result of the "scientistic self-understanding of the sciences," the theory of knowledge was "replaced by a methodology emptied of philosophical thought"[16]; ultimately knowledge was replaced by the "absolutism of pure methodology."[17] Habermas discusses several key German thinkers, beginning with Kant and Hegel and concluding with Freud and Nietzsche, with the intention of "analyzing the connections between knowledge and human interests."[18] We will begin with psychoanalysis, which Habermas states "occupies an important place [within the text] as an example" of critical theory.[19]

The discussion of Freud and psychoanalysis is located in the final three chapters, prepared by an earlier discussion of historicism, the cultural sciences, and hermeneutics, as related to Dilthey's account of life-history, autobiography, and ego identity. Habermas observes the uniqueness of Freud's work insofar as it was the "only tangible example of a science incorporating methodical self-reflection"; that Freud simultaneously "developed a new discipline" and engaged in "methodological discussions."[20] Psychoanalysis is concerned with disrupted patterns such as repression and denial, which are held "behind manifest memory."[21] Subjective consciousness is characterized by its tendency to engage in distorted communication, in which conscious intentions are bound up with omissions, flaws, and "systematic disturbances of memory."[22] These corruptions are not to be disregarded, but rather form the central focus of investigation—they are held to "have meaning as such."[23] Cumulatively, these are understood as "symptoms," the breaking-through of internal distortions, the "scars of a corrupt text that confronts the author as incomprehensible."[24]

Turning to the human faculty of repression, Habermas states that "these conflicts, at first external, are perpetuated intrapsychically; insofar as they are not manifested consciously, this perpetuation takes place as a permanent conflict between a defensive agency representing social repression and unrealizable motives of action."[25] Repression is held to be the transformation of consciousness, publicness, and language into the "delinguisticized"[26] privacy of the unconscious. Defensive strategies consist of repression (directed against one's own self) and disguise (a projective redirection of the self toward the outside).[27] Symbol formations that do not obey the grammatical rules of ordinary language become "incomprehensible symbols,"[28] or "deviant symbol formations," the compromise between "repressed wishes of infantile origin and socially imposed prohibitions of wish-fulfillment."[29] This compromise entails a disruption of the subjects' communication with itself; as a result the "privatized language of unconscious motives is rendered inaccessible to the ego."[30] Psychoanalytic interpretation addresses the communication disturbances within the repressive self, with the intention of "teaching one and the same subject to comprehend his own language."[31] This task takes the form of making deformed private language into a public communication, which "brings to consciousness the persons own self-formative process,"[32] aiming not at understanding as in the cultural sciences, but rather at self-reflection itself.

Self-reflection addresses repression through filling in gaps in memory, and thereby realizing their elimination. A communicative "working-through" is achieved by an archaeological reconstruction of the patients' history and a remembering of that history by the patient. The patient–analyst relationship is characterized by the tendency to repeat repressive conflicts through the phenomenon of transference. However, this tendency is impeded through "the reduction of conscious controls"[33] and "the presence of a reserved partner" within the analytic situation, both of which compel the patient to "learn to reflect on his symptoms."[34] The physician therefore induces self-reflective knowledge in the patient through undoing a "miscarried self-formative process,"[35] which resulted in a splitting-off and detachment of symbols from public linguistic usage into distorted private language. This self-reflective knowledge is realized through initiating the "appropriation of a lost portion of life-history."[36]

Habermas differentiates between the psychoanalytic transference situation and medical treatment on several self-reflective grounds: Psychoanalysis is contingent upon an ongoing interest in self-reflection itself, as health is to be achieved through self-reflection: when the patient "regards the phenomena of his illness as part of his self . . . that the ego of the patient recognize itself in its other, represented by its illness, as in its own alienated self and identity with it."[37] Furthermore, in order that the analyst not project onto the patient, the physician must "make himself the instrument of knowledge"[38] through analytic self-reflection.

The structural model of the psychic apparatus includes the three agencies of the ego, id, and super-ego, the construction of which arose through observing the resistance to making what is unconscious become conscious. This structure also includes the public linguistic communication of consciousness, and unconscious communication, which "creeps into public speech and observable actions through detours, and thus 'urges' towards consciousness."[39] "Flight" functions as a defensive process, whereby the ego both hides from anxiety provoking instinctual dangers and from itself in "the process of internal flight,"[40] which is conducted within a "linguistic framework."[41] Tension and conflict arise from flight and repression on one side, and a simultaneous "strong upward drive"[42] toward consciousness. Internalization is achieved through the activities of the super-ego, the "intrapsychic extension of social authority."[43]

Habermas's Critique of Freud

We can now consider Habermas's critique of Freud and psychoanalysis. First, Habermas asserts that rather than basing his structural model on the communicative and interpretive context of the analytic dialogue, Freud in fact described the analytic dialogue in terms of the structural model: he "construes the interpretive work of the physician in the theoretical expressions of the structural model."[44] As a result, Freud thought that the analytic dialogue ensured the experimental validity of psychoanalysis, and that the psychoanalytic method and its structural model "represented an empirically rigorous scientific formulation."[45] However, problems emerged because the development of psychoanalytic methodology occurred in the context of "specifically sheltered communication,"[46] from the interpretation of distorted texts and communicative patterns. Habermas observes that the analytic dialogue as a transference situation is a "pathological situation,"[47] and the narrative events of a life-history disclosed in a therapeutic relationship are presented as "processes in a drama."[48]

Second, Freud's approach was based on the model of the natural sciences—Freud himself began from physiology, neurology, and medicine, and from his early years was caught in a "scientistic self-understanding"[49] that regressed from self-reflection to positivism. The counterpart of psychoanalysis as self-reflection is the account of psychodynamic activities as pharmacologically and biochemically induced. In fact, Freud held (and hoped) that self-reflective psychoanalysis based on a structural model would one day be replaced: "The future may teach us to exercise a direct influence, by means of particular chemical substances, on the amounts of energy and their distribution in the mental apparatus . . . But for the moment we have nothing better at our disposal than the technique of psycho-analysis."[50] Whereas psychopharmacology "controls functions of the human organism as objectified natural processes,"[51] self-reflection is "the act through which the subject frees itself from a state in which it had become an object for itself." This "must be accomplished by the subject itself."[52] In contrast to Freud, Habermas states that "psychoanalysis does not grant us a power of technical control over the sick psyche comparable to that of biochemistry over a sick organism."[53]

We have observed Habermas's two critiques of psychoanalysis (Freud's scientism and the derivation of psychoanalysis from the distorted communication of the pathological situation of analysis), and can now turn to Freud's social theory. In the final chapter of "Knowledge and Human Interests," Habermas considers Freud's later writings on society, culture, history, and religion, which suggest the possibilities offered by social theory.[54] Freud's "theory of civilization (Kultur)" emerges from what Habermas calls "the diagnosis of communal neurosis," which "takes into account the history of the cultural evolution of the human species, the 'process of civilization'."[55] Freud points toward the place of emancipation or liberation in the correspondence between the inner subjective realm and the external social realm, that "just as in the clinical situation, so in society, pathological compulsion itself is accompanied by the interest in its abolition. [For in] both the pathology of social institutions and that of individual consciousness . . . the interest inherent in the pressure of suffering is also immediately an interest in enlightenment."[56] Freud describes the development of the human species as characterized by the establishment of institutions that "exchanged acute external force for the permanent internal compulsion of distorted and self-limiting communication."[57] Development is driven by the demand to regulate surplus instincts and impulses: Freud "sees even the species' process of civilization as linked to a dynamic of the instincts."[58]

However, Freud's account of these instincts and the "process of civilization" arose from his own observations made from the transference situation itself, which "only *derived* the concept of impulse privately from language deformation and behavioral pathology."[59] Insofar as it was derived from the "sheltered communication"[60] of the transference situation, Freud's social theory falls prey to similar problems as psychoanalysis itself.

Objectivity: The Mythical and Modern Worldviews

We can now turn from the subjective world of the human *psyche*, the realm of psychic forces explicated by Freud's structural model of ego identity and individual development as derived from the transference situation, toward the objective world of externality and publicity, the social and cultural realm of historical development as articulated by sociology. This will indicate the correspondence between developmental dynamics within individual self-formative processes, and the evolution of worldviews as a process of differentiation, enabling criticizability. To do so we turn to volume I of "The Theory of Communicative Action."

Habermas opens this text with a discussion of the importance of sociology, insofar as it originated from a sense of crisis and social anomie, rather than the behavioral pathology observed within the transference situation. Because sociology originated as a discipline concerned with world-historical transitions, it is "most likely to link its basic concepts to the rationality problematic."[61] As a result, "sociology became the science of crisis par excellence; it concerned itself above all with the anomic aspects of the dissolution of traditional social systems and the development of modern ones."[62] These anomic aspects emerge from the processes of modernization and rationalization, or the "rationality problematic." Therefore, unlike psychoanalysis, sociology necessarily incorporated theoretical reflection on this dynamic from its very inception, and has therefore "retained its relations to problems of society as a whole."[63]

We will follow Habermas's discussion of the rise of a modern understanding of the world in his second chapter, titled "Some Characteristics of the Mythical and Modern Ways of Understanding the World."[64] These ways of understanding the world are termed "worldviews," cultural interpretive systems that "reflect the background knowledge of social groups and guarantee an interconnection among the multiplicity of their action orientations."[65] Habermas elaborates mythical worldviews, so that the "basic concepts constitutive of the modern understanding of the world, and thus intuitively familiar to us, begin to stand out."[66] They stand out because mythical worldviews "present the sharpest contrast to the understanding of the world dominant in modern society,"[67] as they are "far from making possible rational orientations of action."[68] Habermas outlines three problems associated with mythical interpretations of the world when compared to the modern worldview.

Critique of the Mythological Worldview

The mythical interpretation of the world processes extensive natural and social information; however it also introduces a mirror-effect by which the image of the human and the world is perpetually reflected and therefore "unified into a totality."[69] The "experience of being delivered up unprotected to the contingencies of an unmastered environment" compels a need to "interpret them away."[70] This is done through the "leveling of the different domains of reality: nature and culture are projected onto the same plane."[71] What emerges is "a nature that is outfitted with anthropomorphic features, drawn into the communication network of social subjects, and in this sense humanized, and on the other hand, a culture that is to a certain extent naturalized and reified and absorbed into the objective nexus of operations of anonymous powers."[72] Therefore, a mythically interpreted world cannot "make certain differentiations that are fundamental to our understanding of the world."[73] This lack of differentiation entails the "mixing of two object domains," a conflation of "physical nature and the sociocultural environment."[74]

Second, mythical worldviews are unable to differentiate "internal relations between symbolic expressions [and] external relations between entities that appear in the world."[75] Instead, the internal subjectivity of self-formative process and the objectified natural world are conflated. In fact, the very domain of subjectivity is theoretically inconceivable from within the mythical worldview: "to the degree that mythical worldviews hold sway over cognition and orientations for action, a clear demarcation of a domain of subjectivity is apparently not possible."[76]

A third problem emerges as a result of the two above conflations. The mythical worldview does not see itself as an interpretation of the world; rather, because it has conceptually integrated both nature and culture as well as internal and external relations, it is a reified worldview and therefore not understood as "subject to error and open to revision."[77] Instead it consists of uncriticizable validity claims, which lack reflectivity. As a result "the world is dogmatically invested with a specific content that is withdrawn from rational discussion and thus from criticism."[78]

In contrast, the modern worldview is characterized by a process of demythologization which corresponds to the three problems Habermas associated with the mythical worldview. First, modernization entails the "desocialization of nature and the denaturalization of society,"[79] and the "conceptual *differentiation between the object domains of nature and culture*."[80] Second, it entails the differentiation between the internal world of subjectivity and the external world of objectivity, which in turn allows the emergence of the subjective realm itself, as "only to the extent that the formal concept of an *external world* develops . . . can the complementary concept of the *internal world* of subjectivity arise."[81] Third, in permitting the above differences, demythologization facilitates critical reflection, such that worldviews can be "understood by members as interpretive systems that are not attached to cultural traditions, constituted by internal interrelations of meaning, symbolically related to reality, and connected with validity claims—and thus exposed to criticism and open to revision."[82]

Three Hypotheses

I now posit three of my own hypotheses regarding Habermas's analysis of psychoanalysis and sociology. First, I consider the correspondence, latent in Habermas's theories within these two texts, between development within the inner realm of subjectivity, as found in Freudian psychoanalysis, and modernization, conceived as a process of demythologization, within the objective realm of worldviews. We can now consider the parallels between the mythical worldview and the inner realm of subjectivity prior to undergoing psychoanalysis; however, this is not a straight forward and direct correspondence, but a more fluid series of parallels. We begin with this final point concerning validity and criticizability. Just as the mythological worldview was characterized by a lack of reflectivity, so too is the psychic state of the subject unreflective prior to psychoanalysis. The uncriticizability of the mythical worldview, arising from its inability to see itself as an interpretation of the world, can therefore also be found in the subjects' self-objectivation and resulting tendency to deceive itself and become inaccessible and incomprehensible to itself prior to psychoanalysis. A correspondence has emerged between modernization as demythologization and the psychoanalytic project of "bringing to conscious the persons own self-formative process,"[83] thereby enabling the "appropriation of a lost portion of life-history."[84] Just as the evolution of worldviews enabled the critical reflection required so that worldviews could be "understood as interpretation systems,"[85] the psychoanalytic process enables "the ego of the patient to recognize itself in its other."[86] While the evolution of worldviews facilitates world-historical development apparent in a meta-narrative of emancipation, self-reflection is aimed at filling in gaps in memory and a reconstruction and recollection of a patients' life history, thereby "undoing a miscarried self-formative process."[87]

This hypothesis is strengthened through considering the original text of Freud, specifically his essay "Anxiety and Instinctual life."[88] Thus my second hypothesis emerges concerning the correspondence between the evolution of worldview and the structural model of the *psyche* as outlined by Freud. In linking the id with instincts, Freud stated that "the theory of instincts is so to say our mythology. Instincts are mythical entities . . ."[89] The mythological worldview then appears as an underlying and integral component of the *psyche* itself, closely linked with the primordial id. The id as the locus of undifferentiated and repressed desires, fantasies, and impulses, is not inherently criticizable or open to revision; it too is "withdrawn from rational discussion."[90] Just as modernity is a process of demythologization, psychoanalysis effects a working through of repressed instincts and impulses, thereby permitting ego development.

In my final hypotheses resulting from this analysis of Habermas's perspective on psychoanalysis and sociology, several reasons now become apparent why sociology holds greater promise for Habermas than psychoanalysis. First, modern socio-pathologies cannot be addressed from the inner realm of subjectivity as articulated through psychoanalysis, but only through the external realm of the evolution of worldviews. Emancipation through self-reflective knowledge was deemed unsuccessful within the subjective realm through psychoanalysis; however, the evolution of worldviews as the differentiation of objective realms and the demarcation of subjectivity enables the criticizability of worldviews as contingent interpretations open to discussion and revision, and therefore the possibility of a metanarrative of emancipation. Second, because within the mythical worldview a "domain of subjectivity is not possible,"[91] without an evolution of worldviews there could be no subjective realm as we understand it, and therefore no psychoanalysis. This is a new way of understanding Habermas's emphasis on sociology: that not only is it the study of this world-historical transition and its anemic consequences (as we observed in the opening pages of "The Theory of Communicative Action") but also the very process that gave rise to the subjectivity for psychoanalysis to diagnose and treat.

We followed Habermas's lead and have cast a wide net; what has emerged is a new way to consider the correspondence between subjectivity and objectivity as it relates to the notion of a metanarrative of emancipation. Several possible avenues for future exploration have been opened by these considerations. First, one could undertake a comparative analysis of Habermas's notion of differentiation with Derrida's *differance*. This would challenge the viability of the dialectical tendency of making distinctions that imply a prior unity, and instead proposes alterity and incommensurability. Second, one could consider the consequences of the modern differentiation of nature and culture. The natural world around us has increasingly become an object of conquest and exploitation, and cultural increasingly commodified. Thinkers such as Martin Heidegger and his discussion of technology would help such an undertaking.[92] So too would further work on Habermas: while this chapter has been selective in its textual considerations, Habermas's work as a whole examines various threats to communicative action, and points toward a rethinking of the positivist and dehumanizing elements of modernity.

Notes

1. Jurgen Habermas, *Modernity versus Postmodernity*, trans. Seyla Benhabib, *New German Critique* 22 (Winter 1981): 3–14.
2. Plato, *The Republic*, trans. Allan Bloom (New York: Basic Books, 1968), pp. 544d–e.
3. Plato's *The Charmides*, trans. West & West (Indianapolis: Indianapolis Hackett Publishing Company, 1986).
4. Frederick Peters, *Greek Philosophical Terms: A Historical Lexicon* (New York: New York University Press, 1967), pp. 38–40, 179–180.
5. This following the translation by Allan Bloom. Cf. pp. 389e, 430e, 568b.
6. Jean Francois Lyotard, *The Postmodern Condition: A Report on Knowledge*, trans. Geoff Bennington and Brian Massumi (Minneapolis: University of Minnesota Press, 1979), p. 37.
7. See for example, Herbert Marcuse, *Eros and Civilization* (New York: Beacon Press, 1962).
8. David Held, *Introduction to Critical Theory: Horkheimer to Habermas* (Los Angeles: University of California Press, 1980), p. 276.
9. Ibid., footnote 60, p. 459.
10. Ibid., p. 278.
11. See "Towards a Reconstruction of Historical Materialism," and "Historical Materialism and the Development of Normative Structures," in *Communication and the Evolution of Society* (Boston: Beacon Press, 1979).
12. See Freud "Moral Development and Ego Identity," in *Communication and the Evolution of Society*, (Heinemann, 1979).
13. Jurgen Habermas, *Knowledge and Human Interests* (Boston: Beacon Press, 1971).
14. Jurgen Habermas, *The Theory of Communicative Action*, volume I, *Reason and the Rationalization of Society*, trans. Thomas McCarthy (Boston: Beacon Press, 1984).
15. Habermas, *Knowledge and Human Interests*, p. 276.
16. Ibid., p. 4.
17. Ibid., p. 5.
18. Ibid., p. vii.
19. Ibid., p. viii.
20. Ibid., p. 214.
21. Ibid., p. 216.
22. Ibid., p. 217.
23. Ibid.
24. Ibid., p. 219.
25. Ibid., p. 223.
26. Ibid., p. 224. Habermas's account of language and the unconscious differs dramatically from postmodern psychoanalytic thinkers. For example, Jacques Lacan argues that language is prior to the unconscious, which is itself structured like a language. Jacques

Lacan, "The Function and Field of Speech and Language in Psychoanalysis," in *Ecrits*, ed. A. Sheridan (New York: Norton, 1953), pp. 30–113.

27. Ibid., p. 225.
28. Ibid., p. 226.
29. Ibid., p. 227.
30. Ibid.
31. Ibid., p. 228.
32. Ibid.
33. Ibid., p. 231.
34. Ibid., p. 232.
35. Ibid.
36. Ibid., p. 233.
37. Ibid., p. 235.
38. Ibid., p. 237.
39. Ibid., p. 238.
40. Ibid., p. 240.
41. Ibid., p. 241.
42. Ibid., p. 243.
43. Ibid.
44. Ibid., p. 245.
45. Ibid., p. 253.
46. Ibid., p. 252.
47. Ibid., p. 254.
48. Ibid., p. 260.
49. Ibid., p. 252.
50. From Sigmund Freud, *An Outline of Psychoanalysis*, The Standard Edition of the Complete Psychological Works of Sigmund Freud, trans. James Strachey (London: The Hogarth Press, 1967), volume 23, p. 182.
51. Habermas, *Knowledge and Human Interests*, p. 247.
52. Ibid., p. 247.
53. Ibid., p. 271.
54. Specifically, these include *Civilization and its Discontents*, and *Future of an Illusion*, trans. James Stratchey, Penguin Freud Library, volume 12 (New York: Penguin, 1991).
55. Habermas, *Knowledge and Human Interests* p. 274.
56. Ibid., p. 288.
57. Ibid., p. 282.
58. Ibid., p. 285.
59. Ibid.
60. Ibid., p. 252.
61. Habermas, *The Theory of Communicative Action*, volume I, *Reason and the Rationalization of Society*, p. 3.
62. Ibid., p. 4.
63. Ibid., p. 5.
64. Ibid., p. 43.
65. Ibid.
66. Ibid., p. 45.
67. Ibid., p. 44.
68. Ibid.
69. Ibid., p. 46.
70. Ibid., p. 47.

71. Ibid.
72. Ibid.
73. Ibid., p. 48.
74. Ibid.
75. Ibid., p. 49.
76. Ibid., p. 51.
77. Ibid., p. 50.
78. Ibid., p. 51.
79. Ibid., p. 48.
80. Ibid.
81. Ibid., p. 49.
82. Ibid., pp. 52–53.
83. Habermas, *Knowledge and Human Interests*, p. 228.
84. Ibid., p. 233.
85. Habermas, *The Theory of Communicative Action*, volume I, *Reason and the Rationalization of Society*, p. 53.
86. Habermas, *Knowledge and Human Interests*, p. 235.
87. Ibid., p. 232.
88. Sigmund Freud, "Anxiety and Instinctual Life," in *An Outline of Psychoanalysis*, pp. 113–144.
89. Ibid., p. 127.
90. Habermas, *The Theory of Communicative Action*, volume I, *Reason and the Rationalization of Society*, p. 51.
91. Ibid., p. 51.
92. Martin Heidegger, *A Question Concerning Technology and Other Essays*, translated with an introduction by William Lovitt (New York: Harper Torchbooks, 1977).

References

Freud, Sigmund. (1967). "Anxiety and Instinctual Life." In *An Outline of Psychoanalysis*, The Standard Edition of the Complete Psychological Works of Sigmund Freud, Volume 23, trans. James Strachey. London: The Hogarth Press.

———. (1979). "Moral Development and Ego Identity." In *Communication and the Evolution of Society*. : Heinemann.

Habermas, Jurgen. (1971). *Knowledge and Human Interests*. Trans. Jeremy J. Shapiro. Boston: Beacon Press.

———. *Modernity versus Postmodernity*. Trans. Seyla Benhabib. *New German Critique* 22 (Winter 1981), pp. 3–14.

———. (1984). *The Theory of Communicative Action*, volume I, *Reason and the Rationalization of Society*. Trans. Thomas McCarthy. Beacon Press: Boston.

Held, David. (1980). *Introduction to Critical Theory: Horkheimer to Habermas*. Los Angeles: University of California Press.

Lacan, Jacques. (1983). "The Function and Field of Speech and Language in Psychoanalysis." In *Ecrits*, ed. A. Sheridan. New York: Norton.

Lyotard, Jean Francois. (1979). *The Postmodern Condition: A Report on Knowledge*. Trans. Geoff Bennington and Brian Massumi. Minneapolis: University of Minnesota Press.

Plato. (1968). *The Republic*. Trans. Allan Bloom. New York: Basic Books, pp. 544d–e.

Chapter 8 ⁓

Freirean Literacy: Difference that Makes a Difference

Carlo Ricci

This chapter looks at ways that we need to engage in dialogue about difference with our students to make a difference. In our contemporary world literacy cannot be limited to learning to read words, but it must connect to the world and our everyday lived experiences. Using Freirean pedagogy as a guide we can start to think about what a system of education that teaches literacy to include difference that makes a difference looks like. This is not meant to be what Freire critiques as a "how-to recipe" for teaching literacy (*Literacy*, p. 134), but it is meant as an example of a fluid approach that others can then re-create and rewrite for use in their own context.

First, as educators we need to give our students the opportunity to engage in dialogue along *with* others in a comfortable nonthreatening environment. Second, teachers need to use what Freire calls a problem-posing method of teaching rather than a banking system. Problem-posing pedagogy forces students to think critically, to reflect, and to act. Of problem-posing education, Freire says,

> They must abandon the educational goal of deposit-making and replace it with the posing of the problems of human beings and their relations with the world. "Problem-posing" education, responding to the essence of consciousness—*intentionality*—rejects communiqués and embodies communication. It epitomizes the special characteristic of consciousness: being conscious of, not only as intent on objects but as turned in upon itself in a Jasperian "split"—consciousness as consciousness of consciousness. (*Oppressed*, p. 60)

A problem-posing system of education is one that offers students the opportunity of engaging in meaningful dialogue about questions and issues that are genuine. Teachers and students need to talk *with* each other, as opposed to having the teacher talk *to* the students. Of course the teacher can and is encouraged to share his or her opinion; however, the teacher should not manipulate or authorize the students to take on the teacher's position. The dialogue must be a genuine inquiry into a substantive issue that is meaningful to the students' lives. A banking system of education, on the other hand, is one whereby the teacher deposits information into the student's head. hooks defines it as, "that approach to learning that is rooted in the notion that all students need to do is consume information fed on them by a professor and to be able to memorize and store it" (p. 14).

In a chapter in *Literacy: Reading the Word, and the World* titled "The People Speak Their Word: Literacy in Action" Freire shows us an example of an emancipatory literacy in practice that focuses on teaching literacy and difference that makes a difference. The chapter is about adult literacy in the context of the republic of Sao Tome and Principe. The texts that are used to teach adult literacy are *The Popular Culture Notebooks:* Freire tells us that this is a generic name given to a series of books and primers. By examining a few of the passages in the text, the political nature of the text quickly becomes apparent. Recall that Freire insists that all teaching is political and that teaching in a directive way is not problematic, but it is only when teaching is done in an authoritarian and manipulative way that it becomes problematic. Here are some sample passages from the texts:

> We all know something. We are all ignorant of something. For this reason, we are always learning.
>
> *Let's read, think, and discuss.*
>
> Working with perseverance, we produce more. Producing more, on the land that is ours, we create riches for the happiness of the people.
>
> With the MLSTP (Liberation Movement of Sao Tome and Principe) we are building a society in which everyone participates for the well-being of all. We need to be watchful against those who are trying to bring back the system of exploitation of the majority by a dominant minority.
>
> Now try to write about what you read and discussed. (Freire, *Literacy*, p. 72)

And,

> *Let's read.*
>
> We become independent at the cost of many sacrifices. With unity, discipline, and work we are consolidating our independence. We repel those who are against us and we gather together those who demonstrate their solidarity with us.
>
> You the colonists, you were wrong to think that your power of exploitation was eternal. For you, it was impossible to believe that the weak, exploited masses would become a force in the struggle against your power.
>
> You took with you almost everything that was ours, but you couldn't take with you our determined will to be free.
>
> Maria, Julieta, and Carlos—they struggled to increase production. They always bring with them the certainty of victory.
>
>> We, us, with us.
>> You, you, with you.
>> They, they, themselves, to themselves, of themselves, for themselves, with themselves, to them, them, them.

Write sentences with:
  Us, to them, with us. (Freire, *Literacy,* p. 73)
The political nature and messages championed in these passages are poignant examples for how in teaching literacy the approach is not academic, utilitarian, cognitive development, nor romantic, but definitively emancipatory.

Just like in the *Popular Culture Notebooks,* we need to focus on an emancipatory literacy that begins with the students' everyday lived experiences. We need to challenge them to read the word and the world in a way that will challenge the oppressive pressure and practices that are racist, sexist, and/or homophobic; we need to challenge them to question the status quo and aim for transformation, rather than merely affirmation. Along with Freire we must engage in literacy and difference that makes a difference.

Furthermore, as teachers are engaging in dialogue *with* their students they need to focus on what Paulo Freire refers to as right thinking. In *Pedagogy of Freedom,* Freire tells us that part of "right thinking" is to decidedly reject any and every form of discrimination. "Preconceptions of race, class, or sex offend the essence of human dignity and constitute a radical negation of democracy" (p. 41). Right thinking, therefore, is an attempt to make society less racist, less sexist, less classist, less homophobic, and more environmentally conscious. In short, right thinking aims to encourage each of us to do our part and transform the world into a more socially just place. Are students and teachers ready for this challenge? Can students and teachers teach and learn to engage in literacy that focuses on difference that makes a difference rather than on a literacy that focuses on Phonics Readers?

In order to answer the above question I read the world by sharing some contemporary examples of stories in today's news (Saturday, December 21, 2002) that offer evidence for how teachers and students can make a difference. Using contemporary news stories is a valuable way of teaching students about the world. It is a useful way of making students aware of substantive issues and to get them to become active citizens that feel empowered enough to transform the world. I argue that literacy is about encouraging students to engage in transforming the world and in contributing to making the world a more just place for all. The first news item I share with you is from British Columbia, Canada. Anybody who has been in the school system recently will attest to the need for dialoguing about homophobia. Many students use language that refers to homosexuals in a derogatory way. This injustice needs to be challenged and students need to reflect on why these citizens have traditionally been marginalized within our society. Using a story that made the front page of many of the major papers in Canada (Saturday, December 21, 2002) is a good way to get students to engage in a meaningful dialogue about the issue. The following news story is a true testament to how we can engage students in literacy that focuses on difference that makes a difference. James Chamberlain, a primary teacher, and four other litigants spent $400,000 of their own money and are now $175,000 in debt to successfully challenge a British Columbia school board for banning three books (*Asha's Mums; Belinda's Bouquet;* and *One Dad, Two Dads, Brown Dad, Blue Dads*) depicting same-sex parents. The Supreme Court of Canada said that, "no age is too tender for children to learn the value of tolerance" (Makin, A1). In his article, Kirk Makin quotes Chief Justice Beverley McLachlin saying, "children cannot learn [tolerance] unless they are exposed to views that differ from those they are taught at home" (A1). Mr. Chamberlain makes a stronger case when he argues for acceptance rather than merely for tolerance. Makin quotes Mr. Chamberlain as saying that "It sends a message to school boards that they need to teach acceptance of same-sex families and have their educators teach kids about homophobia" (A1). A sign of hope is that of the 300 students Mr. Chamberlain taught since the case began only one set of parents has denounced him. We, as educators, must teach texts that encourage right thinking and like Mr. Chamberlain we must challenge unjust decisions and thereby contribute in transforming society for the better.

While at a friend's home several weeks ago she brought out several children's books that she had recently purchased for her two-year-old daughter. She explained how she noticed them on display as she was browsing through the bookstore. She picked up two of the books and proceeded to walk to the cash register ready to pay. The clerk mentioned to her that they have other books in the series and a tape that goes along with it—she purchased the four-volume set. My friend assures me that these books and books like them are very popular and widely used even in schools, and that partly motivated her to buy them. When she took them home and reviewed them before deciding whether to expose her daughter to them she quickly realized that they were not what she had expected or hoped for. She embarrassingly admitted that the purchase was impulsive. The books in question were Dr. Maggie's Phonics Readers. The books (*I Spy; Hap and Cap; Top Job, Mom!; Pom-Pom's Big Win*) were written by Dr. Margaret Allen and illustrated by Priscilla Burris. These books try to teach literacy by using what Paulo Freire refers to as syllabification, rather than by using engaging texts that deal with substantive issues that connects to students' lived experiences, social justice, and democracy. In this chapter I argue that teaching literacy cannot simply be about syllabification but that it must deal with substantive issues. Teaching literacy must be about difference that makes a difference. A literate person is not someone who can decipher phonetic skills, but a literate person is someone who can actively participate in and transform the world they live in.

Both Phonics Readers and the banned books are tools that teachers have to teach literacy. The Phonics Readers are focused on syllabification and sentences like "Spy, spy. I spy. I spy the cat in the hat on a mat" (Allen, *Spy*, pp. 8–9). The banned books, alternatively, deal with issues that are of a more substantive nature. They readily allow for teachers and students to think about, question, challenge, dialogue with each other and transform the status quo in favor of a more right-thinking democratic position. As educators we must offer our students the opportunity to engage with texts that deal with substantive issues.

To those who have Phonics Readers in their rooms and insist on using them I suggest that as teachers we need to teach our students to critically challenge the stereotypes that many of these texts depict. For instance, in Allen's *Top Job, Mom!* the mother is often wearing an apron and cooking while the father is lying on the couch reading a newspaper. Students need to be trained to challenge these stereotypes. The book tries to pass itself off as progressive by having "Mom put the new tan fan on" (Allen, *Top*, p. 5). Mom is pictured with a ladder and tool box; unfortunately, while mom is doing this as well as cooking and taking care of the children, dad is still pictured lying on the couch reading his newspaper. We as educators must teach our students to read their texts (whether they are words, films, malls, architecture, their homes, schools, communities and so on) critically. Teachers should have students rewrite, challenge, and resist the antisexist, antiracist, anti-homophobic, anti-classist, antienvironmental messages whenever they are presented in texts.

Another example of a news story that can be used to examine homophobic issues aired on December 18, 2002. Connie Chung interviewed a gay teen who was banned from gym class, her mother, and their lawyer. The teen, Ashley Massey, was banned from gym class and made to spend over a week in the principal's office during that period. The school claims that she was banned from class because the other students felt uncomfortable about having a gay teen in the locker room. When the teacher called Ashley's mother, Amelia Massey, Amelia asked if Ashley was removed because of misconduct. The teacher responded that there was no misconduct and that Ashley is doing what she is supposed to do in gym class. Although, the teacher added that the other girls felt uncomfortable. Ashley, however, says that she asked the other girls, many who are her friends, and they all assured her that they do not feel uncomfortable by her presence. Connie Chung makes clear that the school, the teacher, the superintendent, and the principal have not given their side of the story.

Martha Matthews, Ashley's attorney, explains that what they are trying to achieve by this lawsuit is that Ashley's constitutional right to equal treatment in a public school classroom be protected. Matthews refers to a fairly recent California state law, Safety and Violence Prevention Act of 2000, which prohibits school districts from discriminating against students on the basis of real or perceived sexual orientation. Matthews discloses that what they want to gain from the lawsuit is an injunction that would require the school to have clear and written policies and training for teachers and administrators. Ultimately, the hope is that this will not happen to any other student. Matthews concludes that just because someone is uncomfortable others do not have a right to exclude them from a public space like a school that everyone has the right to be in. After all, Matthews reminds us that students might have felt uncomfortable by having students of a different race during the early days of integration.

Jeffery Tobin who is the CNN Connie Chung Tonight show's legal analyst paints a bleak picture by revealing that the federal courts under the U.S. constitution have by and large said sexual orientation is not something that they protect. Fortunately, California state law does say that discrimination in a school setting because of sexual orientation is grounds for damages. So, Jeffery predicts that if their allegations are true they could win under California state law. Jeffery concludes that even though the federal courts might let people get away with discrimination resulting from sexual orientation, California state law will not.

This case is another good opportunity for teachers to expose students to literacy that focuses on difference that makes a difference. Teachers can easily use this as a part of their curriculum and allow students to talk *with* each other about the implications of this case. Ultimately, the hope would be that students would side with democratic principles and right thinking. The aim is not to force students to accept right thinking, but to trust that through dialogue students will come to understand that discrimination is not acceptable, that difference must be accepted.

I recently witnessed a group of high school students engaging in a dialogue with their elder family members about interracial marriages and same-sex marriages.

The young high school students did a laudable job of dialoguing with their elders. The elders insisted that interracial and same-sex marriages were wrong, while the high school students passionately argued against this racist and homophobic position. It is shocking that going into 2005 there are still members of our community that are not accepting of interracial and same-sex marriages but not surprising when we consider how high-power community leaders have the audacity to make racist, sexist, and/or homophobic comments in public. Today's news also includes Trent Lott's comments, which are an obvious example of this type of racially inexcusable language.

Another story that has played large in both the United States and Canada is Senate Majority Leader Trent Lott's resignation. In his article, Paul Koring says,

> "Mr. Lott sullied that effort [Mr. Bush's attempts to reach out to minorities who have traditionally felt ignored by the Republican Party] when he recalled that his state of Mississippi had backed Mr. Thurmond's presidential bid in 1948. 'We're proud of it,' he [Mr. Lott] said. 'And if the rest of the country had followed our lead, we wouldn't have had all these problems over the years.'" (A18)

The "our lead" that Mr. Lott is referring to is his wish that Strom Thurmond who "launched his 1948 bid for president on a platform of the 'segregation of the races and the integrity of each race'" (Saunders, A18) would have won the election. In essence Lott is supporting racial intolerance. Students need to be given the opportunity to engage in dialogue about politics and racial intolerance so that they can make informed decisions during elections and hopefully side with acceptance of difference and not with intolerance. They must feel empowered and realize that they can make a difference.

In our visual culture reading pictures is another invaluable form of literacy. The *Globe and Mail* has a poignant and visceral picture of Vice President Dick Cheney, President George Bush, Senator Trent Lott, daughter Julie Thurmond, and wife Nancy Thurmond with Senator Strom Thurmond on December 6, his hundredth birthday. This picture can inspire students to think about the president's attempts to reach out to minorities on the one hand, and his posing with Senator Strom Thurmond who launched his 1948 bid on a platform of the segregation of the races on the other. Students can discuss whether the racial intolerance that the American South is so well known for is alive in the Republican Party and the American presidency? Students must be allowed to engage in a dialogue about the racist ideologies still evidenced in Canada and the United States and they must be encouraged to take their antiracist messages to the community. Just like the example above where the high school students passionately challenged their elders' misguided views, students can take what they learn in the classroom and spread right thinking.

Throughout this chapter, I have tried to offer examples of pedagogy that teaches literacy by focusing on difference that makes a difference. By using contemporary media, Paulo Freire's dialogical approach, his emphasis on problem-posing education, and his notion of right thinking we can see how our education system can go beyond teaching students to accept the status quo and instead to challenge society to struggle to eliminate oppression. We need to encourage students to go beyond the words and to transform the world. We must teach literacy and difference that makes a difference. Students need to read, write about, watch and produce works about difference that make a difference and aim to approach right thinking.

References

Allen, Margaret; Illustrated by Jeannie Winston. (1999). *I Spy.* Cypress, CA: Creative Teaching Press, Inc.

———; Illustrated by Susan Banta. (1999). *Hap and Cap.* Cypress, CA: Creative Teaching Press, Inc.

———; Illustrated by Priscilla Burris. (1999). *Pom-Pom's Big Win.* Cypress, CA: Creative Teaching Press, Inc.

———; Illustrated by Susan Banta. (1999). *Top Job, Mom!* Cypress, CA: Creative Teaching Press, Inc.

CNN. Cable News Network. December 21, 2002. <http://www.cnn.com/TRANSCRIPTS/0212/18/cct.00.html>.

Elwin, Rosamund and Michele, Paulse; Illustrated by Dawn Lee. (1990). *Asha's Mums.* Toronto: Women's Press.

Freire, Paulo. (1993). *Pedagogy of the Oppressed.* Trans. Myra Bergman Ramos. New Revised 20th Anniversary Edition. New York: The Continuum Publishing Company.

———. (1998). *Pedagogy of Freedom.* Trans. Patrick Clarke. Boston: Rowman & Littlefield Publishers, Inc.

Freire, Paulo and Donaldo, Macedo. (1987). *Literacy: Reading the Word, and the World.* South Hadley: Bergin & Garvey Publishers, Inc.

hooks, bell. (1994). *Teaching to Transgress: Education as the Practice of Freedom.* New York: Routledge.

Koring, Paul. "Lott Resigns as U.S. Senate Majority Leader." *The Globe and Mail.* December 21, 2002: A18.

Makin, Kirk. "Schools Can't Ban Gay Books, Court Rules." *The Globe and Mail.* December 21, 2002: A1.

Newman, Leslea; Illustrated by Michael Willhoite. (1991). *Belinda's Bouquet.* Boston, MA: Alyson Wonderland.

Saunders, Doug. "The South's Dominance of Politics May Suffer Same Fate as Senator Lott." *The Globe and Mail.* December 21, 2002: A1, A18.

Valentine, Johnny; Illustrated by Melody Sarecky. (1994). *One Dad, Two Dads, Brown Dad, Blue Dads.* Boston, MA: Alyson Wonderland.

Chapter 9

Crossing the Postmodern Conditions that Divide: Theorizing Difference and the Cultural Politics of Emancipation in Critical Pedagogy

Peter Pericles Trifonas and Effie Balomenos

Postmodernism is the precarious condition of our times. Despite the "post" phase of modernity the prefix of the neologism implies, the social injustices of the previous age have left indelible marks on the solvent ethics of postmodernity and the theorization of difference. The distressing signs of the historical legacy of modernism are to be found in the material domain of discriminatory social practices instituted by the cultural politics of an exclusionary agenda in the name of neoliberal conceptions of an autonomous subject. Difference or deviation from the accepted "norms of being" has been accorded a pejorative connotation in relation to highly arbitrary criteria of judgment based on the ever so problematic categories of race, ethnicity, class, gender, and sexuality. This conscious disenfranchisement of alternate subjectivities or "otherness" is in effect the empirical ground of marginalization within the social sphere of community. It is the material results of the societal production of the meaning of representation that rationalizes the social value placed on acts of inclusion and exclusion. Difference therefore comes to be measured practicably in relation to the acceptable configuration of cultural ordinances of aspect—being like others means being acceptable to a closed conception of community as the taking up of arms against the radicality of difference. Any deviation from standardized images of "normality" is figuratively conceived in terms of narrowly defined criteria and the fixed, qualitative scaling of personal or group characteristics. Marginalization ensues. Consequently, the question of difference has come to be elided with the question of the effects of dominant ideologies upon what are the identity politics of the representation of selfhood within community.

Broaching the Epistemological Culture of Modernity and
Critical Pedagogy

Louis Althusser posited the transversal function of an amassing of diverse ideologies and independent interests under the overarching panoply of a single "controlling culture" with the power to reproduce itself has been a key factor for reactionary theories of subjectivity attempting to explain the social interpellation of the individual into "subject" through the apparatus of the State. It is not surprising that for the so-called reproduction theorists of Structural Marxism, the educational institution represents the speciousness of indoctrination. Or an efficient system for cultivating the repression of identity and difference through the symbolic violence of its curricular strategies and practices of knowledge representation (see Bourdieu and Passeron, 1979). And yet—leaving this issue of the productive sphere of pedagogy temporarily aside—there has also been a current of strong reaction against this "relative autonomy" given ideology to freely tame the irreverence of difference. The theoretical belief in its ability to efficiently deploy, in- and of-itself, the conditions for insuring the concrete manifestations of an unimpeded and, hence, automatic reproducibility of meaning reconstructions within the symbolic realms of the (un)consciousness of the subject has been severely tested. For, this conception of a transmutable ideology presupposes a powerless subject, one unable to resist the intransigence of such procedures of control at work, be they active or passive, overt or covert.

Various educational and curricular reform projects with an emancipatory impetus have risen-up to protect the agency of the subject against what is tantamount to a willfull regimentation of "Truth." Such an instrumentalist value promoting a homogeneous concept of identity could only serve to bolster the already well-wrought fetters of social inequality. The educational movement subsumed under the proper name of "critical pedagogy" has "a nascent disciplinary trajectory within education that has its roots in Marxian analyses of class" (McLaren, 1994, p. 319). Its premises promote the liberatory hope of initiating radical teaching–learning strategies that could enable the epistemological and political subject to reflect upon its complicity with the onerous symptoms of a "false consciousness" that have been arbitrarily imposed upon it. Critical pedagogy is about raising questions about the grounding of knowledge and what is taken for granted. And by so doing, to allow the difference of subjectivity the opportunity to self-consciously reinscribe the meaning of itself in the difference of a newly achieved awareness of possible world structures. The hope is that dialogue, critical analysis, and reflection will motivate the subject to ethical and political action against oppressive social institutions.

To aim at realizing such a thing, the major theorists of critical pedagogy—Henry Giroux and Peter McLaren—succeeded in crafting the minimal basis of its open methodology from a selective admixture of first-generation Frankfurt School social theory, Antonio Gramsci's idea of hegemony (coupled with the intellectual application of a counter-hegemonic resistance to the avid perpetuation of ideology), and Paulo Freire's educational theory/action of *conscientization*. More recently, however, there has been a vitalizing reconceptualization of the operative premises of critical pedagogy, theoretical and practical. Poststructuralism—the theoretical discourses driving the idea of postmodernity—provides a backdrop for finding new ways to continue to rethink the implications of difference for education and community that can inform a post-critical pedagogy.

The Critical Difference of French Philosophy: Sources for a Post-Critical Pedagogy

If there is a principal connection to be made between poststructural theorizing and critical pedagogy, it lies in the all-but-sudden awakening of contemporary scholarship to the inherent limitations and the repressive inadequacies of the modernist paradigm of science. A foundationalist logic has traditionally informed the curricular content of pedagogy and the institution of education. To teach one must have some degree of certainty regarding the truth of content. Otherwise the educational act would be both arbitrary and disingenuous. The transmissive goals of the educational process that a curriculum demands as proof of pedagogical and knowledge objectives would be doomed to failure. This is the major problem of a postmodern view of education: reconciling the precarious degree of certainty relating to truth with the necessity of curricular and pedagogical outcomes.

Postmodern discourses regarding knowledge—thanks to poststructuralism— refute the methical certainty of the conceptual dualism constituting knowledge claims as "right" or "wrong." Educational certainties are rendered suspect. Along with the epistemological grounds that articulate the autotelic unity of a Cartesianist, rationalist subjectivity and the experiential proofs of scientific empiricism undergirding educational research. Through poststructural theory, postmodernism questions the modernist belief in the possibility of describing the determinate rules and systems of reality a posteriori perception. Doubt and skepticism cloud the depiction of truth as a generalizable universal of experience independent of bias, prejudice, or the ideological attributes of tradition and history (Harvey, 1990; Lyotard, 1984).

The New Nietzscheans: Foucault, Derrida, Lyotard, Baudrillard

The critical groundwork for an opposition to the modernist teleology of knowledge was arguably laid out in the latter half of nineteenth century by the German philosopher Friedrich Nietzsche (1844–1900) (see Best and Kellner, 1991). Nietzsche was perhaps the first philosopher to vehemently dispute the legitimacy of Western metaphysics as an empty edifice of claims to knowledge that amounted to nothing more than the weak ideology of a correspondence theory of truth. He denied the univocality of meaning so crucial to establishing an epistemological prerequisite for the rationalizable empiricality of science. Self-explanatory systems of cause–effect relations result from an autotelic experiencing of real-world phenomena by a self-reflexive, unified, and all-knowing subject. Attacking the absolutism of such an uncharitable position to be illusory, Nietzsche established an important precedence for looking beyond what Martin Heidegger later called the onto-theo-logy of an ethnocentric mythology permeating Western philosophical discourse, essentially by seeking to explore how the confluence of ideological interests within a society or culture motivate knowledge constructions.

The epistemological battlefields of contemporary French philosophy have, by and large, provided the integral influences upon what are the ethics and the politics of postmodern thinking—Richard Rorty being perhaps the most notable North American exception. Many French philosophers of the postmodern age, for example, Jacques Derrida (1990), Michel Foucault (1970), Jean-François Lyotard (1984), and Jean Baudrillard have furthered the iconoclastic impulse of Nietzsche's audacious brand of antihumanism, sustaining for a new generation the radical flair of a long overdue critique of Western epistemology and its epistemological certainty. Foucault, Derrida, and Lyotard have addressed the ethical implications of the Enlightenment mentality–morality of modernism for the institution of education and critically gauged the complex problems of knowledge, power, and language in relation to the construction of discipline and disciplinarity (Trifonas, 1995b). The hierarchical schema of densely prescriptive knowledge structures that is the basis for educational practices and curricular formations is supported by of a modernist exemplar of epistemology as transmissive knowledge. It is grounded on an empirical research base that is an immutable archive of science and its laws. What is officially recognized as "knowledge" *orders* and *is likewise ordered* by the institutional formation of the disciplines (Apple, 1993). The system of valuations/devaluation is based in the immediate contingencies of a binary logic: that is, the reductive interpretation of real-world phenomena as "true" or "false." This opposition forms the Western foundation and certainty of knowledge. It is a simplistic pattern of thought and a way of thinking whose effects are congealed within the totalizing medians of an easily transferable logic of culture and science. Truth becomes the effect of a discourse supported by the prevailing structures of power. The cultural politics of knowledge reinforces and naturalizes the ideological basis of socio-historical meaning constructions. The production of truth permeates the discursive habitus of the subject as the semiotic outworking of forces intrinsic to the communication of concepts through which a consciousness of self, or subjectivity, is induced (Bourdieu, 1984).

Along these lines of theoretical demarcation, Foucault (1970, 1980) conducted remarkable genealogical researches into the archeology of the discursive ordering of meaning and sense within the human sciences. The historicity of Western episteme is illuminated throughout his work as the synchronic and diachronic structuring of language usage and form that constitutes a nexus of power/knowledge relations. Foucault identifies how discourse is codified by the cultural expropriations of language, via its production and its reception. Power is instituted through linguistic means as a theory of praxis to be performed. In short, for Foucault an "ethics of knowledge" is born of discourse practices. From the ordering of vague concepts in the mind to the surreptitious workings of language upon the culture of society, the discursive nature of human existence is analyzed by Foucault through an archi-tectonic mode of conceptual reconstructions. His arche-ology is a method for defining the expanding regions of an array of belief systems that function to inform subjectivity through the disciplining of the subject. In this context of its usage, the word "discipline" specifically refers to the active process of training or educating the body for docile subserviance (e.g., a master and a disciple), a meaning that is brought out in the Latinate origins of its root. Foucault (1980) tried to reveal the operative features of this cruel force of institutional domination by analyzing how the surveillance techniques used in schools and prisons (taking exemplary form in the model for the Panopticon developed by Jeremy Bentham) are internalized by a willful subject functionally capable of dissent. The linguistic essence of the representation of subjective identity subsumes the difference between being and milieu, humanity and socius. The desire to "respect such differences, and even try to grasp them in their specificity" (Foulcault, 1973, p. xii) of construction is what fascinated Foucault. Even more to the point was the question of why a subject would seek to be dominated that is a theme running through his work. This line of inquiry enabled him to reflect upon the obvious ideological inconsistencies within the macrology of institutionalized systems of thought and how readings of subjectivity may be conducted from the microscopy of an intense questioning of attitudes toward language.

Even more radically anti-foundationalist in scope than the de-archiving methods of Foucault, Derrida (1976) has theorized a conception of difference that is an ironic reversal of the laws of speculative idealism governing Western philosophy from the Ancient Greek thinking to Hegel and afterward. Even in deconstruction, difference is an epistemological benchmark of "the Other." But Derrida moves beyond the idealization of identity to signify the (non)ended of absolute knowledge or the self-effacement of dialectical totalities that can never be resolved. He extends the Hegelian imperative for a strict negativity to the quasi-semantics of meaning deferrals that suspend closure. This is an iterability articulated by the affective differences of the trace of repetition displacements, or *différance*. What Foucault and Derrida have both clarified are the dangers of liberal humanist arguments for the "singularity" and "particularity" of subjective identity. It is their contention that projects intending to regularize the cognitive, the affective, and even the bodily behaviors of individuals within the field of a society or culture can no longer be condoned by promoting "the truth" of knowledge through a dialectical symmetrization of subjective identity as either positive or negative in nature. To suggest that there can be such an equationing of subjectivity through interventive means is a very troubling hypothesis. There is difference in similarity, similarity in difference. There are differences within subjectivities correlating to differences within perception that must be taken into account. As Charles Jencks (1992, p. 11) explains the epistemological implications of this originary difference, "the uncontested dominance of the modern world view has definitely ended. Like it or not the West has become a plurality of competing subcultures where no one ideology and episteme dominates for long." Valorizing the fragmentation of subjectivity or acknowledging the openness of difference warrants an appreciation for the plurality of discourses or alternative configurations of legitimate meaning sources that embrace the contexts of society and culture. Foucault suggests that "we must not imagine a world of discourse divided between accepted discourse and excluded discourse . . . but as multiplicity of discursive elements that can come into play in various strategies" (cited in Martusewicz, 1992, p. 147). In identifying the need to be open to a plethora of subject positions, what postmodern theorizing forthrightly discourages is the recuperation of "otherness," an objectification of identity leading either to a rejection or an "exoticization" of the other (see McLaren, 1994). Such a differentiation of subjectivities reconstitutes a stereotypical metaphor of "cultural authenticity" and ignores the reality of individuals as existing within communities of difference.

Modernist knowledge claims in relation to the historicity of "Reason" grant primacy to Western epistemological "edicts" while suppressing the capacity to reinforce the ideological differences of marginalized group identities. Especially, insofar as a reliance upon an introspective normativity is entrench within a monodimensional view of subjective consciousness. Postmodernism provides the critical means for facilitating a hermeneutic shift in the discursive means for upholding regimes of power/knowledge and that critical act of resistance would offer much needed respect to the dissonance of voices kept at the border lines of a "general culture" (Giroux, 1988c). Jencks (1992, p. 36) elucidates the ethical ramifications of perpetuating the logic of a one-sided epistemological background characteristic of the dominance of one culture by another to illustrate how the prospective effects of this myopia can be opposed with what a postmodern education expects of its participants:

> It is crucially important that free communication be safeguarded and a good education provided for everyone. Otherwise, it is quite certain, we will create more vicious divides within society and between cultures, and deepen the shame of a post-industrial society—the permanent underclass. Such moral points are not out of place . . . since every post-modern discourse emphasizes the interconnectedness of things.

In explaining the purpose of recognizing varying viewpoints to consolidate an aura of community, Jencks converges upon the unifying aspect of postmodernism that would foster an appreciation for otherness and difference through concentrating upon the contextual dependency of human understandings relative to the multivariate nature of experience (Giroux, 1990). A noncoercive environment in which to initiate genuinely intersubjective dialogues between perspectives is crucial to the familiarization of differences for the enrichment of society overall. Acceding to differences of alternative domains within the communicative substrata of "Culture" could lead to a sublimation of the axiomatics for upholding an hierarchy of privilege by defusing the institutionalized logic of an enforced unity of identity through either visible or invisible means of discipline, training, and correction designed to "normalize" subjectivity (Foucault, 1977). What entitles the subalterned or disenfranchised to a voice denies the reification of subjectivity that a general culture depends upon. Its radical ethics protects the inherent differences of subjective identity against the consensus and consistency of a dominant discourse (Spivak, 1992).

A corollary effect of establishing a semiosphere of cultural communication is the psychological necessity of coping with the effects of a lack of determinacy in meaning-making. Or, what is the aftermath of a fissuring of rigid moral orders of discourse arising from an approbation of otherness or of difference. This relativistic type of social bonding requires a more "open" than "closed" interpretative matrix through which to renegotiate the cultural politics of a critical awareness and subjective differences. Within postmodernism, poststructural theories of signification proffer such flexible critical tools for analyzing the cybernetics of institutional knowledge constructions in order to reveal how the ideological presuppositions within the textualized forms of a discursive expression of content mediate to systemically neutralize the freedom of subjective conclusions by a reconstruction of the conceptual conditions of "truth" through writing (see Kellner, 1988). Sometimes described as needlessly cynical or just "playful," poststructuralism suspends the finality of an idiosyncratic reading by resisting the terminating values of signification within a text. Meaning is taken to a subjective plateau of situationally viable, but potentially variable interpretative choices that cannot appeal to objective measures or standards for a verification of "truthfulness" (Derrida, 1976). Poststructuralism destabilizes the disinterestedness of knowledge. It grounds texts firmly within the literary contexts or the situations of their constructions to expand the intersubjectivity of world to the variegated dimensions of "possible worlds" (Eco, 1979). Poststructuralism denies objectivity within perception. It places perception within the affectivity of discourse so as to account for the effectuation of consciousness from linguistic contexts and practices. The validity of arguments is shown not to be self-evident in language, but contiguous to a presentation of contextually discerned phenomena that are both faithful and unfaithful to the constructions of their own logic (Derrida, 1976).

Jean-François Lyotard (1984) and Jean Baudrillard (1981) align the postmodern arena of information exchange to the spectacle of computer-simulated graphics and the images of techno-pseudo presentation that are multiplying within the symbolic field of cultural production. The effects of these "new" visual-based media fetishize the sense of otherness or of difference within community. They implode and fix the conceptual limits of identity in a ready-made format for a globally disseminated intersubjective networking of fictional realities. According to Baudrillard, the swift meta-statization of available technologies for modeling simulations of real-world phenomena have so permeated contemporary society through the proliferation of "virtual media" (e.g., television, video, computers, and the like) that the boundaries separating "the real" from "the fabricated" are no longer distinguishable, just disguised in the glossy formulaic alternatives of an idyllic *hyperreality* (Baudrillard, 1981). These *simulacra* of the real transgress the subjective experience of the world as real. Having been refurbished and recoded, the essential qualities of reality consequently shape the subjective understanding and knowledge in a newly self-conscious way. A more intricate and sophisticated system of information de-archiving is now required by the discerning subject (see Baudrillard, 1981). Baudrillard identifies parody as the critical lens. Seeking the existence of a transcendental referent or signified in technological dissimulations of the real is no longer possible. There are no limits to what can or should be thought in the parameters of simulated realities because there are no limits to what can be produced. It is because the generic or normative archetypes of fictionalizations of phenomena are fed back into the real that "truth" therefore loses all plausibility within the infinite permutations of meaning-making propagated through the cross-mediality of a visual semiotics of cultural literacy. Lyotard (1984, p. 75) echoes the postmodern stance Baudrillard puts forward apropos representation by refuting the commensurability of meaning across incompatible ideologies or competing epistemologies and modernist metanarratives from postmodern discourses:

> Consensus does violence to the heterogeneity of language games. And invention is always born of dissension. Postmodern knowledge is not simply a tool of the authorities; it refines our sensitivity to differences and reinforces our ability to tolerate the incommensurable.

The application of the Wittgenstienian phrase "language games" to discourse refers to, at least, a partial incommenserability of understandings among subjects or a nonpractical consensus of intersubjectivity. The reconcilability of meaning-making emanates less from genuine agreement than from the pragmatic suppression of differing ideological orientations maintained relative to individual belief systems. What Lyotard would seem to suggest is that claims to knowledge can only be approached through a self-critical consciousness, whereby dissent is the questioning of the difference of concepts in a constantly malleable state of flux. It is a prototype of reading for broadening a subjective acquaintance of the likelihood of alternative semantico-stylistic prospects within expression. Scrutinizing the astructural "depths" of the interplay of these discursive potentialities fuses the interpretability of content with "textualizations" of experience by harnessing the critical power of the subject to unearth the ideological undertones that influence the recording of a perspective and the means to attempt to comprehend it.

Postmodern Education?

The break of postmodern theorizing with the representational foundationalism of modernity has been much celebrated. But where this "epistemological rupture" leads, remains a highly contested issue. On the one side, the more apophatic factions within the postmodern debate envision the presently confused critical condition as the result of an apocalyptic resignation looking forward in space and time to the end of history: all options will soon be exhausted in *toto,* leaving no "tangible" future from which to realize the human progression of a history of meaning (Kellner, 1988; see also Best and Kellner, 1991). On the other, more optimistic factions view the current condition of postmodern critical collage as an extension of interpretative differences denied modernism and portray the alterity of the re-representation of ideas by a linking of the cultural sphere of knowledge to an intertwining of discourses exhibiting an endless intertextuality of expressive forms (Hutcheon, 1992; see also Bennington, 1986). Linda Hutcheon (1992), for example, points out that the fractured pluralism of our times has given rise to the need for a revitalization of theorizing and of expression, for example, she posits a metafictive anti-genre of writing that might successfully cohabitate with the ideological vicissitudes of a postmodernist politics of knowledge. The critical subtlety of a postmodern consciousness engenders an acceptance, if only a relative one, of the very belief systems it attempts to subjugate and to problematize by incorporating them within the boundless textuality of its pliant corpus. In this fashion, perspectival standards are immanently assessed so as to permit for "aesthetic forms and social formations to be problematized by critical reflection" (Hutcheon, 1992, p. 77). Relating the postmodern dilemma of difference more specifically to the growing discipline of cultural studies, Stuart Hall (1986) believes individuals can no longer subscribe to critical absolutes within such a magnitude of contradictory understandings of reality pervading societies. Systematized traditions can offer insights for a critical consumption of their relative value as discourses of difference or examples of otherness so as to change the force of "old arguments" in light of more original and more radically open perspectives. Whereas theoretical absolutism has offered a "series of uneven developments that have emerged out of conflicts between traditional economic models and new cultural formations and modes of criticism" (Giroux, 1988c, pp. 10–11), a postmodern perspective would, more often than not, embrace an acceptance of plurality and of difference within hermeneutic frameworks. But, through a self-critical analysis of the discursive structuring of the conceptual lay-out of arguments related in order to bring to the surface any "blind-spots" (i.e., contradictions of position, ideological hierarchies, and the like). Such a "deconstructive reading" would play the language or themes of a text against itself to test the solidity of the logic of its conceptual foundations (Derrida, 1976). Deconstruction reveals the argumentative means organizing the authority of a subject position taken up in a text by evaluating the preoccupations of discourse that follow the linguistic structuring of a perceived reality. Derrida (interviewed in Kearns and Newton, 1980, p. 21) warns of the dangers of instrumental uses of deconstruction to unilaterally reject all claims to knowledge:

> I would never say that every interpretation is equal . . . The hierarchy is between forces and not between true and false. . . . I would not say that some interpretations are truer than others. I would say that some are more powerful than others. The hierarchy is between forces and not between true and false. There are interpretations which account for more meaning and this is the criterion.

The external and internal interaction of the "system of forces" acting to generate meaning-making potential (to which Derrida has often referred to as the outcome of the cumulative effects of psychologically motivated factors) are never identical for any two individuals (see Derrida, 1976, 1981). Every individual brings to an act of reading the mental differences of a subjective identity drawn from experiences that have inculcated the (un)conscious formation of a personalized psychic reality. Derrida (also from Kearns and Newton, 1980, pp. 21–22) comments further upon the role of the difference of subjectivity in deconstruction:

> No-one is free to read as he or she wants. The reader does not interpret freely, taking into account only his own reading, excluding the author, the historical period in which the text appeared and so on. . . . I think that one cannot read without trying to reconstruct the historical context but history is not the last work, the final key, of reading.

Derrida's explanation, at odds with the hyperrelativism attributed to deconstruction by its critics, leaves open a hermeneutical space or "gap" in which to explore the significance of the intentionality of meaning (re)constructions to be derived from the reading, while simultaneously suggesting that such considerations are to be seen as but a single agent coloring the discursive mediation of experience resulting in the textualization of "reality." Perspectives may not be consciously "selected," but differences within the discursive conditions of experience forefront a variety of subject stances that therefore concede a surplus of positional definitions.

Postmodern theoretical discourses engage in criticism removed from nurturing the isolation of personal meaning-making by constantly searching for "the possible" in "the unlikely" or "the improbable." And the iconoclastic experimentalism of this epistemological adventurousness is valorized by the gravity of Jencks's (1992, p. 11) post-metaphysical observations: "The uncontested dominance of the modern world view has definitely ended. Like it or not the West has become a plurality of competing subcultures where no one ideology and episteme dominates for long." Rather than helping to create an adversely competitive environment that would deny "subcultures" the right to be heard over the monologue of dominant metanarratives, accepting the heterogeneity of perspectives within contemporary societies requires legitimating the postmodern interplay among a variety of differing voices (Lyotard, 1984).

A Critical Pedagogy after Poststructural Theory

The term "critical pedagogy" relates to and originates from within the material conditions of the epistemological effects that poststructural theorizing has attempted to critique. It does so by focusing upon contextualizing the basis of the possibilities for social change to bring about a more equitable "new-world-picture" through the education of the subject. Because the term "critical pedagogy" possesses obvious semantic connotations associated with conceptual analysis, the early interpretations of it were taken to imply a method of pedagogy used to involve students in overtly critical exercises. The adjective "critical" within "critical pedagogy" refers to "critical theory"—the Marxist philosophical tract, upon which, its theoretico-methodological ends are founded. Critical theorists, such as Theodore Adorno and Herbert Marcuse, have argued that subjects should strive for social and intellectual emancipation from the circumstance of political and economic domination enshrined by the powers-that-be (Stanley, 1992). A critical pedagogy must take up the urgency of this core Marxian tenet by seeking to maximize the subject's capacity for a revolutionary move to such a state of freedom through deconstructive exercises that clarify ideology and exude the potential for an interpretative plurality within hegemonic discourses by an illumination of the conditions of the oppressive power of the educational institution (Giroux, 1987, 1988d; McLaren, 1991). But it must also displace the metanarratives governing the ethical and political dimensions of subjects and institutions. The idea of a de-reification of power through a negative critique, or "negative dialectics," aims at de-subjectifying the "false consciousness" of the self. This estrangement of the incorporate shell of subjective identity is a fundamental step to the individual's emancipation from the hegemony of ideology infusing the site of unabashed exploitation. A counter-hegemonic practice is also well versed in the limitations of negative critique as the intellectual instrument for a sustained resistance to the imposition of meaning from ideologically overdetermined sources outside the self. To liberate subjectivity, in this sense, does not mean to deny self-identity, but to assert independence and control over the homeostatic effects of ideology that enslave the subject to a living-through of the interests and desires of the system.

Much of the theoretical premises of critical pedagogy can also be traced to the writings of the Brazilian philosopher of education Paulo Freire. Freire (1970) maintained that educational systems should foster an ability for autonomous thought and independent action by encouraging students to actively take part in the development of their own *active paideia,* or an ethical logic of praxis dealing in practical and ideological terms with the knowledge claims thrust upon them. Showing how the subordinated groups of a dominant cultural orientation become alienated within educational system supporting the interests of the *status quo*, Freire advocated teaching–learning environments that would be conducive to critical reflection by teachers and students alike, hence, enabling the cultivation, in individual subjects, of the ability to fervently realize the legitimacy of honoring differences, especially ideological ones, by not subscribing *a priori* experience to the oppressive structural arrangements of institutions often organized according to austere doctrines of manipulation. The necessity of developing teaching–learning situations responsive to the essential reflexivity of such a "critical literacy" for self-liberation is then realized by encouraging students to relay personal experiences to one another so as to incite thought and discussion upon their own discourse and those of others, through which, could be actualized provisional but intelligibly framed arguments that are not governed solely by a dictated percipience (Freire and Faundez, 1989). For Freire (1970), reality is not "concrete" or "static," but a relentless enmeshing of the contextual factors reshaping its construction in the conscious and unconscious axiology of the subject's perception. Concomitantly, it is admitted that interpretations of experience are troublesome if qualified by the justifiability of each claim to knowledge as a contingent language of possibility and not as a dictatorial language of imposition (see McLaren, 1991, 1994). Phenomenological analysis is the critical resource to broaden knowledge. Differences of perception are expressed as dialogic constructions of differences relating to experiences. Deconstructive/reconstructive exercises are used to synthesize the subject's return to self-awareness, or "conscientization" (Freire, 1970). Through employing critical discourse to question and to challenge the assumptions of selfhood and the difference of otherness, students are expected to gravitate toward fresh understandings that can circumvent the need to reproduce institutionally endorsed ideologies. Students engage in critical activities to uncover more options for themselves as equal members of society and to develop the skill or breadth of a more penetrating insight of the cultural remnants of past myths, through which, the knowledge gained from institutionalized systems of teaching–learning is augmented.

It may be said that a critical pedagogy arises from within a sociocultural milieu that has been insensitive to the reality of the postmodern condition in which a torrent of differences simply exist (Stanley, 1992; Giroux, 1988c). On one level, the subjects of contemporary societies are characterized in terms of a "world of difference" where individuals are considered to be identities constructed from an unceasing exposure to a diverse array of images, discourses, codes, and the like (Spivak, 1992). On another level, the heterogeneity of identity is exemplified in communities of otherness inhabited by individuals who further embellish this primary difference of subjectivity in complex affiliations of integrating an endless combination of gender, class, race, ethnic or sexual orientations. A critical pedagogy needs to recognize that this abundance of individuality, mapped both within and on the "fringes" of society, is not always given the freedom to organize and to assert a sense of personalizeable or personalized identity within school systems; moreover, educational institutions are inclined to enforce subscription to prefabricated norms and authorized policies. In this case, individual freedoms and rights are predisposed to the "governmentality" of prescriptive knowledge structures regulated through the juridical strategies of supposedly democratic systems that exclude participants because of inherent or inherited differences to the common system.

This attitude is taken by a number of critical pedagogy theorists (i.e., McLaren, 1991; Kanpol, 1991; Giroux, 1988a; Smyth, 1987) and critical educators who have questioned the "commonizing rituals" through which the arrangement of schooling structures or educational systems exculpate conformist intellectual or behavioral expectations without showing sensitivity to the knowledge students hold in relation to personalized subcodes of meaning-making and forms of discourse production (Giroux and McLaren, 1992). We have to see students as being forced to comply with the commodification of knowledge, their intellectual potential having to be re-aimed at the realization of a predesignated "cultural capital" so as to ensure success within the hegemony of the school order and its "official knowledge." Michael Apple (1990) and Pierre Bourdieu (1984) have persuasively argued that a dominant culture both overtly and covertly transmits a code of value structures within the practical implementation of curricular discourses as educational programs endorsing certain knowledges and behaviors facilitating the reproduction of the mean by championing its superiority over other forms of understanding to thereby create an hierarchy of identities based upon ideological conformity. Individuals from groups of lower social and economic status entering the school systems are at an obvious disadvantage from the beginning of the educational process due to a relatively limited exposure of dominant forms of cultural knowledge and literacy that have the status of a higher learning or canon not rooted in everyday popular culture (Apple, 1992). In short, the cultural knowledge and literacy that subordinated groups bring to the traditional school setting are not necessarily supported by the cultural hegemony of an ideological ordering of school syllabi and curricula. And an individual's class, gender, racial identity, ethnicity, or sexual preference can work against the attainment of optimum educational benefits from participation in a schooling system that does not embrace forms of knowledge that are rooted within nondominant worldviews. Because societies and communities are amalgams of differing populations and peoples, such a phenomenon in the educational enterprise is destructive and inequitable, due to the fact that it fails to offer an effective form of pedagogy for a great portion of nondominant groups represented within and representing society. School systems often exhibit little appreciation for and sensitivity to the potentially divergent interests of lowered or marginalized status groups (Giroux and McLaren, 1992).

Kanpol (1992) stresses that critical pedagogy has a right and responsibility to expand the cultural ideals of difference that dominate educational contexts by bringing attention to the need to supersede pedagogical theories that locate knowledge within exclusionary totalizations of subjectivity. Individual differences are celebrated only if the recognition of difference is unconditional. The existence of alternate subjective identities or "otherness" relative to stable group membership must be engaged on their own terms. We all have a responsibility to be open to the difference of others while reserving judgments that cut off the possibility of engaging in dialogue that is predicated on the responsibility we have to understand the difference of the other without condition. It is in the other that we see ourselves reflected as another. That does not mean that difference disappears or is subsumed in the notion of a homogeneous community. Kanpol (1992, p. 220) states, "Of course what must be established within schools are personal struggles that are not only separate and different—by race, class, or gender—given their discursive nature, but also intimately connected by their commonalities." A critical pedagogy has to value the ethos of singularity of difference upon which the concept of intersubjectivity rests within the diaspora of communities of difference and a community of differences. The mien of educational practices that pervade the intellectual and ethical environment of the subject should inculcate an empathy for the recognition of difference and not a tolerance of otherness through critical reflection upon the cultural sites of discourse production. To illuminate a rhizome of existing realities, critical educators have to facilitate this analytic exploration of differing perspectives by way of ongoing dialogues on experience and its representations as real-life and media images (Bromley, 1989). Through dialogues on the meaning of representation, the meanings of difference and differences of meaning are more likely to be negotiated, their ground apprehended, and then woven into interpersonal schemata or codes of meaning-making we all engage in that stretch our individual perceptions of "possible worlds." For the reconstructive phase of this genre of intercommunicative learning to take place via a critical engagement with pedagogy, the subjective nature of reality rendered by students and teachers as empirical and epistemological subjects must be reflected within the institutional scene of teaching–learning. Education must in the sense be based on content that is relevant to the personal experiences and lives of both: that is, in a knowledge not encased within the pedagogical agendas of modulated syllabi handed down through preplanned and prepackaged curricula appealing to a general culture or a general community postulated to exist outside of difference.

Toward this end, a critical pedagogy cannot indicate "clear-cut" or "definitive" learning outcomes *per se*, but yields to the interpretative interests of individuals not necessarily communities, from which, the central logic of educational concepts is structured and presented in areas of study superseding the confines offered by a given "dominant group" reading. Michael Apple (1990) has identified the indoctrinating power of the institution by analyzing the practice of how school systems adhere to readymade instructional packages that bypass any critical role the teacher or student might play in selecting materials for the teaching–learning process. This common strategy of "best practices" and "authorized curricula" makes teachers and students appear as monodimensional cogs lost in a tangled lattice of intra-institutional paraphernalia and fit only to be governed by managerial organizers external to the reality of the classroom environment. The trend toward pedagogical accountability or excellence in education has reinstated standardized syllabi and measurable curricular outcomes of teaching–learning that enforce student and teacher conformity for meeting the technocratic goal of the commercial productivity of "sustainable economies" (Stanley, 1991; see also Giroux, 1988a). Critical pedagogy has to engage how the mainstream approaches of a "back-to-basics" education tend to undermine the sociopolitical interests of marginal groups because the competitive edge of any quest for "educational excellence" secures the teaching–learning of official knowledge as a form of "cultural capital" worth having—its reproduction has social and economic rewards (Bourdieu and Passeron, 1977). A narrow evaluation of curricular knowledge and academic achievement can limit the opportunity to education for those on the margins while claiming that higher standards ensure that educational objectives are met. The question is: "Whose objectives are met and how?" The quest for educational excellence does not provide equal access to education for all, nor does it assure that all students can attain or want to possess the knowledge that is privileged as valuable to a general culture. Critical pedagogy is founded on the hope that education can be emancipated from a curricular system that is founded on the idea of an ideal student capable of apprehending and reflecting an ideal knowledge.

Henry Giroux, a theorist who has offered the most systematic theoretical and practicable outline of the parameters and merits of critical pedagogy after Freire, accents the educational importance of unveiling the oppressive element of the institutional control of knowledge. Critical pedagogy supports critical citizenship through education and it aims at actualizing within individual subjects the active potential of their natural abilities to counter domination. Giroux has advocated a pedagogical sense of reflexivity situated within the experiential frameworks of knowledge drawn from popular culture. Critical pedagogy has to engage education as a form introspection into the effects of media representations on the formation of subjectivity. Teachers can heighten student awareness of the influences of popular culture—its images and discourses—on subjective desires. Critical pedagogy is grounded on the analysis of the interests of knowledge in direct relation to the communicative act of teaching–learning. It envisions the means for a more equitable institution of education that crosses the boundaries of culture and undoes the distinctions between "high," "middle," and "low." The egalitarian premises of critical pedagogy look forward to providing students with the discursive and conceptual tools to formulation truly original ideas through an analysis that would protect their democratic right to voice opinions without having to hide under a veil of commonality to suppress tacit knowledges. This process of "applied reasoning" or "critical thinking" can be, as Blatz (1989, p. 107) notes, "understood as the deliberate pursuit of well supported beliefs, decisions, plans, and actions." The "genuineness" of these pursuits is displayed in any critical pedagogy by the accountability of political actions to the tain of logic constructing one's own subjective understandings as influenced by race, ethnicity, class, gender, or sexuality. By expanding the capability to elaborate upon or to amplify a unique critical voice or analytic perspective with which to add to the classroom presentation, previously "subordinated" group understandings and perceptions are given the opportunity to be realized in full. Critical pedagogy, as a result, has to actualize the ability of teachers and students to be open-minded to an acceptance of a variety of differing viewpoints, including their own, by affirming knowledge through a problematizing of its discursive possibilities. As McLaren (1988, p. 73) suggests, "Critical pedagogy is positioned irreverently against a pedantic cult of singularity in which moral authority and theoretical assurance are arrived at unproblematically without regard to the repressed narratives and suffering of the historically disenfranchised." Criticalists are not interested in using to "effective methods" for the efficient and manageable consumption of a content of self-mirroring knowledges. Knowledge does not reside in the materiality of "real-world" resources or commodities so as to be given out, "consumed," and verily reproduced for the sociocultural or politico-economic benefit of the subject, but is an entity requiring the painstaking rigors of involved intellection—an understanding that stems from a highly personalized grounding of experience and interpretation (see Giroux, 1987, 1992).

The summative goal of critical pedagogy is to empower students with the ability to think and act reflectively as individual subjects of a society or a culture who have formed a conscious self-awareness of the meanings of their multiple affiliations and the significance of their worldly transactions with the other. That a platform for the creative exchange of student experiences must be maintained within the practicable components of a theory of learning is vital to criticalists. Giroux (1988d, p. 53) correctly explains,

> . . . students have experiences and you can't deny that these experiences are relevant to the learning process even though you might say that these experiences are limited, raw, unfruitful or whatever. Students have memories, families, religions, feelings, languages and cultures that give them a distinctive voice. We can critically engage that experience and we can move beyond it. But we can't deny it.

The unevenness of experience alters subjectivity through the repetition of difference and of changes in the states of relation of the subject to it, that, in turn, influences the modality of "rational" stances the subject ascribes to. Subjectivity changes just as the experience of the subject changes over space and time. Criticalists aspire to elevate the consciousness of students to the translatability of these "living-changes" so as to inspire the self-confidence to actively question concepts and themes set in relation to an ever expanding difference of understandings (Kaplan, 1991). This does not imply that teachers are stripped of the right to voice and to convey the experience of their own understandings, for as Giroux and Simon (1988, p. 16) put it:

> Indeed, the pedagogical struggle is lessened without such resources. However, teachers and students must find forms within which a single discourse does not become the locus of certainty and certification. Rather, teachers must find ways of creating a space for mutual engagement of lived difference that does not require the silencing of a multiplic-ity of voices by a single dominant discourse; at the same time, teachers must develop forms of pedagogy informed by a substantive ethic that contests racism, sexism, and class exploitation as ideologies and social practices that disrupt and devalue public life.

Discourse serves as the medium through which students can practice the critical power to interrogate concepts for the sake of learning more about the self while keeping in mind the exploitation or alienation that may arise when knowledge claims are taken to be absolute and not interpretations to be enriched by the creative adding of the differ-ence of experience to a rational possibility. To this end, teachers and students work together to appreciate otherness and to simultaneously bridge the discursive abyss of an untranslatability of difference through patient rereading and self-critical rationality. In a multicultural society, there is a need to develop a sensitivity for otherness over a willful submission of the self to cultural metanarratives that castigate difference in the everyday conditions that house the living realm of our aspirations as students and teachers within the uncomplicated concept of a unified community.

For an Ending

In recent applications of philosophical research to educational problems, there has been an increasing interest in the re-theorization of pedagogical methods for the purpose of empowering students with the intellectual capabilities demanded for the engenderment of a confident self-expression of subjective identity cognizant of the value of otherness and of difference (i.e., Luke and Gore, 1992; Giroux, 1992; McLaren, 1994). Multiculturalism and gender issues having become a focus of the critical outlook of such pedagogies of difference, the rapid growth of these areas of educational inquiry further demonstrates the postmodern exigency to preserve and appreciate the differences of culture (widely construed) in the proliferation of social diversity among a global community. In the end, the pluralism of a postmodern interpretation of difference, as reconceptualized through the educational lens of critical pedagogy, contains the promise to release the subject by freeing the power of identity unto a knowledge of the truth of self. Yet one is still wont to ask, is this enough or can it ever be?

Bibliography

Althusser, L. (1971). *Lenin and Philosophy and Other Essays*. Trans. B. Brewster. London: New Left Books.

Apple, M. W. (1990). *Ideology and Curriculum*. Routledge: New York.

————. Education, Culture, and Class Power: Basil Bernstein and the Neo-Marxist Sociology of Education. *Educational Theory* 42:2 (1992): 1–27.

Baudrillard, J. (1981). *Simulcres et Simulation*. Paris: Galilée.

————. (1983). *For a Critique of the Political Economy of the Sign*. St. Louis: Telos Press.

Bennington, G. (1986). "Postmodernism." In *Postmodernism,* ed. L. Appignanesi. London: Institute of Contemporary Arts, p. 5.

Best, S. and Kellner, D. (1991). *Postmodern Theory*. New York: The Guilford Press.

Blatz, C. V. (1989). "Contextualism and Critical Thinking: Programmatic Investigations." *Educational Theory* 39:2 (1989): 107–119.

Bourdieu, P. (1984). *Distinction: A Social Critique of the Judgement of Taste*. Trans. R. Nice. Massachusetts: Harvard University Press.

Bourdieu, P. and Passeron, J. C. (1977). *Reproduction in Education, Society and Culture*. Trans. R. Nice. London: Sage.

Bromley, H. "Identity Politics and Critical Pedagogy." *Educational Theory* 39:3 (1989): 207–223.

Cherryholmes, C. H. (1988). *Power and Criticism: Poststructural Investigations in Education*. New York: Teachers College Press.

————. "Reading Research." *Curriculum Studies* 25:1 (1993): 1–32.

Corson, J. D. "Social Justice and Minority Language Policy." *Educational Theory* 42:2 (1992): 201–216.

Derrida, J. (1976). *Of Grammatology*. Trans. G. C. Spivak. Baltimore: Johns Hopkins University Press.

————. (1981). *Dissemination*. Trans. B. Johnson. Chicago: University of Chicago Press.

Doll, W. E. (1989). "Foundations for a Postmodern Curriculum." *Journal of Curriculum Studies* 21:1 (1989): 243–253.

Eco, U. (1979). *The Role of the Reader: Explorations in the Semiotics of Text*. Bloomington: University of Indiana Press.

Foster, H. (1983). "Postmodernism." In *The Anti-Aesthetic,* ed. H. Foster. Port Townsend: Bay Press, pp. ix–xvi.

Foucault, M. (1973). *The Order of Things*. New York: Vintage Books.

————. (1979). *Discipline and Punish: The Birth of the Prison*. Trans. A. Sheridan. New York: Vintage Books.

————. (1980). *Knowledge/Power*. Trans. C. Gordon. New York: Pantheon Books.

Freire, P. (1970). *Pedagogy of the Oppressed*. Trans. M. B. Rames. New York: Seabury Press.

Freire, P. and Faundez, A. (1989). *Learning to Question: A Pedagogy of Liberation*. New York: Continuum.

Giroux, H. A. "Critical Literacy and Student Experience: Donald Graves' Approach to Literacy." *Language Arts* 64:2 (1987): 175–181.

————. (1988a). *Schooling and the Struggle for Public Life*. Minneapolis: University of Minnesota Press.

————. "Postmodernism and the Discourse of Educational Criticism." *Journal of Education* 170:3 (1988b): 5–30.

————. Border Pedagogy in the Age of Postmodernism. *Journal of Education* 170:3 (1988c): 162–181.

————. "The Hope of Radical Education: A Conversation with Henry Giroux." *Journal of Education* 170:2 (1988d): 91–101.

————. "The Politics of Postmodernism." *Journal of Urban and Cultural Studies* 1:1 (1990): 5–38.

————. (1992). *Border Crossings: Cultural Workers and the Politics of Education*. New York: Routledge.

Giroux, H. A. and Simon, R. I. "Schooling, Popular Culture, and a Pedagogy of Possibility." *Journal of Education* 170:1 (1988): 9–26.

Giroux, H. A. and McLaren, P. "Writing from the Margins: Geographies of Identity, Pedagogy, and Power." *Journal of Education* 174:1 (1992): 7–29.

Goodman, J. "Teachers as Intellectuals: Toward a Critical Pedagogy of Learning." *Journal of Education* 170:2 (1988): 143–149.

Guba, E. G. "Relativism." *Curriculum Inquiry* 22:1 (1992): 17–23.

Hall, S. "On Postmodernism and Articulation: An Interview." *Journal of Communication Inquiry* 10:2 (1986): 45–60.

Harvey, D. (1990). *The Condition of Postmodernity*. Cambridge, MA: Blackwell.

Hutcheon, L. (1992). "Theorizing the Postmodern." In *The Post-Modern Reader*, ed. C. Jencks. New York: St. Martin's Press, pp. 76–93.

Jameson, F. (1989). *Postmodernism, or, the Cultural Logic of Late Capitalism*. Durham: Duke University Press.

Jencks, C. (1986). *What is Postmodernism?* New York: St. Martin's Press.

————. (1987). *Post-Modernism: New Classicism in Art and Architecture*. New York: Rizzoli.

————. (1992). "The Postmodern Agenda." In *The Post-Modern Reader*, ed. C. Jencks. New York: St. Martin's Press, pp. 10–39.

Kanpol, B. "Postmodernism in Education Revisited: Similarities within Differences and the Democratic Imaginary." *Educational Theory* 42:2 (1992): 217–230.

Kaplan, L. D. "Teaching Intellectual Autonomy: The Failure of the Critical Thinking Movement." *Educational Theory* 41:4 (1991): 361–370.

Kearns, J. and Newton, K. "An Interview with Jacques Derrida." *Literary Review* 14 (1980): 21–22.

Kellner, D. "Reading Images Critically: Toward a Postmodern Pedagogy." *Journal of Education* 170:3 (1988): 31–52.

————. (1989). *Critical Theory, Marxism and Modernity*. Baltimore: The Johns Hopkins University Press.

Lather, P. "Ideology and Methodological Attitude." *JCT* 9:2 (1989): 7–26.

————. (1991). *Getting Smart: Feminist Research and Pedagogy with/in the Postmodern*. New York: Routledge.

Luke, C. and Gore, J. (eds.) (1992). *Feminisms and Critical Pedagogy*. New York: Routledge.

Lyotard, J. F. (1984). *The Postmodern Condition: A Report on Knowledge.* Trans. G. Bennington and B. Massumi. Minneapolis: University of Minnesota Press.

———. (1986). "Defining the Postmodern." In *Postmodernism*, ed. L. Appignanesi. London: Institute of Contemporary Arts, pp. 6–7.

———. (1992). "What is Postmodernism?" In *The Post-Modern Reader*, ed. C. Jencks. New York: St Martin's Press, pp. 138–150.

Martusewicz, R. A. (1992). "Mapping the Terrain of the Post-Modern Subject: Post-Structuralism and the Educated Woman." In *Understanding Curriculum as Phenomenological and Deconstructed Text*, ed. W. F. Pinar and Reynolds. New York: Teachers College Press, pp. 131–158.

McLaren, P. "Schooling the Postmodern Body: Critical Pedagogy and the Politics of Enfleshment." *Journal of Education* 170:3 (1988): 53–83.

———. (1991). "Critical Pedagogy, Postcolonial Politics and Redemptive Remembrance." In *Fortieth Yearbook of the National Reading Conference.* Ohio: The National Reading Conference, Inc., pp. 33–48.

———. "Critical Pedagogy, Political Agency, and the Pragmatics of Justice: The Case of Lyotard." *Educational Theory* 44:3 (1994): 319–340.

Siegel, H. (1988). *Educating Reason.* New York: Routledge.

Smyth, J. W. (1987). *A Rationale for Teachers' Critical Pedagogy: A Handbook.* Victoria: Deakin University.

Spivak, G. C. "Acting Bits/Identity Talk." *Critical Inquiry* 18:4 (1992): 770–803.

Stanley, W. B. (1992). *Curriculum for Utopia.* New York: State University of New York Press.

Von Glassersfeld, E. "Cognition, Construction of Knowledge, and Teaching." *Synthese* 80 (1989): 121–140.

Wittgenstein, L. (1953). *Philosophical Investigations.* Trans. G. E. M. Anscombe. New York: MacMillan.

Part 3 ~

Technology, Difference, Community

Chapter 10 ~

The Technology of Difference: ASCII,[1] Hegemony, and the Internet

Jason Nolan

Saturday night. My partner, Yuka, is translating *Orphan at My Door* by Canadian Children's author Jean Little into Japanese[2] (Little, 2001). Her plan is to translate it into a web-page diary in a format known as a *blog* (Cooper, 2001; Power, 2001). Blogging will allow her to maintain an on-line journal, where each entry is not just a static web page, but forms part of a chronologically ordered interactive database. A group of Japanese scholars, friends, and her editor will be able to follow the progress and make suggestions, and the finished product will be downloaded by the publisher and printed. A novel approach, to translate an orphan's diary using an on-line diary-writing tool.

All of the code we looked at—Blogger, Livejournal, Wikiweb, and GreyMatter[3]—however, are either monolingual or privileges English to the extent that functioning in Japanese is virtually impossible. I settled on GreyMatter because the code is open-sourced, and can be run on my Internet server (achieve.utoronto.ca). This way, I could see if it could force the code to "do Japanese." I located a half dozen locations where the code needed to be *modified*, to tell the script "Hey, there are more languages than English, eh?," and to allow both the input and display of Kanji, Hiragana and Katakana, and Romanji (roman characters); the four alphabets that are used in written Japanese, by adding the code: "<META HTTP-EQUIV = 'Content-Type' CONTENT = 'text/html;CHARSET = x-sjis'>" (Lunde, 1993).

Yuka's next complaint was somewhat obvious. None of the environments (software/programs) had any way to save your work. All these environments allow you to post your messages to the Internet, and you can edit previous posts, but there is no way to save your work to ensure that if you get disconnected from the Internet, you do not lose everything. No programmer thought of adding one, it seems. There are a myriad of ways to work around this, but Yuka does not take well to *work-arounds*; an attitude that has informed much thinking about user compliance and the whims of the programmer (Cooper, 1999; Nolan, 2001; Nolan and Hogbin, 2001).

Thus Emma Jane Hogbin. With the promise of dinner, she arrives to hack a save button. Self-motivated and self-taught, Emma is a Hacker. Her bookshelves inspire fear in the non-digiterati (Gray, 2001, p. 48). We all talk through dinner (my job) as the printer processes the 200 plus pages of code/text that make up GreyMatter. She reads the printout, making notes, and I conduct keyword searches for lines of code at her direction. Suddenly she looks up with a laugh and announces, "Sheeeeeeeeeeet. This guy needs a life!" in shock at the featuritis of the code (Raymond, 2001). I am unsure if the comment is one of admiration. And we continue to work.

Program of Inquiry

This scenario occurred just as I was settling down to write this chapter. The ideas have been percolating for half a decade, and this experience was just another in a long list of experiences where we are confronted by the arbitrary whims of a technologically positivist metanarrative that decenters people, cultures, language, gender, orientation, and most of all locates power and privilege within the grasp of a small group of individuals; generally those participating in the white male North American English discourse that informs postmodern technology (Cooper, 1999; Noble, 1997; Wertheim, 2000).

The intention of this chapter is to engage the deep structures of the hegemony of the digital technology revolution as represented by the Internet, levels beneath those addressed by most of the contemporary critical discourses. This time, I am not working with more obvious examples of the Technology of Difference, such as the relationship of access to safe drinking water and basic rights of women's education to global attempts to bridge the digital divide (Nolan, 2000), the future of educational technology in North America (Nolan and Hogbin, 2001), or the potential for zero-cost computing and telephony technologies and indigenous language software environments. The goal is to extend the dialogue of difference and access to locations of communication and community to a consideration of the locations of control over which disadvantaged groups of users and nonusers of communication technologies have little or no control, and even less information or understanding. I am looking not at the content/information/data that is presented through the various media of the Internet, but at the bias inherent in the medium itself (Jones, 2000).

The Internet is first and foremost a learning environment in both formal and informal learning contexts (Nolan and Weiss, 2002). It is, of course one that presents itself as value neutral; a manifestation of McLuhan's global village where bias and difference all meld into a stream of bits (McLuhan, 1995). There is a great deal of pedagogy and curriculum about the Internet that both challenges and reinforces difference (Cummins and Sayers, 1995; Harasim et al., 1995; Haynes and Holmevik, 1998). But there is very little curriculum or curriculum theorizing that engages the software, code, discourse, and metanarrative of the Internet itself, leaving current pedagogy to function in a sea of assumptions about what can be done and said and accomplished online. There is an "anti-intellectualism" similar to what Giroux describes as present in the classroom, or lack of interest in the subsurface discourse of the code and software of the Internet (Gray, 2001; Giroux, 1992, p. 116).

McLuhan's *medium is the message* mantra is ever current in our thoughts as we are infected with the latest rash of technological developments. However, as educators and researchers confront the dominant and subversive ideologies presented on-line, very few are willing or aware of the need to critique the imposition of the locations of power that have brought the Internet into existence. There is a need for us all to be aware of the levels of implicit colonialization that accompanies the proliferation of Internet-informed culture (Said, 1993). There are a variety of layers that must be unpacked and brought into the light of inquiry, "to know as much as possible about the house that technology built, about its secret passages and its trapdoors" (Franklin, 1992, p. 12). First and foremost is the foundation and genesis of the Internet itself, located in the Cold War desire for a computer network designed to withstand nuclear war (Krol, 1992). Who made the Internet? Who are its informal architects? What culture was this creation located in? Second, we have to look at the software that runs the Internet, the servers that move information, and the software that extends its purview to our desktops at home and in our workspaces. Third, there is the post-1994 World Wide Web that opened this brave new world to both the general public and to the commercial influences that followed them (Berners-Lee, 1998). Fourth, we are faced with the Internet representing technology and discourse as the informing metanarrative of the new global economy. Finally, I suggest some strategies to help educators encounter difference in our pedagogy, practice and inquiry. This will serve to point to locations, the potential avenues, for radical repositioning of the discourse at the nexus of the educator and her performative/transformational capacity as creator of learning environments (Nolan, 2001).

The Foundation and Genesis of the Internet

Most of us are aware of the genesis of the Internet at the hands of the Advanced Projects Research Group, of the U.S. Department of Defense which, in late 1960s founded research that led to the linking of computers at university in the Southwestern United States (Cailliau, 1995; Gray, 2001; Krol, 1992; Mitchell, 1998). This foundation has morphed into an ostensibly uncontrolled and uncontrollable global phenomenon that has exploded the opportunities for voice and communication around the world. It has gone down in Western history alongside Gutenberg and Caxton's moveable type revolutions, which propelled text out of the Medieval modes of production and privilege (McLuhan, 1995). And just as the print revolution was about the technology of the printing press, the Internet is as much about the software code and Internet Protocols (originally TCP/IP, Telnet, SMTP, FTP, and recently HTTP) that bring the Internet into existence, as it is about what we do on it. Those who controlled the printing presses still controlled what could be and was said. Someone needed to control a printing press in order to have voice; as time went on more people had access, and differing voices could make themselves heard. Of course, concomitant with this means of production, one needed to have access to networks of distribution, a limitation that still restricts the diversity of voices that are heard both in media-rich and media-poor cultures/languages. Today, access to public consciousness via the medium of print is seen as widespread, but in many situations individuals and groups are still voiceless (OECD, 2000).

The Internet stands now as a force within our collective worlds. But control is still located in corporate and government institutions. In 1992, the U.S. government released the rules governing acceptable use of Internet resources, opening the Internet up to business, and since then corporations have taken over much of the Internet (Cerny, 2001; Hochheiser and Ric, 1998). Individuals must purchase or rent time on expensive machines made by an ever-shrinking number of multinational corporations. Organizations such as the various Freenets (Scott, 2001), FIDOnet (Vest, 2001), and the Free Software Foundation (Stallman, 2000) are still challenging the hegemony of institutional and corporate interests, but their influence is small and localized.

Technologies of Resistance

The Internet is not the free-for-all anarchic space that business, the media, Libertarians, and cyborgs would have us believe (Gray, 2001). Though chaotic and anarchic activities do exist, and these are very important locations of resistance, every act of resistance or conformity occurs under the graces of the protocols of the Internet. These protocols are governed by various institutions, governments, and administrative agreements. The most fundamental of these it the TCP/IP protocol, invented by Vinton Cerf and Bob Kahn. Almost all Internet traffic must conform to the TCP/IP protocol or it is rejected by the servers that pass information from computer to computer. All traffic must pass along telephone lines, from the plain old telephone (POT) lines in our homes to major Internet backbones maintained by Telcos (Krol, 1992). How that information is encoded is governed by standards developed and maintained by various groups such as World Wide Web Consortium (WC3), Internet Corporation for Assigned Names and Numbers (ICANN), Institute for Electrical and Electronic Engineers (IEEE), and Joint Photographic Experts Group (JPEG) (Champeon, n.d.). These regulatory bodies, organizations, and protocol standards control what can and is done on the Internet. Many of these groups are transnational, and do have representation from institutions around the world. But they contain a very narrow selection of interests that are contiguous with the goals of the West.

There is no question that the software and hardware we use is primarily informed by multinational corporations; Microsoft, Sun Microsystems, Intel, AMD, AOL Time Warner, Apple Computer, IBM, Yahoo, Hewlett-Packard, Sony, and the like, along with their support companies and organizations, control at the most basic level how we communicate on-line. Even putting aside the hardware manufacturers in this discussion, and focusing on the software with which we do what we can do with computers, every keystroke invokes a software response that mediates our communication. This software is not value-neutral. It is culturally and linguistically embedded in a technologically positivist metanarrative that sees the technology itself, and those who create it and use it, at the apogee of human cultural experience (Lyotard, 1984). This predisposition is encoded in the software itself.

There are a number technologies and movements that challenge the consumerist/ corporatist profit-driven models of the Internet, positing a somewhat prosumerist[4] model; "As prosumers we have a new set of responsibilities, to educate ourselves.

We are no longer a passive market upon which industry dumps consumer goods but a part of the process, pulling toward us the information and services that we design from our own imagination" (Finely, 2000). The open source movement is the key idea that brings otherwise competing interests together; it is one of the most important in computing in the late 1990s, and will probably be one of the dominant forces into the next century (Scoville, 2000; Raymond, 1998; O'Reilly and Associates, 2000). Open Source Initiative and the GNU Project are two organizations influenced by specific individuals; GNU by Richard Stallman, and Open Source by Eric Raymond (Scoville, 2000). In general terms, they both want to promote software that is free, freely available, and open to the Hacker community. These projects both support the traditional notion of sharing resources among members of a community.

The Free Software Foundation is clearly immersed in the Hacker philosophy that information wants to be free. I can and have put my own invention V.A.S.E. under a Free Software Foundation GPL license (Nolan, 2000). I did not need to ask for permission. I only need to include the text that would identify this license in my code, and abide by the license myself.

The Free Software Foundation's GNU General Public License (GPL) was first brought forth in 1991:

> The licenses for most software are designed to take away your freedom to share and change it. By contrast, the GNU General Public License is intended to guarantee your freedom to share and change free software—to make sure the software is free for all its users. This General Public License applies to most of the Free Software Foundation's software and to any other program whose authors commit to using it. (Some other Free Software Foundation software is covered by the GNU Library General Public License instead.) You can apply it to your programs, too. When we speak of free software, we are referring to freedom, not price. Our General Public Licenses are designed to make sure that you have the freedom to distribute copies of free software (and charge for this service if you wish), that you receive source code or can get it if you want it, that you can change the software or use pieces of it in new free programs; and that you know you can do these things.
>
> To protect your rights, we need to make restrictions that forbid anyone to deny you these rights or to ask you to surrender the rights. These restrictions translate to certain responsibilities for you if you distribute copies of the software, or if you modify it. For example, if you distribute copies of such a program, whether gratis or for a fee, you must give the recipients all the rights that you have. You must make sure that they, too, receive or can get the source code. (Stallman, 1998)

The Linux operating system builds on this open source philosophy. It is both a software and a conceptual revolution that has changed computing in a way that we cannot have imagined. Because of its success, it is also an important pedagogical signpost, showing an alternative direction from the commercialization of online exploration of difference. "Linux is a free Unix-type operating system originally created by Linus Torvalds with the assistance of developers around the world. Developed under the GNU General Public License, the source code for Linux is freely available to everyone" (Online, 1994–2000). As such, it represents a movement that critical education can follow, through vehicles such as the GNU, to allow individuals and organizations to maintain ownership, while freely sharing of their work with a larger community. Linus created Linux while a student at the University of Helsinki. While Linus Torvalds is world-famous, he does not directly make money from his Linux Kernel (Online, 1994–2000).

Due to the very nature of Linux's functionality and availability, it has become quite popular worldwide and a vast number of software programmers have taken Linux's source code and adapted it to meet their individual needs (Online, 1994–2000). Most major computer companies have recognized the importance of Linux. Dell, IBM, Apple, and others have Linux compliant hardware. Intel, who makes the CPUs for the Windows operating system, actually owns a large amount of stock in RedHat, the most popular version of Linux (Raymond, 1999).

The rise in importance of Linux (www.linux.org) is predicated on the fact that it is an open-source operating system. The dynamic potential of the CVEs (Collaborative Virtual Environments) I work with is fundamentally due to their open source existence. This means that the raw source code of the system is publicly available under a license that allows anyone to use it and modify it for their own purposes under relatively flexible conditions as laid out in the license (Nolan and Weiss, 2002; Nolan, 2001). The result is that many thousands of users are motivated not only to modify and add to Linux for their own purposes, but also to share what they have created with the entire Linux community. The strength of Linux comes from the openness of the system and the community that surrounds it. This does not mean that Linux is necessarily always free, but that it is freely available. Redhat (www.redhat.com), one of the most important companies in the Linux movement, repackages Linux and creates its own flavor and support which they then sell. Though all the components are freely available from places like www.redhat.com, www.linux.org, and other sites, even the entire Redhat release can be downloaded for free, although it is easier and more convenient to spend the money for their packaged version on CD-ROM.

There are obvious advantages to hundreds of independent and corporate programmers adding their little bit to a product that can then both be made available without charge on-line and compiled and variously packaged by any company to be resold to those users who want to purchase a particular distribution such as those Redhat, Corel, and other companies offer. In this scenario we are moving beyond the present notion of consumerism, a shifting series of intersections between programmer, distributor, and user where an individual or company can participate in one, two, or three roles simultaneously. They become, many of them, prosumers—both producer and consumer—in concert with the company like Apple or the Linux meta-organization, which is itself no longer merely a producer, but also a consumer of the products produced by its users. This circular relationship is obviously appealing in terms of challenging control over the means of production, because the production of technology is a cultural production first and foremost.

Cultural Production

These initiatives and software do not challenge the Western bias outlined in this chapter. They do, however, challenge the multinational corporations' ability to control what software we use, and how software can be modified for our own uses.

Open-source initiatives offer individuals and groups interested in social justice not only valuable allies who are often underutilized, but most importantly a model of resistance that seeks to transform debates and relocalize them within social, as opposed to corporate, purviews.

There are other communities of resistance, but they would not be positioned as communities of difference in the terms set out for this edited collection. I am not sure if I can or want to make an argument for their inclusion either, but they exist, and should be considered by communities of difference as potential allies. These groups—geeks, radicals, digerati—think that information and knowledge should be free. Warez sites, 2600.com, alt.2600, MOOs, and the GNU, are all children of the early Hacker communities (Anonymous, 2000; Babcock, 2001; Curtis and Nicols, 1993).

Hackers are the first community of the Internet. Many of the original members are the programmers who hacked the Internet together in the first place. They were the first to subvert the dominant discourse of the Internet to human, communicative, social ends (Ruffin, 2001; Sterling, 1993). Hackers are not the malicious Crackers and virus programmers that strike fear into corporations and are vilified in the popular media (e-cyclopedia, 1999; Raymond, 2000; Stoll, 1989). They are not destroyers, but travelers, seekers, and creators of alternatives and solutions to barriers to accessing knowledge and information. Their mantra is that information wants to be free (Gray, 2001, pp. 48–54). They are also predominately the ultra-privileged young educated heteronormative white males, but they are philosophically opposed to the hegemony of corporate and governmental interests. I work with queer Hackers, cyborgwomen and cybergirls, and the work of Stone on the transgendered body (Stone, 1992), and Harraway's cyborg (Harraway, 2000), and Hayles post-human (Harraway, 2000; Hayles, 1999) collectively reveal how the interfacing of women and technology are relocalizing the discourse of hacking in gendered spaces. As the technologies and influence of technology on the body are engaged by women, they are staking territory in the realm of the Hacker. The roots of the community, however, are located in this opposition to institutions that want to control information and access to resources.

The Warez movement is a more nefarious offshoot that makes available commercial and copyright protected commercial software, serial numbers and passwords; it is the black market or Pirates of the Internet (Tetzlaff, 2000). This illegal activity—one that most philosophically conscious Hackers eschew—exists using the various technologies that make the Internet impervious to domination and control or destruction. It is difficult to locate Warez sites on the Internet as they appear wherever unprotected holes and nodes are located, and disappear as soon as authorities find them. But it is possible to trace their existence through search engines and archived references to sites that no longer exist. Information is passed through IRC (Internet Relay Chat) servers, and content appears on web services that allow for free websites such as geocities.com. At their most subversive they use pre-WWW technologies such as Gopher, Archie, and Veronica servers (Krol, 1992; Nolan, 1994), and Warez sites have recently become havens for illegal materials such as child pornography. But they remain examples of an active subculture that actively opposes Western commercial and governmental interests, and uses all the tools that are situated deep within the woof and warp of the Internet.

2600: The Hacker Quarterly is the Hacker's bible. With writers including Noam Chomsky, and famous Hackers Kevin Mitnick and Phiber Optik, *2600* (named after 2,600 Hz, the frequency AT&T used to indicate an unused phone line) is the public window onto this otherwise hidden world. Hackers, or Phreaks as Telco Hackers are called, exploited this frequency to make free long-distance phone calls. The journal is full of radical philosophy, how-to-hack guides, and a forum for Hackers to describe their latest exploits in exposing the attempts of institutions to thwart the desire of information to be free. Though *2600* has its roots in telephony, the fact that voice and data communication travel the same wires means that *2600* is the public domain of an element of the Hacker community that is a must read for anyone interested in maintaining or compromising computer security. *2600* is about digital mastery and machismo, but it also represents, in the manner of cattle ranchers of nineteenth-century America, resistance to the enclosure, commercialization, commodification of the virtual free range. This range is an important potential location for homesteaders of difference who want to stake out territory beyond the ken of Western commercial interests.

Hacking is not all a shady underworld act that can result in security services carting off your PC in a predawn raid. There are social learning environments, collectively called Collaborative Virtual Environments (CVEs) such as MOOs, where individuals and groups construct/program/hack out virtual spaces and communities (Bruckman, 1997; Cicognani, 1998; Fanderclai, 1995; Nolan and Weiss, 2002; Rheingold, 1993; Schank et al., 1999; Turkle, 1995; Wertheim, 2000). I have been involved in CVEs since the late 1980s, and developed two MOOs. MOO is an acronym for Object Oriented MUD, itself an acronym often unpacked as Multi-User Domain/Dungeon/Discourse (Curtis, 1992; Curtis and Nichols, 1993). My MOOs—MOOkti and Project Achieve—are virtual places where participants from as far away as Taiwan, Iceland, Brazil, and Russia "create representations of people, places and things and share them with others" (Nolan, 2001). The key to these constructionist, polysynchronous[5] (integrated synchronous and asynchronous communication) spaces is that people not only communicate on-line in a multimedia, open-source software environment, but that they can collaboratively create and program these spaces according to whatever criteria they choose to conceptualize and describe (Nolan, 1995; Davie et al., 1998; Davie and Nolan, 1999). Though MOOs still suffer from their English-only roots, we can and have worked simultaneously in English, Chinese, Japanese, Russian, Icelandic, German, French, and we are conceiving a MOO dedicated to polylingual programming, construction and communication environment. A polylingual space, versus multilingual, suggests that not only can many languages be accommodated, but that no one language reigns supreme; that multiple, intersecting language events and spaces can be created, and participants can work within the language(s) of their choice without being mediated by an overall dominant language.

In MOOs, identity and gender are not only performed but constructed and experimented with (Bruckman, 1992; Stone, 1992). Identity is liquid and continually open to rethinking, reconstruction, and negotiation. Among our many activities on Project Achieve (http://achieve.utoronto.ca), we have been running annual workshops on gender and identity with the Triangle Project, of the Toronto District

School Board, Canada's only school for Queer Youth. Many of their projects are publicly viewable, allowing visitors to experience their work. But all aspects of their self-representation and the presentation of their ideas are under their control, negotiated with their teacher in accordance with mutually agreed upon curriculum. They maintain ownership of their work and govern how it is viewed. If they find something missing or required, they can create it themselves, collaborate with others, or interact with the wider community to access resources important to achieving their goals. Many of the hundreds of the public CVEs across the Internet allow for this level of construction and governance. As such, they are important and powerful tools that offer communities of difference the potential to represent themselves beyond external control and influence.

The Internet is Written in English

These three strands, the Internet infrastructure, mega-corporations, and technologies/ groups that challenge them, are primarily English/male/Western-dominated discourses. All strands are Western in voice. Linux with its roots in Linus Torvald's Finland is an example of one of the rare innovations that enters the popular consciousness that is not of G7 genesis. More importantly, software is written in programming languages such as C, C++, ObjectC, Java, and or scripting/markup languages like Perl, PHP (PHP Hypertext Preprocessor), HTML (HyperText Markup Language), XML (eXtensible Markup Language), SGML (Standard Generalized Markup Language). Though it is possible to use these languages to express written languages other than English through various encodings, these languages were created by speakers of English to be used by speakers of English. You cannot participate in the creation of software without *using* English in the programming, scripting or markup of content, without participating in the hegemony of English, even if you do not have the ability to speak or write English.

What does this mean in terms of issues of difference in technology? Simply put, it means that it is practically impossible to participate in the world of technology without privileging English. The Internet is written in English. A programmer who wants to write a word processor for Icelandic writes the word processor in English using a language like Java or C++. The software is installed into, say, a Windows, Linux, or Apple-operating system that has been *localized* into Icelandic. But files created still require, in most instances, a .doc, .txt., html suffix; all derived from English. These *localized* versions are localized as an afterthought. The major operating systems, and the various software packages, are most all written for English consumers first, tested and made available to English consumers, and then *ported* to other languages, *if* the software company feels that it is profitable to do so. In 1997, Microsoft was pressured into porting one of their versions of windows to Icelandic by the Icelandic government highlighting the fragility of languages in the face of English and corporate interests (Ford, 2001).

Though many operating systems, such as Macintosh's OSX and Linux, now are sufficiently international to ship with multi-language package options and as localized versions for a few major language markets, there is very little available that is not Anglo-centric. There are non-English environments in which one can work, such as the Assembler programming language, which predates the C language on which the Internet and most commercial software is based, and there are embedded proprietary languages that are not directly available to the public or working on the Internet. The hegemonic influence of English in the computer languages running the Internet, however, means that concerted effort by educators of difference who are willing to work toward the creation of alternative language spaces is required.

The 26 letters of the English alphabet form the basis of how most content moves across the Internet, encoded as ASCII (American Standard Code for Information Interchange) text. The Internet functions primarily using the 94 printable characters that make up the ASCII character set.

```
abcdefghijklmnopqrstuvwxyz
ABCDEFGHIJKLMNOPQRSTUVWXYZ
0123456789
!"#$%&'()*+,-./:;<=?@[\]^_`{!}~ (Lunde, 1993, p. 36)
```

And when Japanese is displayed on your computer, the characters look and act like Japanese, but the encoding method still involves ASCII characters in the background.

かな漢字
82A9   82C8   8ABF   8E9A

In this example the two groups of characters, *ka na* and *kan ji*,[6] are presented with the ASCII encodings shown below. These *characters* which represent words that describe the two main writing scripts in Japanese (*ka na* and *kan ji*) are each encoded into four ASCII characters in order to be processed by computer and to be communicated over the Internet. That is, the Japanese language must be encoded through the agency of the ASCII to be communicated to another computer, even within Japan.

When you write a program, script, or electronic document, it must be written using an English-based programming language, such as Java, C, Perl, HTML. This following example from MOOca.java describes connecting to our MOO and setting the parameters for encoding non-English characters:

```
outputWriter = new OutputStream Writer(mSocket.getOutputStream(),
    mRequestedEncoding);
s = new String(inputBuffer, 0, byteCount, getEncoding());
```
(Nolan and Goulden, 1996–2001)

Where mRequestedEncoding is taken from the applet parameters and is a string such as "SJIS" "ASCII" "UTF8" [Unicode] which tells Mooca how it should encode the characters to send it to the Moo. Where getEncoding() usually is the same as mRequestedEncoding above. The only time it would be different is if someone tried to ask for an encoding that didn't exist, such as "japlish," in which case it would fall back to the user's default encoding. (Goulden, 2001)

It is possible to see this form of encoding as unproblematic. A minor price to pay for global communication, but the hegemony of English is even more profound: "Does the interiorization of media such as letters alter the ratio among our sense and change mental processes?" (McLuhan, 1995, p. 119). When you send an e-mail message, regardless of the language in which you compose your text, your e-mail program must talk to a server. A message is sent to a server on port 25 and the first message it says is "HELO," an abbreviation of "hello" in order to initiate a process that gets your e-mail moving on its way (commands sent to initiate communication are in bold):

> **telnet achieve.utoronto.ca 25**
> Trying 128.100.163.159 . . . Connected to achieve.utoronto.ca.
> Escape character is '^]'. 220 achieve.utoronto.ca ESMTP Sendmail 8.9.3/8.9.3;
> Tue, 6 Nov 2001 14:36:15 -0500
>
> **helo achieve.utoronto.ca 25**
> achieve..utoronto.ca Hello envvirtual.utoronto.ca [128.100.163.131], pleased to meet you

This means that every e-mail ever sent on the Internet by anyone in any language to any country, is couched in, or bracketed by, English. Communication is initiated in English and concluded in English. As language theorist George Steiner notes, in *After Babel:* "So far as language is the mirror or counter statement to the world, or most probably an interpretation of the reflective with the creative along an 'interface' of which we have no formal model, it changes as rapidly and in as many ways as human experience itself"(Steiner, 1998, p. 468). Steiner's ideas, in the context of the problematic dominance of English throughout the woof and warp of the Internet, suggest that what we can do and think with technology is forever informed by a language that, though in flux itself, forces the expression of human experience to conform to the influence of a single language and perhaps the metanarrative of those who thus situated it. The phenomenon that is the Internet has come upon the human species fast and unanticipated. Educators are playing catch up in their critical awareness of the foundations of the Internet, with the result that aspects of this revolution that should be challenged and problematized have slipped by, perhaps unnoticed.

The Educator as a Creator of Learning Environments

I am writing this chapter in English, as it is the only language to which I can claim fluency, but I choose to code this chapter in raw html, the hidden background scripting language that forms the background of all web pages. What I have written looks to me like this:

```
</blockquote>
<p>The educator as a Creator of Learning Environments</p>
<blockquote>
<p>I am writing this chapter in English . . .
```

I am also writing this using programs such PICO and BBEditLite, free and simple word processors. These choices remove, even if just temporarily, a level of commercial influence over the production of text, and a level of isolation from what goes on behind the location of the presentation of text. In order to participate in the publication of this book, however, I will have to convert my text into Microsoft's

Word program, but I will e-mail it to the editor using open-source software. These vaguely symbolic acts do highlight how an educator can position herself within alternatives to corporatist agendas, and model a practice that can be both emulated by students and stimulate awareness and inquiry into alternatives.

These are, however, the most superficial locations of resistance, and an entire volume such as this would be required to engage the possible examples and experiences of CVEs, MOOs, Cyborgs, and Hackers (Gray, 2001; Stone, 1992). Technology and computer literacy as it is taught in our faculties of education, and in the classroom, rarely takes even this stance. Review any curriculum, and you will see that it is largely infused with corporate technologies and corporate interests. The goal of technology-based curriculum is that of teaching users to be consumers of products in the name of global competitiveness and efficiency. Often the technologies are no more than computer-assisted learning and evaluation tools. When the technologies are used for expressive communication, the teaching is limited to what is proscribed in the manual. Rarely do even the most pedagogically aware educators, informed by critical pedagogy and aware of the need to promote alternative voices, critique the technologies in which the voices are located. And if/when they are aware, they lack the time or resources to really explore the options that are hidden away by security-conscious systems administrators (Nolan, 2001). Today most decisions as to what technologies are used in learning environments are made by technology specialists and administrators, and are given to educators with little or no consultation. There is even less awareness on the part of the educators and students that alternatives exist.

This is an untenable position. If valid and sustained strides are to be made to embed alternative choices in the global culture, they must be found within the technologies we use. These technological alternatives are something that cannot be done for us either. They must be done with us, and by us in community with our peers and students. To control the conceptualization, creation, development, implementation, cohabitation, and governance of these spaces we must learn to code, program, create our own software and environments that reflect our diverse needs and goals, and we must share them freely with others; allowing others to revise and relocalize what we share according to their own criteria and needs. This must be undertaken with the same vigor as the alternative press who have given voice to their own communities and experiences. There really is no other alternative. For if we do not actively participate in the creation of our discursive spaces, they are created by someone else, and we are at the most disempowered end of the power relationship (Foucault, 1991; Illich, 1970). If we do not govern our own spaces, our pedagogy, curriculum, writing, and thinking are open to commodification, and we are no longer creators, but consumers.

As a first step, transforming ourselves from consumers into prosumers where we are involved in communities of discourses, technologies, and narratives that we cocreate and inhabit, allows us to share and interact with stories of difference. The much vaunted and rarely experienced virtual community becomes a potential reality when we are able to (re)construct and embrace both collective and infinitely differentiating representations of ourselves, as we see ourselves, and reflect upon how we see others and are seen by them (Fernback and Thompson, 1995; Rheingold, 1993). The potential dialogues are, however, only realizable when we control (or consciously yield control over) the means of our own representation. The situation is hazardous simulation when dialogues are mediated by technologies over which we have minimal understanding and scant influence (Baudrillard, 1988; Fernback and Thompson, 1995; Stone, 1992; Turkle, 1995).

The influence of the Internet on the diverse languages and cultures of the world, those represented and underrepresented by technology, is in many instances an act of relocalization of culture(s) from the real to the virtual. Cultural topologies are (re)constructed, and cultural experience must find new strategies of expression and resistance to survive and thrive (Nolan, 1998; Ostrom, 1990; Rheingold, 1993). But more importantly, this relocalization is an act of translation of cultural experience (Steiner, 1998). And without the concerted effort of educators informed by the ideas of the pedagogies of difference—educators who are able to engage and dialogue with the Englishness of the Internet below the surface level of written texts, down to the level of the code and encodings that make the Internet happen—we are situating struggles within colonializing dialogues, aware of whose hands we are playing into, but unaware of how deeply the cards are stacked against us (Giroux, 1992). Where Steiner hypothesizes that "the proliferation of mutually incomprehensible tongues stems from an absolutely fundamental impulse in language itself [and] that the communication of information, of ostensive and verifiable 'facts', constitutes only one part, and perhaps a secondary part, of human discourse" I think that we are not only engaged in a struggle to liberate Internet discourses from the hegemony of English, but are engaged in a struggle fundamental to the defense of all aspects of difference (Steiner, 1998, p. 497). There is nothing that can be done to exorcise English as the fundamental language informing all communication on the Internet, but it is incumbent on all educators engaged in struggles to defend or demarginalize communities of difference to extend their program of inquiry and resistance to an engagement of how language and cultural influences inherent in the structure of the Internet translate/encode discourse and experience within a dominant cultural ideology.

Notes

1. ASCII stands for American Standard Code for Information Exchange, and is the encoding method by which most text-based information moves around the Internet.
2. I use Japanese as the example of a non-English language because it is one in which I have the greatest fluency. It is also that language which makes up 9.2% of all web pages on the Internet (Reach, 2001).
3. http://www.blogger.com; http://www.livejournal.com; http://c2.com/cgi-bin/wiki? Wiki WikiWebFaq; http://www.noahgrey.com/greysoft/.
4. Prosumer, in general, is an individual who partakes in both production and consumption.
5. Polysynchronous is a term coined to describe the nature of MOOs where communication is an embedded combination of both synchronous and asynchronous communication (Davie and Nolan, 1999; Nolan, 1998). An IRC chat group is completely synchronous. Users communicate in real time, and there is usually no record kept of the communication unless one member personally creates a transcript of the interaction as a log. Asynchronous communication refers to what happens on bulletin boards and via e-mail where a message is composed and transmitted to another individual or group. In a MOO, communication can be synchronous or asynchronous, but it can also be a

combination of both. A conversation can be encoded into an object for others to read. MOO objects can be programmed to listen to conversations between members and generate responses that become part of the MOO-space itself for other participants to listen to later. As well, a conversational interaction may take the form of direct synchronous speech *and* the co-manipulation of MOO objects. It is possible to talk with another person, hand her virtual objects for her to look at, co-program MOO objects, and record the conversation for a third party to read later. This type of polysynchrony is particular to MOO-type environments, but reflects the direction that collaborative virtual environments are anticipated to follow in the future (Nolan, 2001).

6. The *ka na* and *kan ji* characters and their encodings have been created by Ken Lunde for this publication.

Bibliography

Anonymous. (2001). *alt.2600 FAQ Revision .014 (1/4)* [HTML], May, 29, 2000 [cited October 1, 2001]. Available from http://www.faqs.org/faqs/alt-2600/faq/.

Babcock, Jim. (2001). *2600- a what is definition* [HTML], July 21, 2001 [cited October 1, 2001]. Available from http://whatis.techtarget.com/definition/0,,sid9_gci211496,00.html.

Baudrillard, Jean. (1988). Simulacra and Simulations. In *Selected Writings*, ed. M. Poster. Stanford: Stanford University Press.

Berners-Lee, Tim. (2001). *Tim Berners-Lee: A Short History of Web Development.* 1998 [cited August 2, 2001]. Available from http://www.w3.org/People/Berners-Lee/ShortHistory.

Bruckman, Amy. (1998). *MOOSE Crossing: Construction, Community, and Learning in a Networked Virtual World for Kids.* [Web page, PhD Dissertation] 1997 [cited 1998]. Available from http://www.cc.gatech.edu/fac/Amy.Bruckman/thesis/index.html.

———. (1999). *Identity Workshop: Emergent Social And Psychological Phenomena in Text-Based Virtual Reality* [Postscript document]. Amy Bruckman, Friday, September 3, 1999; 1992 [cited December 12, 1999].

Cailliau, Robert. (1999). *A Little History of the World Wide Web* [HTML]. W3C, October 3, 1995 [cited August 4, 1999].

Cerny, Jim. (2001). *Who Runs the Internet?* [HTML], 2000 [cited November 1, 2001]. Available from http://www.unh.edu/Internet/web/whoruns.html.

Champeon, Steve. (2001). *RTFM: A Guide to Online Research* [HTML]. Wired Digital Inc. n.d. [cited November 1, 2001]. Available from http://hotwired.lycos.com/webmonkey/templates/print_template.htmlt?meta=/webmonkey/00/08/index2a_meta.html.

Cicognani, Anna. "On the Linguistic Nature of Cyberspace and Virtual Communities." *Virtual Reality* 3 (1998): 16–24.

Cooper, Alan. (1999). *The Inmates are Running the Asylum: Why High-Tech Products Drive Us Crazy and How to Restore the Sanity.* Indianapolis, IN: SAMS.

Cooper, Charles. (2001). *When Blogging Came of Age.* CNN 2001 [cited September 20, 2001]. Available from http://news.cnet.com/news/0-1272-210-7242676-1.html?tag=bt_bh.

Cummins, Jim and Dennis Sayers. (1995). *Brave New Schools: Challenging Cultural Illiteracy through Global Learning Networks.* Toronto: O.I.S.E. Press.

Curtis, Pavel. "Mudding: Social Phenomena in Text-Based Virtual Realities." *Intertrek* 3:3 (1992): 26–34.

Curtis, Pavel and Doug Nichols. (1993). *MUDs Grow Up: Social Virtual Reality in the Real World.* Paper read at Third International Conference on Cyberspace, at Austin, TX.

Davie, Lynn, Hema Abeygunawardena, Katherine Davidson, and Jason Nolan. (1998). *Universities, Communities, and Building Sites: An Exploration of Three Online Systems.* Paper read at Educational Computing Organization of Ontario, at Toronto, ON.

Davie, Lynn and Jason Nolan. (1999). *Doing Learning: Building Constructionist Skills for Educators, or, Theatre of Metaphor: Skills Constructing for Building Educators.* Paper read at TCC, at Maui, Hawaii.

e-cyclopedia. 2000. *BBC News | e-cyclopedia | Cracking: Hackers Turn Nasty* [HTML]. e-cyclopedia@bbc.co.uk, Tuesday, August 31, 1999, 12:34 GMT 1999 [cited April 19, 2000]. Available from http://news.bbc.co.uk/hi/english/special_report/1999/02/99/e-cyclopedia/newsid_434000/434498.stm.

Fanderclai, T. L. "MUDs in Education: New Environments, New Pedagogies." *Computer-Mediated Communication* 2:1 (1995): 8.

Fernback, Jan and Brad Thompson. (1999). *Virtual Communities: Abort, Retry, Failure?* [HTML] 1995 [cited August 16, 1999]. Available from http://www.well.com/user/hlr/texts/VCcivil.html.

Finely, Michael. (2000). *Alvin Toffler and the Third Wave.* www.mastersforum.com, Mon, Jan 31, 2000 10:17:18 PM GMT 2000 [cited April 18, 2000]. Available from http://www.mastersforum.com/toffler/toffler.htm.

Ford, Peter. (2001). *Need Software in, say, Icelandic? Call the Irish* [HTML]. Christian Science Monitor, February 6, 2001 [cited October 15, 2001]. Available from http://www.csmonitor.com/durable/2001/02/06/fp1s3-csm.shtml.

Foucault, M. (1991). "Governmentality." In *The Foucault Effect: Studies in Governmental Rationality*, ed. G. Burchell, C. Gordon, and P. Miller. Hertfordshire: Harvester Wheatsheaf.

Franklin, Ursula. (1992). *The Real World of Technology.* Toronto: Anansi.

Giroux, Henry A. (1992). *Border Crossings: Cultural Workers and the Politics of Education.* New York: Routledge.

Goulden, David. (2001). *Raw MOOca.* Toronto, November 7, 2001.

Gray, Chris Hables. (2001). *Cyborg Citizen: Politics in the Posthuman Age.* New York: Routledge.

Harasim, Linda, Starr Roxanne Hiltz, Lucio Teles, and Murray Turoff. (1995). *Learning Networks: A Field Guide to Teaching and Learning Online.* Cambridge, MA: MIT Press.

Harraway, Donna. (2000). "A Cyborg Manifesto: Science, Technology and Socialist-Feminism in the Late Twentieth Century." In *The Cybercultures Reader*, ed. D. Bell and B. Kennedy. London: Routledge.

———. (2000). *How Like a Leaf.* New York: Routledge.

Hayles, Katherine. (1999). *How We Became Posthuman: Virtual Bodies in Cybernetics, Literature, and Informatics.* Chicago: University of Chicago Press.

Haynes, Cynthia and Jan Rune Holmevik. (1998). *Highwired: On the Design, Use and Theory of Educational MOOs.* Ann Arbor: Michigan.

Hochheiser, Harry and Robin Ric. (2001). *Who Runs the Internet?* [HTML]. Computer Professionals for Social Responsibility, May 3, 1998 [cited November 1, 2001]. Available from http://www.cpsr.org/onenet/whoruns.html.

Illich, Ivan. (1970). *Deschooling Society.* New York: Harper & Row.

Jones, Steve. (2000). "The Bias of the Web." In *The World Wide Web and Contemporary Cultural Theory*, ed. A. Herman and T. Swiss. New York: Routledge.

Krol, Ed. (1992). *The Whole Internet User's Guide & Catalog.* Sebastapol: O'Reilly.

Little, Jean. (2001). *Orphan at My Door: The Home Childe Diary of Victoria Cope Guelph Ontario 1897.* Toronto: Scholastic.

Lunde, Ken. (1993). *Understanding Japanese Information Processing.* Sebastapol: O'Reilly.

Lyotard, Jean François. (1984). *The Postmodern Condition : A Report on Knowledge, Theory and History of Literature. v. 10.* Manchester: Manchester University Press.

McLuhan, Marshall. (1995). "The Gutenberg Galaxy." In *Essential McLuhan*, ed. E. McLuhan and F. Zingrone. Toronto: Anansi.

Mitchell, William. (1998). *City of Bits: Space, Place and the Infobhan.* Cambridge, MA: MIT Press.

Noble, David. (1997). *The Religion of Technology: The Divinity of Man and the Spirit of Invention.* New York: Knopf.

Nolan, Jason. (1999). *Educators in MOOkti: A Polysynchronous Collaborative Virtual Learning Environment,* February 28, 1999; 1995 [cited April 25, 1999]. Available from http://noisey.oise.utoronto.ca/jason/dissertation-proposal.html.

————. (1999). *The Dark Side of the Internet* [HTML], 1998; 1994 [cited August 5, 1999]. Available from http://noisey.oise.utoronto.ca/gbut/.

————. (2000). Project Achieve & VASE: Virtual Learning Environments. Paper read at TEACHING, LEARNING AND RESEARCH IN TODAY'S UNIVERSITY: Information Technology and the University Professor, at University of Toronto, Toronto, Ontario.

————. "Unpacking Transnational Policy: Learning to Bridge the Digital Divide." *Educational Technology & Society* 1:1 (2000).

————. (2001). "The Techneducator Effect: Colliding Technology and Education in the Conceptualization of Virtual Learning Environments." Ph.D Dissertation, Curriculum Teaching and Learning, Ontario Institute for Studies in Education, University of Toronto, Toronto.

————. (2001). *Vase: The Virtual Assignment Server Environment* [HTML], 2000 [cited September 27, 2001]. Available from http://achieve.utoronto.ca/vase.

Nolan Jason, and David Goulden. *MOOca.java* (3.0) [Java Applet]. Project Achieve 1996–2001 [cited]. Available from http://www.zanid.com/mooca/.

Nolan, Jason and Emma Jane Hogbin. (2001). *Internet Literate: A Report on Future Trends for Online Learning Environments in North America.* Toronto: Vivendi.

Nolan, Jason, Jeff Lawrence, and Yuka Kajihara. (1998). "Montgomery's Island in the Net: Metaphor and Community on the Kindred Spirit's E-mail List." *Canadian Children's Literature* 24:3/4 (1991/92): 64–77.

Nolan, Jason and Joel Weiss. (2002). "Learning Cyberspace: An Educational View of Virtual Community." In *Building Virtual Communities: Learning and Change in Cyberspace,* ed. K. A. Renninger and W. Shumar. Cambridge: Cambridge University Press.

O'Reilly and Associates, Inc. (2000). *Welcome to the O'Reilly Open Source Center* [HTML]. O'Reilly & Associates, Inc., Thursday, April 13, 2000 4:10:53 PM GMT 2000 [cited April 18, 2000]. Available from http://opensource.oreilly.com/.

OECD. (2000). *Learning to Bridge the Digital Divide, Schooling for Tomorrow.* Paris: OECD Publications.

Online, Linux. 2000. *The Linux Home Page at Linux Online.* Linux Online Inc. 1994–2000 [cited April 18, 2000]. Available from http://www.linux.org/.

Ostrom, Elinor. (1990). "Governing the Commons: The Evolution of Institutions for Collective Action". In *The Political Economy of Institutions and Decisions* ed. J. A. D. North, Cambridge: Cambridge University Press.

Power, Edward. (2001). *Joe Blogs on the Internet* [HTML]. Irish Times, Dublin, October 28, 2000 [cited October 31, 2001]. Available from http://www.ireland.com/newspaper/features/2000/1028/features4.htm.

Raymond, Eric S. (2000). *Open Source: Software Gets Honest* [HTML], 1998 [cited April 18, 2000]. Available from http://www.opensource.org/.

————. (2000). *The Rampantly Unofficial Linus Torvalds FAQ* [HTML]. Eric S. Raymond, Wednesday, December 22, 1999 5:01:41 PM GMT 1999 [cited April 18, 2000]. Available from http://www.tuxedo.org/~esr/faqs/linus/.

————. (2000). *How to Become a Hacker* [HTML], March 24, 2000 [cited April 18, 2000]. Available from http://www.tuxedo.org/~esr/faqs/hacker-howto.html.

————. (2001). *Creeping Featuritis* [HTML], 2001 [cited November 1, 2001]. Available from http://www.tuxedo.org/~esr/jargon/html/entry/creeping-featuritis.html.

Reach, Global. (2001). *Global Internet Statistics (by Language)* [HTML], September 30, 2001 [cited November 1, 2001]. Available from http://www.glreach.com/globstats/index.php3.

Rheingold, Howard. (1993). *The Virtual Community.* New York: Harper.

Ruffin, Oxblood. (2001). *The Hacktivismo FAQ v1.0* [HTML]. cDc communications 2001 [cited October 20, 2001]. Available from http://www.cultdeadcow.com/cDc_files/HacktivismoFAQ.html.

Said, Edward. (1993). *Culture and Imperialism.* New York: Vintage Press.

Schank, Patricia, Jamie Fenton, Mark Schlager, and Judi Fusco. (2000). *From MOO to MEOW: Domesticating Technology for Online Communities* [HTML]. SRI International, Center for Technology in Learning 1999 [cited April 7, 2000]. Available from http://kn.cilt.org/cscl99/A64/A64.HTM.

Scott, Peter. (2001). *Free-Nets and Community Networks* [HTML]. Lights.com, unk 2001 [cited October 15, 2001]. Available from http://www.lights.com/freenet/.

Scoville, Thomas. (2000). *Whence the Source: Untangling the Open Source/Free Software Debate* [On-line]. O'Reilly & Associates, Inc., Thursday, December 9, 1999 7:10:38 PM GMT 1998 [cited April 18, 2000]. Available from http://opensource.oreilly.com/news/scoville_0399.html.

Stallman, Richard. (2000). *GNU's Not Unix!—the GNU Project and the Free Software Foundation (FSF)* [HTML]. Free Software Foundation, Inc., Saturday, April 8, 2000 4:04:17 AM GMT 1999 [cited April 18, 2000]. Available from http://www.fsf.org/.

Steiner, George. (1998). *After Babel: Aspects of Language and Translation*, 3rd ed. New York: Oxford University Press. Original edition, 1975.

Sterling, Bruce. (1993). *The Hacker Crackdown: Law and Disorder on the Electronic Frontier.* New York: Bantam.

Stoll, Cliff. (1989). *The Cuckoo's Egg: Tracking a Spy through the Maze of Computer Espionage.* New York: Pocket books.

Stone, Allucquere Rosanne. (1992). "Will the Real Body Please Stand Up?: Boundary Stories about Virtual Cultures." In *Cyberspace: First Steps*, ed. M. Benedikt. Cambridge, MA: MIT Press.

Tetzlaff, David. (2000). "Yo–Ho–Ho and a Server of Warez." In *The World Wide Web and Contemporary Cultural Theory*, ed. A. Herman and T. Swiss. New York: Routledge.

Turkle, Sherry. (1995). *Life on the Screen.* New York: Schuster.

Vest, Frank. (2001). *FidoNews—The FidoNet Dialup BBS Community Weekly Newsletter* [HTML]. FidoNews Editor, October 15, 2001 [cited October 15, 2001]. Available from http://www.fidonews.org/.

Wertheim, Margaret. (2000). *The Pearly Gates of Cyberspace: A History of Space from Dante to the Internet.* New York: Norton.

Chapter 11 ∿

The Phoneur: Mobile Commerce and the Digital Pedagogies of the Wireless Web

Robert Luke

Freedom—that's the promise of mobile phones. Already in Europe and Japan and set to hit the North American market next year, m-commerce phones let users surf the web, send email and pay for stuff all from the palm of their hand. A convenience you can't do without? Perhaps. But subscribing to the next generation of mobile services makes you an unwitting participant in an experiment that eavesdrops on everything you do. It may seem like a great deal, but there's a hidden cost to living in the wireless world.[1]

Introduction: The Habit@

Corporate data collectors track every move you make on the electronic landscape, recording your m-commerce phone habits only to sell them back to you through advertising that entices you to spend more. Think of these phones as a kind of remote-controlled radio collar—like the ones scientists use to monitor the behaviour of the animals they study.

The move toward mobile commerce, or m-commerce, still nascent in North America, is an attempt to create a worldwide datastructure built on the premise of consumption. The habit@ is the electronic environment—and the sociocultural conditions—of the wireless and worldwide webs (W4 and W3). Within it, "The structures constitutive of a particular type of environment . . . produce *habitus*, systems of durable, transposable dispositions, structured structures predisposed to function as structuring structures" (Bourdieu, 1977, p. 72; 1990). These structures are the invisible data collection mechanisms that track user habits through the data flows of electronic identity formation, and sell these habits back to the user in the form of "push" advertising.[2] "There is no fixed self, only the habit of looking for one" (Wise, 2000, p. 303), and this habit of looking is our habit@on-line. The wireless habit@ is constituted in the patterns of our mobile browsing behavior, which is in turn repackaged and re-presented as a demographic representation of how we will engage the spending process, how we will actualize ourselves as desiring-machines (Deleuze and Guattari, 1983). The habit@ is becoming the marker of social distinction. Where once social difference was measured by the possession of a cell phone, the ubiquity of these devices now means that there is no distinction in having one. Social difference is now measured by the *type* of mobile phone service a person consumes.

These commodified network relationships represent the transformation of commodity and capital into the realm of the purely symbolic: information about users in the habit@ becomes a way to track as well as lure the user within the commercial datastructure of on-line shopping. The Internet is a medium by which symbolic capital is at home: "In the vectorial space of the Internet the special quality of both information and money—that unlike other commodities they have no use value in their own right but only as items of exchange—is naturalized" (Stratton, 1996, p. 259). Information about users in the habit@ is an item of exchange; the collection of personal information enabled by phones equipped with Global Positioning System (GPS) software becomes the locus of identity formation within the vectors of mobile commerce. Users exchange personal information for the commercial privilege of using the networks, information that is then used to sell other commodities to the user even while this information becomes an object of exchange in the market(ing) of demographic information. The ephemeral flow of production/consumption within the habit@on-line is one digit of the invisible hand of capitalism, serving our commodities in exchange for an identity-as-consumer capitulation.

With the new mobile phone service my-iD.com (my-id.com, 2001), Rogers Wireless seeks to create a culture of its user base. Rogers would enculturate users into its phone service habit@ as a site of social difference, a place to be heard, to participate, to belong. The my-iD.com service offers an avenue of self-expression and concomitant control over the presentation of digital identity, but it does so under very strict controls that are really limiting parameters on just what constitutes this identity in the first place. This sense of belonging and identity is based on the panoptic surveillance of movement through the dataflows. The digital pedagogy of the wireless world teaches consumption and commodification: the location of W4 culture as the home of capital construes the digital citizen as consumer. The postmodern city, punctuated by the peremptory sounds of cell phones ringing, now has its own home. The habit@ is the location marked by the territorializing impulse of the postmodern primitive who dances to the tribal sounds of the McLuhanesque mantra of media saturation. The affective investment in the desire to own a cell phone and, now, to participate in a culture of *phonerie* (Morgan, 2000),[3] is a pedagogy of liberation (from landlines) concurrently caught in the mobile Net.

From the Flâneur to the Phoneur: The Mobile (S)Talker

> Our wily e-urbanite emerges from his lair and makes his way to the local coffee shop. On the way, he pre-orders his latte with his cell phone. The venti-sized beverage with a sprinkle of chocolate is waiting for him when he arrives. Payment is automatically processed from his m-commerce phone, scanned as he walks in the door.

The phoneur is the postmodern flâneur: a mobile phone user strolling the cityscape. The flâneur, implicated within modernist scopophilia (Benjamin, 1999; Ferguson, 1994; Frisby, 1994; Mazlish, 1994; Shields, 1994), is "the spectator of the modern world" (Mazlish, 1994, p. 43). Likewise, the phoneur is a commentator on the postmodern world, speaking from the mobile phone's commercial capabilities. Ursula Kelly, in outlining the differing concepts of literacy that punctuate the postmodern age, says

> The directive question in this relationship [between literacy and cultural forms] is how cultural practices of representation and meaning court desires and mobilize identities: in other words, are pedagogical. Of particular importance in addressing this question is the cultural work of the popular, the site on which dominant habits of desire are circulated, reiterated, and challenged. (Kelly, 1997, p. 69)

This site is the postmodern habit@ of the phoneur, the cell phone sporting, incessantly talking, e-urbanite whose identity is articulated within the mediated space of the mobile phone and the ensuing enculturation processes of the wireless web.

Just as "the flâneur's vision of life, based on his peripatetic observations, creates reality" (Mazlish, 1994, p. 53), so too do the commercial grids and communication vectors (the sociotechnical constructs of communication) create the reality for the phoneur. An identity is mobilized as the phoneur wanders, observed while (s)talking the city streets. Kelly reminds us that as we engage in reading the sites of popular culture, we must pay particular attention to "the lived engagements of media and meaning through how desires, dreams, identities, and social relations are shaped" (Kelly, 1997, pp. 70–71). These engagements constitute the enculturation into telephonerie, or simply phonerie, within the digital networks and virtual terrain of information.

If "space is composed of intersections of mobile elements" (de Certeau, 1984, p. 117), then these mobile elements are the composite parts that overlay the real with the logic of mobile capital. Castells tells us that we live in an informational era wherein "the emphasis on interactivity between places breaks up spatial patterns of behaviour into a fluid network of exchanges that underlies the emergence of a new kind of space, the space of flows" (Castells, 1996, p. 398). For Castells, this space of flows is the larger geopolitical dimensions of capital movements: interconnected globalized manufacturing and distribution systems all contained within a network of production and consumption. The micro version of this space of flows is refracted in the logic of the phoneur, to whom "The phone is an object and a technology. But it is also part of a system of ideas, even a way of looking at everyday life" (Myerson, 2001, p. 9). Examining this way of life and the affective investment into which users are enticed through this phonerie enculturation reveals a digital pedagogy of consumption, and an identity made up of assemblages of commodities that flow through the ether into handheld market proxies.

The mass "mobilization" of desire and affect (Myerson, 2001) is the *vox populi* of the phoneur punctuating the post-metropolis. Benjamin tells us that " 'the colportage phenomenon of space' is the flâneur's basic experience" (1999, p. 418), and this is an apt descriptor of the phoneur's relationship to the mediated commercial grid. Colportage, "to hawk, carry for sale" (OED), is the basic experience of the phoneur in the habit@on-line, where "Communication is being increasingly measured in terms of money, becoming 'metered' " (Myerson, 2001, p. 60). The phoneur is the mobile tele-talker, stalked by corporate hunters who datamine the habit@ and place the social relations of phonerie amidst flows of commodity and desire.

Portals, Panoptics, and Personalized Information Space

> While at work, he "accidentally" surfs onto a porn site. It takes his cookie and processes his ID. "Enlarge your penis" spam begins to fill his email inbox which is synchronized to his phone. A call to the service provider and payment of a "nominal" fee means the spam is successfully filtered.

Web portals are web sites that enable users to personalize or customize a public site based on personal preferences.[4] Users log on and create the datastructure that will be presented to them according to the preferences registered in their "user profile." Portals such as America Online (AOL), CompuServe (CompuServe), Traffick (Traffick), Yahoo! (Yahoo), Netscape (Netscape), Excite (Excite), and Microsoft (Microsoft; Microsoft) offer users the ability to personalize their own portal datastructure in exchange for submitting personal information. The next generation of web portals are auspiciously labeled with the first-person possessive pronoun "My" (myTO; My Yahoo!; My Netscape; Microsoft Passport). Users are encouraged to "become" their portal identity and to identify directly with the information presented within these pockets of data.

Wireless portal providers seek to bring the portal directly to the user with WWW-enabled mobile phones, deploying rhetorical strategies that encourage users to develop proprietary feelings toward their mobile portal identity. This is especially true of the wireless portal my-iD.com (my-id.com, 2001). Another mobile phone service provider, Bell Mobility, offers a service called "My Time," which is a personalized phone payment plan based on user preference ("some restrictions apply," of course). Bell is currently running a series of advertisements in support of this program that uses a glib humor to inspire an individualist ethos within the "My Time" service. Using slogans such as "Make as many 3 am 'I love you' calls as you feel like," Bell attempts to appeal to a self-deprecating sense of observational humor. Other slogans, including "Careful. You could sprain a lip" and "Doing our part to support gossip everywhere," encourage the consumer to identify with the "My Time" service as one that is in keeping with a popular conception of human nature: a contrived recognition of what we have in common that can best be served with a personalized phone service such as "My Time."

Users submit to the subtle collection of data in order to personalize a portal page or to participate in the ebb and flow of m-commerce, resulting in a data collection and target marketing according to registered and observed preferences. M-commerce phone users are seduced into complicity with the desiring-machine of capitalism and its concomitant surveillance of the activity of commercial networks. This desiring-machine thus constitutes its own panoptic as the mobile phone is insinuated and interpolated into everyday life. The mobile phone as desiring-machine—if not a desired machine—takes this surveillance into the streets with the advent of GPS-enabled phones that literally track user movements through the informational city. The mobile phone becomes a "panoptic mechanism . . . a point of exchange between a mechanism of power and a function; it is a way of making power relations function in a function, and of making a function through these power relations" (Foucault, 1997, p. 365). The functional power relations of capitalist production and consumption are articulated by the willful submission to panoptic surveillance of activities within the wired and the wireless network, as well as the desire to possess the technology of mobile commerce and communication. This "desire is a process, a synthesis of machines, a machinic arrangement—desiring machines. The order of desire is the order of *production*; all production is at once desiring-production and social production" (Deleuze and Guattari, 1983, p. 296). Within the logic of m-commerce, the phoneur is attached to a machine (the cell phone) which is in turn attached to other machines (the networked datastructure) in a machinic arrangement that produces social relations based on commodity production and consumption. This "machinic arrangement" is a social process (Wise, 1997; Agre, 1994; Clarke, 1994): "The mobilization of the phone isn't really a technological process—it's cultural. The problem isn't to *invent* the machine, but to get us all to *adopt* it, to feel we need it" (Myerson, 2001, p. 7). To produce desire is to produce consumption, of capital flows, of information, of communication as commodity. The social relations of desire and affect are the effects of phonerie.

Mobile phone-enabled consumption renders the sites of consumerism as polymorphous, ubiquitous, and pervasive. W4 portal providers seek to be the point of access for the mobile crowd, the hinge between the commercial datastructure of the habit@ and the lived environment of social relations, the milieu of the phoneur. Web portals are the fortified enclaves of the Internet and the WWW (Luke, 2004), and the logic of the on-line fortified enclave is now being extended to the mobile phone: "the mobile phone promotes a verbal gated community; you can shut out everyone around you. It's become a personal accessory that allows the oblivious to live in their own world" (Goodman, 1999). But this obliviousness extends to the invisible data collection of the habit@, as it is based on the sophisticated move toward an invisible and participatory panopticism enabled by the "trace technologies of the habit@online" (Luke, in press). The citizen-consumer is seduced into partaking of these flows by the emancipatory promise of new technologies: the wireless web and the premise of a digital citizenry. This notion of citizenship is predicated on an ability to covertly trace the datatrails of the digital individual (here the phoneur):

> Technological developments linking surveillance with societal simulation [m-commerce phones as the latest and greatest gadget, for example], and the increasing horizontal co-ordination between "dossiers" and sites of surveillance (credit bureaus, banks, retailers, utilities, media firms, transport operators, state and correctional agencies), seem likely to prefigure a rapid intensification of co-ordinated, comprehensive surveillance. (Graham, 1999, p. 142)

With the addition of m-commerce GPS-enabled phones, these "geographies of surveillant simulation" (Graham, 1999) are part of the collection and collation of habit@ data that operates within a panoptic paradigm of consensual surveillance. The "cultural technologies" (Giroux, 2000, p. 123) of media and the iconography of culture affect the ways in which people are encouraged to use cell phones within the learned behavior of phonerie.

My id:entity

> He punches in a GPS request for that new restaurant he read about in yesterday's userNews feature. He finds out it is within walking distance and gets a 10% discount coupon sent to him as he heads there. As he strolls through the shopping strip on his way back from lunch, each store he passes sends an e-coupon to his phone. Communications jam up until he gets through the shopping district.

Digital citizenship is more and more being articulated within the rubric of consumption and commodity. As Kelly says, "desire and difference intersect in identity" (Kelly, 1997, p. 105). This is especially so within my-iD.com. This service seeks to be both a marker of social difference with the participation in its service (vis-à-vis other phone service providers), as well as within its service, with respect to constructing your personal identity within its portal's pages for others to see. "It is difference that makes identity possible" (Kelly, 1997, p. 108), and the markers of difference within my-iD.com constitute the phoneur's entity. Within on-line or cybernetic grammar, an entity is a stand-in or representation. For example, "A character entity reference is an SGML [Standard Generalized Markup Language] construct that references a character of the document character set" (World Wide Web Consortium). That is, an entity is a representation in code of a particular sign or symbol. It is a way to represent certain signs and/or symbols that do not have a corresponding key on a standard keyboard (e.g., Latin, mathematical symbols, and Greek letters, markup-significant and international characters). With respect to my-iD.com, a user's id:entity is the representation of that user within the network. It is the user's ID—an identifying mark or proxy of identification. It can also be said to be a representation of the id, or underlying psychological profile of desire, as per the psychoanalytic use of the Latin term for "id": "The inherited instinctive impulses of the individual, forming part of the unconscious and, in Freudian theory, interacting in the psyche with the ego and the super-ego" (OED). If we accept that the id is the wellspring of the subconscious and individual desire, then this is an appropriate rendering of the way in which my-iD.com is seeking to operate within the enculturation of the phoneur's identity:

> The fluid nature of the habit@id:entity is a functional representation of online market proxies in constant renegotiation and informational articulation. It is an additive function in which our presence is deferred insofar as we are always mediated and represented by our id:entity, which stands in for our sense of self within online environments. (Luke, in press)

The id:entity, as the stand-in for the person, is a portal proxy and the representation of desire, "a tool for your self-expression and an outlet for your thoughts. It's everything you need to make yourself heard" (my-id.com, 2001). The id:entity is the mediator—both literally and figuratively—between the ego and the super-ego, the individual and the network configuration(s) of desire and commodity exchange: the way to broadcast your self into the ether of the wireless web.[5]

The my-iD.com mobile phone service offers users an enculturation into the experience of participating within a userCulture of like-minded people. Advertising for this new breed of mobile phone asks "What's your iD?" implying that, like your real identity, which is unique and particular to you and only you, this new phone service offers a personalized place or space for the creation, maintenance, and cultivation of your own iD within the constraints of a liberatory capitalism. The my-iD service is the wireless extension of the construction of the on-line persona, itself an essential part of the postmodern consciousness of the Internet generation. Within the habit@ you need a digital tool—a veritable digital soapbox—upon which to stage your "self-expression," and "iD . . . acts as a tool for your self-expression and an outlet for your thoughts. It's everything you need to make yourself heard." Your thoughts can be broadcast throughout the userCulture with your new mobile phone; my-iD.com turns phones from basic senders and receivers into more robust broadcast devices. Transmuted from basic communication devices, these phones allow you to hear and be heard above and beyond the din of all the other cell phones ringing. The iD phone, as "everything you need to make yourself heard," is the ultimate accouterment of the digital citizen that will make you stand above the crowd.

Turning the simple handset into a multimedia broadcast device[6]—or at least selling it with this appearance and cachet—means that the personalized space of web portals (as a place to broadcast your personal tastes and desires) now resides with you at all times. No longer attached to the wires of the web, the wireless revolution pushes the information datastructure out into the streets of the mediated city. New media are being designed to "hear" your phone as you pass by, and send you e-coupons to use in an effort to entice you into stores you encounter as you stroll the city streets (Haskins, 2001). This city—territorialized within the rubric of capital and commodity flows—now reaches out to you as you pass by, interpolating consciousness with every step you take. The construction of the consuming consciousness is reconstituted within the on-line shopping mall of the future (Stratton, 1996, p. 257), now the mobile mall that follows the phoneur through the city street.

The my-iD.com service takes the web portal and makes it portable. This new emergence of the phone portal is advertised as offering the following features: "Exclusive contests, polls, and iVent information; Personalize content and have it sent to your phone; An ongoing, ever growing interactive member area" (my-id.com, 2001). In addition to voice, these phones also offer "2-way Email and Text Messaging." iVents are "events" that only subscribers will be privy to. The locus of network identity is the location of the "I" in an egocentric habit@id:entity. Access to special deals and discounts are intended to entice users to subscribe to the iD service and relinquish their privacy. And this is where the real problem lies. A close reading of the privacy and security regulations reveals a disturbing trend toward corporate ownership of personal data. This data is sold—or rather, the rights to it are—all in the name of consumption within the increasingly over-commodified and corporatized space of network capital.

The privacy policy of the my-iD service acknowledges the tech-savviness of their potential customer base. This policy seeks to circumvent privacy concerns by tackling head-on issues surrounding the use of cookies to track user habits:

How does Rogers/my-id.com use information it gathers about me?

> Rogers/my-id.com collects and uses your name, email address and other personal infor-
> mation, for example, to provide you with product and other information that you
> requested, to respond to your questions, to enter you in and to administer contests,
> to email you updates and news and to contact you respecting polls and surveys.
> Rogers/my-id.com will not use any personally-identifiable information, other than
> contact information, obtained in member polls or surveys without your prior express
> consent. This information also enables Rogers to develop and customize products or
> services to better meet your needs and preferences and to offer you products and ser-
> vices from Rogers, any of its affiliated companies within the Rogers group of companies
> and other companies with whom we have marketing. (my-id.com, 2001, /Privacy.jsp)

The language used here is designed to create the illusion of empowerment. Rogers
will collect private and personal data "to provide you with product and other information that you requested, to respond to your questions, to enter you in and to
administer contests, to email you updates and news and to contact you respecting
polls and surveys." The provision of service in return for users' personal data is meant
to ameliorate the fact that users do lose privacy within the service. Users are told that
they can give up their personal information in order to get something that they may
want. The premise and the promise of this push advertising rely on a sense of proprietary consumption—the idea that you will want to partake of future commodities produced with "you" in mind. This further plays on the "unique iD"—the
id:entity—angle that uses the idea of individuality even as it marshals the technology
to produce an individual profile based on past habits and inputted personal data. "At
heart, the mobile concept is about being in control—as a separate and distinct individual" (Myerson, 2001, p. 20). The irony is that this individual uniqueness is only
made possible by the collection of the habits of mass consumption, as "Countless—
but counted—individuals are seeking their desires separately, and yet unknowingly
they are caught up in a huge system" (Myerson, 2001, p. 21).

What gets really disturbing is the trend toward actual ownership of data that is moved
across the service. Rogers assumes all control over anything that is moved over its service:

> You hereby grant to Rogers a worldwide, royalty-free, perpetual, irrevocable, non-exclusive
> right and license to use, reproduce, modify, adapt, publish, translate, distribute and subli-
> cense, and hereby agree to waive in favour of Rogers all of your moral rights in, any and all
> material, information or content submitted by you to the my-id.com web site and/or to
> incorporate it in other works regardless of form, medium or technology, without compen-
> sation. (my-id.com, 2001, /Privacy.jsp)

Users have no rights to their personal data within the my-iD dataspace. Anything
they upload or transfer over the network becomes the sole property of Rogers, who
can then resell this content for profit with no remuneration to the person(s) who
actually created it. The Terms And Conditions Of Membership for my-iD.com
further stipulates that by signing up for their service users agree to all terms and
conditions, even if these get changed:

> By registering as a member of my-id.com you acknowledge and agree to comply with
> these terms and conditions and all policies and notices on this site (collectively the

"Terms and Conditions"). We reserve the right, at our sole discretion, to modify the Terms and Conditions at any time, and such modifications shall be effective immediately upon posting of the modified Terms and Conditions. You agree to review the Terms and Conditions periodically to be aware of such modifications and your continued use of the my-id.com web site shall be deemed your conclusive acceptance of the modified Terms and Conditions. Registration by any person under age 16 requires consent and agreement by a parent or guardian including without restriction their agreement to comply with the Terms and Conditions. (my-id.com, 2001, /Privacy.jsp)

The assumption is that the user will periodically check back with the terms and conditions (the users agrees "to review the Terms and Conditions periodically to be aware of such modifications" to the rules). Thus Rogers has no obligation to inform users if terms change. How many people will actually reread the Terms and Conditions, and more to the point, how many are going to read these closely the first time? Most people give these kinds of policies a cursory read at best, as they are more concerned with signing up for and on to the system in order to reap the "benefits" of membership.

Within the my-iD.com habit@, service is tailored to the individual—it's a new individualism, a new frontier to be tamed by the reaches of capitalism. The my-iD.com logo (my-id.com 2001) is an approximation or hybrid of the @ symbol but with the "i" in the center. And this is perhaps the point, for within the habit@ the virtual "I" is the most important entity. This is my iD:my identity and my id:entity that seeks a home of and for self-expression within the wireless web offered by the my-iD.com network. Within the habit@, "we no longer have roots we have aerials" (Wark, 1994, p. 64). My entity on the network becomes me, as I become data. I am where it's @.

You Say You Want a ®evolution™

> He sends an email to a friend suggesting they meet at the movies to catch the latest feature flick. The e-phone's mailer scans the outgoing text, picks up the film's keyword, and sends back a coupon for free Coke with purchase of a super-size popcorn. The cinema emails him to say he can reserve his tickets (paid for electronically). By accepting the push advertising, no ticket is necessary—just show the e-coupon to the usher.

The search for meaning in the postmodern world sees the endless repetition and regurgitation of past forms pressed into the service of the present. The enculturation process of the my-iD.com service—this "new kind of wireless service" which is in fact a new way of being in the city—reconfigures the lived experience (or more to the point, the shopping experience, which is now conflated with the lived experience) within "another type of consumption: consumption of the very process of consumption itself, above and beyond its content and the immediate commercial products" (Jameson, 1991, p. 276). Jameson notes that in society, "What is wanted is a great collective project in which an active majority of the population participates, as something belonging to it and constructed by its own energies" (Jameson, 1991, p. 278). But what is happening within Rogers' advertisements for its new wireless services is the total evacuation of this sense of a collective project, as well as the commodification of revolution itself as another rubric under which to sell commodities. This is the ®evolution™.

Rogers' ads play on a complex sense of revolution, belonging, and the iconography of fandom and bring it under the economic alary of mobile networks. A recent Rogers advertising campaign for its mobile phone service featured people holding what appear to be protest signs and smiling as they anticipate the next generation of wireless services. This is the digital citizenry advocating for their consumer empowerment, and getting fulfillment within "Unlimited evening and weekend calling." Another advertisement for limitless evening and weekend calling, free voicemail and text messaging states "This could be the closest thing to free speech." The use of the rhetoric of ®evolution reterritorializes the revolutionary stance within the logic of the mobile market. This is further suggested with another Rogers advertisement that sells the idea of working anywhere—home, office, train, canoe, chair lift, or even the "top of a flagpole." This last point of access alludes to protest and/or "college kid" enthusiasm for antics designed to draw attention (to a cause, etc.). Rogers could be capitalizing on the well-known fact that protesters at the anti–free trade demonstrations in Seattle, Washington, and other cities have all used wireless communication devices to organize and mobilize protest vis-à-vis police actions. The use of the protest semiotic thus reduces it to another aspect of consumption within Rogers' wireless web.

In early 2001 Rogers also ran a series of television ads that use black-and-white footage of a Beatles-esque foursome, running from a hoard of screaming fans, with which to sell the message of "Imagine a better wireless world." Rogers seeks to capture and capitalize on the popular conception of the 1950s and 1960s explosion of mass (consumer and/or political) consciousness and channel this into their new wireless service, which includes my-iD.com. Both the print and television advertisements evacuate the sense of revolution concomitant with this era of popular culture. Rogers uses leftist rhetoric of revolution (which was hailed as protest anthems by groups such as the Beatles), perverting the Jamesonion notion of "a great collective project in which an active majority of the population participates." Rogers wishes this project to be their wireless network. More to the point, this network will be "something belonging to it [the active majority] and constructed by its own energies," in that within my-iD.com, users are given the "ability" to construct their own culture, their own sense of collective identity—their id:entity—within the network habit@ itself.

Users' own energies are channeled into creating a mobile room of their own, "something" they can belong to, identify with, and create. The trouble with this is that their demographic data is collected within this habit@ and sold back at them as they are enticed to spend as part of their identity formation. The cachet of rebellion is successfully co-opted under capitalist market(ing) flows, just as Giroux diagnoses a cultural shift "As the interface between global capital and new electronic technologies refigure and reshape the face of culture" (Giroux, 2000, p. 8).

The Space of Flows and the Logic of Mobile Capital

> As the credits roll, an exit survey of the film is emailed. Our e-urbanite is asked to vote on the movie's merits; his esteemed opinion will be published in tomorrow's user survey and shared with the service provider's customer base.

The commodity-ready mobile phones constitute the new, mobile panoptic, perhaps best rendered as the pan*info*con. Within this habit@, the collection of "transaction-generated information (TGI) . . . is increasingly collected and used to predict and modify consumer behavior" (Samarajiva, 1998, p. 277). The key here is "predict and modify," and digital consumers, stalked in their habit@, are seduced into a commercial web or "new economy based on mass customization" (Samarajiva, 1998, p. 278). The phoneur embodies the acme of individualism within a limited conception of "digital democracy" because "choosing" one's media becomes a way to register voice, albeit within the confines of consumption. The phoneur is a citizen of the digital world, the netizen having personal access to only that which s/he desires to see. The personalized web creates the "Daily Me" that filters out undesirable or unfavorable opinions, making it easier to see and hear only that which accords to your own personal point of view (Sunstein, 2001).[7] This is a danger to democracy and free speech, in that it advocates a kind of myopia that can lead to narrow-minded thinking and the growth of intolerance for social difference (Sunstein, 2001).

This "Daily Me" is the portal logic of personalization that is sold as an avenue of empowerment, though empowerment as defined as the ability to consume that which is presented within the flows of information capital. This definition becomes a restricted habit@, wherein the phoneur is a protected species. A Now Magazine advertisement exhorts users to become "Cell Mates" and "Get Now movie times, restaurant and live music listings on you dot.com ready ClearNet and Bell Mobility phones." This advertisement plays on this paradigm of privilege even as it uses the rhetoric of prisons to mask its panoptic impulse. As Baudrillard says, "prisons are there to conceal the fact that it is the social in its entirety, in its banal omnipresence, which is carceral" (Baudrillard, 1984, p. 25). The "Cell Mates" advertisement alludes to the fortified enclave of phonerie, and in fact sells itself with this as a virtue, repurposing the rhetoric of incarceration under the rubric of free access to information (only insofar as the information itself is free; the access is not, strictly speaking, since users pay for the phone service). If digital pedagogies are implicated within notions of citizenship based on consumption, then the learned behavior within digital networks is limited first to that which is broadcast over the media networks themselves, and second by the process of choosing which version of information (news, stock tips, horoscopes, etc.) in which to invest.

The phoneur constructs id:entity as part of the flows of mobile capital. Thus, media vectors—trajectories of media that "can connect enormously vast and vaguely defined spaces together and move images, and sounds, words, and furies, between them" (Wark, 1994, pp. 11–12)—are automatically absorbed into consciousness, not necessarily with any attendant critical analysis. As Wark reminds us,

> The question for vectoral analysis is not what is your identity but where is your nonidentity? What points does it lie between? Along which lines does it oscillate? This is not an abstract question, but a very concrete one: what are the channels, what are the frequencies, what are the sources at your disposal to orient you to the world? What the vector does is make identity oscillate between more and more points. (Wark, 1994, p. 59)[8]

Mobile phones are vectors of capital flows moving in fluid and constant (re)negotiation as per the needs of individual users. The phoneur's place in the habit@ is marked by consumption—the locations of spending habits that are tracked and sold back in an endless cycle of consumption. This is the informational city—the city as information within the logic of mobile market capitalism. To paraphrase Baudrillard, the mobile mall exists to distract us from the fact that the whole world is a mall.

The citizen as consumer construct disrupts the conception of digital citizenry, in that this form of citizenship is (re)constituted solely under the rubric of consumption. As Jameson says, "market as a concept rarely has anything to do with choice or freedom, since those are all determined for us in advance, whether we are talking about new model cars, toys, or television programs: we select among those, no doubt, but we can scarcely be said to have a say in actually choosing any of them" (Jameson, 1991, p. 266). That is to say, we can choose only from that which is offered for us; we cannot choose what is (not) offered. Within the space of flows of postmodern, mobile capital, we consume our identity from a menu of predetermined choices: "Coupled with the general public's increasing loss of faith in public government, public institutions, and the democratic process, the only form of agency or civic participation offered to the American people is consumerism as opposed to substantive forms of citizenship" (Giroux, 2000, p. 3). This conception of citizen is entirely predicated upon our ability to access the technologies that mediate these choices as much as it is dependent also on the ability to pay for this access and the commodities themselves.

To consume our identities such, to be the phoneur within the habit@ of the *homo digitalis*, is to realize the ephemeral flows of mobile capital and to reify the instantiation of capital and consumption itself. We consume to consume, to be consumed, for "in the postmodern, indeed, it is the very idea of the market that is consumed with the most prodigious gratification; as it were, a bonus or surplus of the commodification process" (Jameson, 1991, p. 269). Within this conception of digital literacy, and the digital pedagogy of phonerie in particular, we learn to consume as part of the conception of digital citizenship. A recent press release for an electronic device marketed by Accenture unabashedly uses the rhetoric of empowerment to situate new wireless technologies at the fore of an enlightened digital citizen:

> Score one for Pocket Bargain Finder, a project developed by the Accenture Technology Research and Innovation team. By enabling an intelligent agent to search online stores for the lowest prices, Pocket Bargain Finder is redefining "consumer empowerment"— while vividly demonstrating how technology is changing the relationship between buyers and sellers. (Accenture, 2001)

Our choice is limited to that which is offered on the market: "The force, then, of the concept of the market lies in its 'totalizing' structure, as they say nowadays; that is, in its capacity to afford a model of a social totality" (Jameson, 1991, p. 272). The my-iD phone is this totality: "everything you need to make yourself heard" above the crowds of the urban e-scape. The economic imperative that is the driving force behind technological innovation is affecting the manner in which we conceive of communications within the new, networked reality (Dickson, 2000, p. 120). This imperative has transmogrified the Internet from a communication medium to one of commercial concerns (Rheingold, 1993, pp. 285–286). More and more, media define our conception of "social agency" (Giroux, 2000, p. 109), and this agency is increasingly determined by media manipulation—the ability to have and control the medium and its message. This endless media manipulation and programmatic citizenry operates under "the logic of consumerism" (Giroux, 2000, p. 116). Within this logic, the digital citizen is the phoneur, left to wander the habit@ in search of meaning within the flows of commodity production and consumption.

Within the networked space of flows and the information city we now have the ability to always be in contact with the market economy. Watching the market by way of stock quotes and tips coming over the wireless web is one of the enticements mobile phone service providers offer to potential users. But as these phones become GPS-enabled and track movements through the market(place), the phoneur becomes the market, surveilled by the pan*info*con apparatus of market(ing) media that watches or listens for the trace through the habit@.

Digital Literacy, Digital Pedagogy, and the Self *in formation*

> Having contributed his movie review to the userCulture, our e-urbanite feels important and involved. Not everyone gets to participate within *this* digital democracy—membership does have its privileges. But while he sleeps, corporate "scientists" compile his demographic data. When he awakens, a new set of coupons and commercial enticements greet him as he checks his messages. Where does he want to go today? His handlers have laid a trail of cheese through the city's commercial maze.

Identity formation is a socially determined process rather than a definitive product (Miedema and Wardekker, 1999; Castells, 1997). This is especially so of the habit@id:entity which is a constant and consistent mediated representation of the digital self *in formation*. This self is formed through a "pedagogy of the supplement" (Trifonas, 2000) that has a double nature. The trace technologies of the habit@online continually supplement the id:entity profile of the individual user, and in effect "learn" about individual user preferences in order to serve a market logic. But just as "Identity is not a given, but an activity, the result of which is always only a local stability" (Miedema and Wardekker, 1999, p. 79), we continue to learn as part of the larger process(es) of living in general. The local stability of identity is continually negotiated and supplemented in dialogic relationship to the mediated environment (Miedema and Wardekker, 1999; Bakhtin, 1996). Education as process produces an interactive pedagogy that represents the constituent and iterative local adaptations and informal learning situations that punctuate daily life. If the digital citizen is constructed as the phoneur without any attendant critical awareness, the key pedagogical question to ask is to what extent are we aware of our habit@on-line? Are we cognizant of the fact that our movements of and in consumption are being sold back at us? Are we comfortable living a life lived in formation, as lived information? What strategies for awareness can we cultivate to combat the appropriation of our communication as linked to consumption?

The danger of constituting a digital literacy (a term that encompasses the critical skills needed to decode and work within the networked, digital environment) within consumerism means that we do not teach people how to critically analyze the mediated world around us.[9] Digital literacy encompasses teaching the "multiple, critical literacies" that encourage critical reflection on all aspects of culture (Kellner, 2000; Luke, 2000; Giroux, 2000). Being digitally literate means having the skills required to access the technology, but also the skills required to decode the cultural apparatuses of power that form the subsurface of this technology as it is put into practice within everyday contexts. We must read—and be able to read—all sites of cultural production within our mediated habit@: "A healthy suspicion of all media, including print, is essential in the development of a critically literate populace. A critical popular literacy involves reading vigilantly the sociocultural and economic dimensions of our engagements with culture" (Kelly, 1997, p. 82). At issue here is being able to render the cultural contexts within which we live transparent to true democracy, and the democratization of knowledge. "A politician is now a commodity, citizens are consumers, and issues are decided via sound-bites and staged events" (Rheingold, 1993, p. 285), as digital citizenship is more and more being articulated within the rubric of consumption and commodity (Kelly, 1997; Rheingold, 1993).

Within the capitalist gestalt, the icons of capitalist desire constitute and refer to commodities as being that which brings completion. These commodity forms are aggregates, conglomerates of a unity that is constantly deferred; "a structural unity is imposed on the desiring-machines that joins them together in a molar aggregate; the partial objects are referred to a totality that can appear only as that which the partial objects lack, and as that which is lacking unto itself while being lacking in them" (Deleuze and Guattari, 1983, p. 306). This molar aggregate (a supplemental pedagogy) is the demographic data collected in the habit@ that marks our place within the flows of capital. The phoneur lives a life in formation, as lived information, never complete, always deferred. The danger is that users are being seduced into thinking they have democratic access to knowledge when in fact they are passive consumers and collectors of "points of view" within the political and commodity landscape (Appadurai, 1996, p. 42).

New, digital media change our conception of our relationship to information (The New London Group, 2000), and the wireless web and the logic of mobile commerce teach consumption as a basic component of literacy and agency within the digital world. This digital pedagogy of desire and affect is not imbued with a critical component; rather, "Both subjectivity and agency are wrapped up (knotted) in technological systems. To have 'power' and 'prestige' is to possess or to be able to possess the most advanced of technological systems (whether a private jet, CD player, or laptop)" (Menser and Aronowitz, 1996, p. 21). Those who desire to possess the technology learn to do so as consumers, and not producers, even though they are producers of demographic data that they then re-consume in a kind of coprophagic discourse uroboros that feeds on the materiality of itself in an *ex stasis* cycle of desiring machine production and consumption: "Producing is always something 'grafted onto' the product; and for that reason desiring-production is production of production, just as every machine is a machine connected to another machine" (Deleuze and Guattari, 1983, p. 6). For the phoneur, entangled in a machinic arrangement of desire and affect, consumption and commodity are grafted onto communication (Myerson, 2001).

The prescriptive digital pedagogies of phonerie seduce the user into a kind of "direct democracy" that allows him/her to vote on what s/he likes to see presented within the on-line space. But this digital democracy is itself caught up within the politics of consumption. This conception of the digital citizen reinforces the concept that "We are who we are, not through an essence that underlies all our motions and thoughts, but through the habitual repetition of those motions and thoughts" (Wise, 2000, p. 303). The phoneur becomes a moving point on a commercial grid, articulating a habit@id:entity within the commercial network. And it is this commercial grid that thus defines the concept of the digital citizen. Phonerie becomes the "common culture" (Willis, 1990) of which those who are not desire to be like, to become the phoneur. These digital pedagogies and conceptions of digital citizenry affect a "purchasing ideology" (Luke, in press); that is, an ideology based on what is purchased, even as these habits of consumption are collated and purchased anew within a cycle of endless consumption. Within the purchasing ideology, a cultural narrative of consumption is written onto the body politic. In the culture of phonerie, this narrative is based on the flows and practices within the habit@: those practises that partake of commercial enterprise, at the same time as they constitute this enterprise.

With the increased homogenization of media—increasingly in the hands of a few conglomerates (Giroux, 2000, p. 108)—and with the ubiquity of mobile phone growing daily, it becomes important to ask where social difference lies in the face of the globalized mobilization. "Beyond the democratic ideal of diversity, the Internet enforces uniformity" (Interrogate the Internet, 1996, p. 127), and this applies equally to W4 environments like my-iD.com. Where resides social difference if we only learn to be consumers? The eradication of social difference and the construction of the digital citizen as a consumer of multinational capital are exacted in the face of the personalization of the on-line, W3 and W4 portalized worlds. Thus while consumer-citizens are given the opportunity to personalize their dataspaces, they may fail to question the homogenization this really entails. The danger is that "Public spheres are replaced by commercial spheres as the substance of critical democracy is emptied out and replaced by a democracy of goods, consumer lifestyles, shopping malls, and the increasing expansion of the cultural and political power of corporations throughout the world" (Giroux, 2000, p. 41). This democracy of goods is the individualization of the mediascape, personalized on your portal, preconfigured and packaged to your personal digital assistant (PDA) or mobile phone. This is a democratization marked by the power to be all for everyone, the demarcation of the Daily Me that belies a dangerous myopia to the world as constructed of capital and commodity flows.

Conclusion: Response Ability and the Digital Citizen

The wireless web has evolved as a subset of capitalism. It is a datastructural extension of the media-dominated space of flows that pushes e-advertising through data portals (phones, PDAs). The act of "voting" on a favorite movie, restaurant, and so on, assumes the guise of democratic voice but under the rubric of consumption, and evacuates the rhetoric of voting by "Reformulating social issues as strictly individual or economic issues, corporate culture functions largely to cancel out the democratic impulses and practices of civil society by either devaluing them or absorbing such impulses within a market logic" (Giroux, 2000, p. 41). Recent fears over globalization and free trade (April 20–22, 2001 Quebec City Summit of the Americas protest is just one example; Seattle, Washington, Windsor being others) are congruent with the narrow conception of digital citizenry outlined above.

If our choices as digital citizens are limited to what we can purchase on the dot.com horizon, then our roles as citizens are severely limited, curtailed, and reduced to a progressive paternoster of consumer goods. "Democracy is not synonymous with capitalism, and critical citizenship is not limited to being a literate consumer" (Giroux, 2000, pp. 59–60), but as U.S. president George W. Bush remarked during the Quebec trade summit, "Trade brings freedom," illustrating clearly that the U.S. government, for one, sees its citizens as consumers. In the aftermath of September 11, Bush acknowledged openly that the United States considers its citizens as consumers when he exhorted Americans to "go out and shop" as a way to do their part for America during its time of crisis.[10] The equating of citizenship with consumerism is not new, but if "communications technologies . . . become such a part of our functioning that they disappear from active view, from critical consideration, they disappear into their content and into our communicative habits" (Wise, 1997, p. 188). Because these technologies are relatively new, we have a unique opportunity to intervene at a critical juncture in their codification into the *habitus* and the habit@on-line.

When we desire *to be like* (cf. Friere, 1970)—to assume uncritically the trappings of the dominant digital culture—we may fail to see the ideology that lurks beneath the surface of contemporary electronic practices. If we do not question the relinquishment of private data, then control over the personal is abrogated in favor of corporate control over identity formation itself. Cultivating a critical, digital literacy and pedagogy means examining the technologies that punctuate our daily lives, and reading these critically in order "to urge redefinition of the world rather than mere participation in it as it is now structured. Such objectives demand the examination of how culture is engaged and how literacies are practiced in specific contexts and for specific purposes" (Kelly, 1997, p. 77). By examining how the habit@id:entity is constructed amidst the imbrications of desire and affect, we can expose what Kelly calls "the pedagogies of persuasion and the persuasions of pedagogy" (Kelly, 1997, p. 74). These persuasions undergird the media available for consumption, and the politics and processes of consumption (Kelly, 1997, p. 76).

Using ubiquitous media in education enlivens debate about its use (Kress, 2000). Ignoring the pedagogical contexts of popular media forms (and the mechanisms for access) is an abrogation of responsibility. Rather, we have a response ability—an ability to respond to how technologies are used in everyday contexts. The symbiotic relationship between the habit@id:entity and consumption will not easily be disrupted. Rather, the issue is how to use this id:entity as part of the pedagogic process of engaging popular culture.[11] By exposing the "the logic of consumerism" (Giroux, 2000, p. 116) latent in electronic discourses of desire and the economy of affect wherein those without the technology simply desire to posses it, we can illustrate how we become in-formed by media representation, encourage critical reflection and promote digital literacies. More importantly, we can fashion an interactive pedagogy that does not simply react to media and new technology, but rather acts within its lived relations and directs the appropriate use of technology with attendant critical awareness. This interactive pedagogy is education *in formation*: a foundation of active and engaged digital citizenship.

Notes

1. The italicized excerpts are from Luke (2001).
2. For an overview of these data tracking mechanisms (see Peters, 1999).
3. I am indebted to Robert Morgan for the term "phonerie" and its connection to the flâneur and flânerie.
4. See (Luke, in press) for a discussion about the habit@on-line and its relation to web portals.
5. The id:entity is currently being taken to a new level with the introduction of Intelligent Agents (IA). An IA is a sophisticated software program that acts as a proxy for a user under set parameters. The latest advances in the IA field are in Japan (where technology is a full three years ahead of North America). NTT (Japan's National Telephone Service) offers the popular i-mode DoCoMo service, which now includes i-chara, interactive characters that literally stand in for users. I-chara find information and shopping deals based on consumption habits, and even go out and meet other i-chara agents: "Living in mobile devices, i-chara are highly evolved, highly personalized digital agents, guiding their owners through an electronic social and informational matrix" (Galloway, 2001, p. 39). This matrix is the habit@, and in Japan, mobile phones are integral parts of identity formation and "rank second only to a wallet in things a person will not leave behind" (Binsted, 2001). The i-chara act as "social filters," preventing user–user interaction (by interacting only with other i-chara) so that personal information and privacy is protected for other users; this makes people more comfortable about entering risky social situations (meeting new people, etc.) (Binsted, 2001). However, "as agents become more efficient and fade into the woodwork, we will lose the opportunity to interrogate some of the social actors making the greatest impact on our lives" (Wise, 1998, p. 423). While Wise is speaking specifically of intelligent agents with respect to W3 portals, his analysis is particularly trenchant as agents enter W4 environments and more and more people sign up for a habit@id:entity (see also Wise, 1997, pp. 156–157).
6. So-called 3G (Third Generation) phones will offer high-bandwidth connections over the W4 network, allowing for streaming video and other high-capacity data to be sent and received from mobile handsets. That GPS-enabled handsets also broadcast data-trails is a hidden form of broadcasting enabled by these devices.
7. Sunstein borrows the term "Daily Me" from Nicholas Negroponte. But where the latter extols the Daily Me as a virtue of the online future, Sunstein raises a caution to critically engage this concept as to what it might mean for the development (or lack thereof) of democratic discourse and the engagement of social difference.
8. Wark borrows the term "vector" from Paul Virilio: "It is a term from geometry meaning a line of fixed length and direction but having no fixed position. Virilio employs it to mean any trajectory along which bodies, information, or warheads can potentially pass. . . . Media vectors have fixed properties . . . [but] no necessary position: it can link almost any points together" (Wark, 1994, p. 11).
9. In many respects there is no clear distinction between online and offline activities (Burbules, 2000, p. 340): all form part of the context of daily life in a postmodern world (this does, of course, presuppose familiarity with and access to these cultural notions of meaning).
10. Reported September 27, 2001 on CNN (http://cnn.com).
11. It should be pointed out that on-line learning platforms (integrated courseware systems) use id:entity structures and surveillance mechanisms extensively. This is one aspect of on-line surveillance that is both necessary and positive, as it allows for different kinds of pedagogies to be implemented within on-line learning (tracking cognitive paths through curricular material, for example).

Bibliography

Accenture. (2001). "Imagining the EFuture." Accenture.

Agre, Phil. "Surveillance and Capture: Two Models of Privacy." *The Information Society* 10 (1994): 101–127.

AOL. "Welcome to AOL Anywhere." America Online, Inc. <http://www.aol.com/>.

Appadurai, Arjun. (1996). *Modernity at Large: Cultural Dimensions of Globalization*. Public Worlds, vol. 1. Minneapolis and London: University of Minnesota Press.

Bakhtin, Mikhail Mikhailovich. (1981). *The Dialogic Imagination*. Trans. Caryl Emerson and Michael Holquist. Ed. Michael Holquist. Austin: Texas University Press, 1996.

Baudrillard, Jean. (1984). *Simulations: The Precession of Simulacra*. Trans. Paul Foss, Paul Patton, and Philip Beitchman. London: Foreign Agents.

Benjamin, Walter. (1999). *The Arcades Project*. Trans. Howard Eiland and Kevin McLaughlin. Cambridge, MA: Belknap Press of Harvard University Press.

Binsted, Kim. "Mobile Magic: The Future of Mobile Connectivity." Presented at the Interactive Arena 2000–2001. The Design Exchange, 234 Bay Street, Toronto, ON, May 1, 2001.

Bourdieu, Pierre. (1977). *Outline of a Theory of Practice*. Trans. Richard Nice. Cambridge, New York: Cambridge University Press.

———. (1980). *The Logic of Practice*. Trans. Richard Nice. Stanford, CA: Stanford University Press, 1990.

Burbules, Nicholas. (2000). "Does the Internet Constitute a Global Educational Community?" In *Globalization and Education: Critical Perspectives*, ed. Nicholas Burbules and Carlos Alberto Torre. Social Theory, Education and Cultural Change. London and New York: Routledge, pp. 323–356.

Castells, Manuel. (1996). *The Rise of the Network Society*. The Information Age: Economy, Society and Culture, vol. 1. London: Blackwell.

———. (1997). *The Power of Identity*. The Information Age: Economy, Society and Culture, vol. 2. London: Blackwell.

Clarke, Roger. "The Digital Persona and Its Application to Data Surveillance." *The Information Society* 10 (1994): 77–92.

CompuServe. "My CompuServe." CompuServe Interactive Services, Inc. <http://www.compuserve.com/compuserve/default.asp>.

de Certeau, Michel. (1984). *The Practice of Everyday Life*. Berkeley: University of California Press.

Deleuze, Gilles and Félix Guattari. (1972). *Anti-Oedipus: Capitalism and Schizophrenia*. Trans. Robert Hurley, Mark Seem, and Helen Lane. Minneapolis: University of Minnesota Press, 1983.

Dickson, Peter. "Understanding the Trade Winds: The Global Evolution of Production, Consumption, and the Internet." *Journal of Consumer Research* 27:1 (June 2000): 115–122.

Excite. "My Excite Start Page." At Home Corporation. <http://www.excite.com/>.

Ferguson, Priscilla Parkhurst. (1994). "The Flâneur on and Off the Streets of Paris." In *The Flâneur*, ed. Keith Tester. London and New York: Routledge, pp. 22–42.

Foucault, Michel. (1997). "Panopticism." In *Rethinking Architecture Today: A Reader in Cultural Theory*, ed. N. Leach. London: Routledge, pp. 356–379.

Friere, Paulo. (1968). *Pedagogy of the Oppressed*. Trans. Myra Bergman Ramos. New York: Seabury Press, 1970.

Frisby, David. (1994). "The Flâneur in Social Theory." In *The Flâneur*, ed. Keith Tester. London and New York: Routledge, pp. 81–110.

Galloway, Matt. "Absolute Mobility." *Now* (Toronto) April 26–May 2, 2001: 39.

Giroux, Henry. (2000). *Impure Acts: The Practical Politics of Cultural Studies.* New York and London: Routledge, 2000.

Goodman, Ellen. "Cell Phone Speech Far from Free." *Reporter-News.Com.* <http://www.reporternews.com/1999/opinion/good0323.html>.

Graham, Stephen. (1999). "Geographies of Surveillant Simulation." In *Virtual Geographies: Bodies, Space and Relations*, ed. Mike Crang, Phil Crang, and Jon May. London and New York: Routledge, pp. 131–148.

Haskins, Walaika. "Take It To The Streets." *PC Magazine* 20:8 (April 24, 2001): 63.

Interrogate the Internet. (1996). "Contradictions in Cyberspace: Collective Response." In *Cultures of Internet: Virtual Spaces, Real Histories, Living Bodies*, ed. Rob Shields. London: Sage, pp. 125–132.

Jameson, Fredric. (1991). *Postmodernism, or, The Cultural Logic of Late Capitalism.* Durham: Duke University Press.

Kellner, Douglas. (2000). "Multiple Literacies and Critical Pedagogies: New Paradigms." In *Revolutionary Pedagogies: Cultural Politics, Instituting Education, and the Discourse of Theory*, ed. Peter Pericles Trifonas. New York and London: Routledge, pp. 196–202.

Kelly, Ursula. (1997). *Schooling Desire: Literacy, Cultural Politics and Pedagogy.* New York: Routledge.

Kress, Guenther. (2000). "Design and Transformation: New Theories of Meaning." In *Multiliteracies: Literacy Learning and the Design of Social Futures*, ed. Bill Cope and Mary Kalantzis. Literacies. London and New York: Routledge, pp. 153–161.

Luke, Carmen. (2000). "Cyber-Schooling and Technological Change: Multiliteracies for New Times." In *Multiliteracies: Literacy Learning and the Design of Social Futures*, ed. Bill Cope and Mary Kalantzis. Literacies. London and New York: Routledge, pp. 69–91.

Luke, Robert. (2001). "Dial In, Sell Out." *Shift* (Available on-line: http://www.shift.com/mag/9.2/html/9.2autopsy.asp), pp. 28–29.

———. "habit@online:web portals as purchasing ideology." *Topia* (in press).

———. "Signal Event Context: Trace Technologies of the habit@online." *Educational Philosophy and Theory* (in press).

Mazlish, Bruce. (1994). "The Flaneur: From Spectator to Representation." In *The Flâneur*, ed. Keith Tester. London and New York: Routledge, pp. 43–60.

Menser, Michael and Stanley Aronowitz. (1996). "On Cultural Studies, Science and Technology." In *Technoscience and Cyberculture*, ed. Stanley Aronowitz et al. New York and London: Routledge, pp. 7–28.

Microsoft Passport. "Microsoft Passport." Microsoft Corporation. <http://passport.com/Consumer/default.asp?PPlcid=1033>.

Microsoft. "MSN Canada." Microsoft Corporation. <http://ca.msn.com>.

———. "Welcome to MSN.Com." Microsoft Corporation. <http://www.msn.com/>.

Miedema, Siebren and Willem L. Wardekker. (1999). "Emergent Identity Versus Consistent Identity: Possibilities for a Postmodern Repoliticization of Critical Pedagogy." In *Critical Theories in Education: Changing Terrains of Knowledge and Politics*, ed. Thomas S. Popkewitz and Lynn Fendler. London and New York: Routledge, pp. 67–83.

Morgan, Robert. (2000). Personal Communication.

My Netscape. "My Netscape." Netscape. <http://my.netscape.com/>.

My Yahoo! "Welcome to My Yahoo!" Yahoo! Inc. <http://my.yahoo.com/>.

my-id.com. "My-Id.Com." <www.my-id.com> 2001.

Myerson, George. (2001). *Heidegger, Habermas and the Mobile Phone.* Reading, UK: Icon Books (UK); Totem Books (US).

myTO. "MyTO.Com—Part of the Telus Network." Telus. <http://www.myto.com/>.

Netscape. "Netscape.Com." Netscape. <http://www.netscape.com/>.

Peters, Thomas A. (1999). *Computerized Monitoring and Online Privacy*. Jefferson, North Carolina and London: McFarland and Company, Inc.

Rheingold, Howard. (1993). *The Virtual Community: Homesteading on the Electronic*. Reading, Mass: Addison-Wesley Pub. Co.

Samarajiva, Rohan. (1998). "Interactivity As Though Privacy Mattered." In *Technology and Privacy: The New Landscape*, ed. Phil E. Agre and Marc Rotenberg. Cambridge and London: The MIT Press, pp. 277–310.

Shields, Rob. (1994). "Fancy Footwork: Walter Benjamin's Notes on Flânerie." In *The Flâneur*, ed. Keith Tester. London and New York: Routledge, pp. 61–80.

Stratton, Jon. (1996). "Cyberspace and the Globalization of Culture." In *Internet Culture*, ed. David Porter. London and New York: Routledge, pp. 253–276.

Sunstein, Cass. (2001). *Republic.Com*. Princeton, NJ: Princeton University Press.

The New London Group. (2000). "A Pedagogy of Multiliteracies Designing Social Futures." In *Multiliteracies: Literacy Learning and the Design of Social Futures*, ed. Bill Cope and Mary Kalantzis. Literacies. London and New York: Routledge, pp. 9–38.

Traffick. "Traffick – The PORTAL Portal." Traffick.com. <http://traffick.com/>.

Trifonas, Peter. "Derrida and Rousseau: Deconstructing the Ethics of a Pedagogy of the Supplement." *The Review of Education/ Pedagogy/ Cultural Studies* 22:3 (2000): 243–265.

Wark, McKenzie. (1994). *Virtual Geography: Living with Global Media Events*. Bloomington and Indianapolis: Indiana University Press.

Willis, Paul. (1990). *Common Culture: Symbolic Work at Play in the Everyday Cultures of the Young*. Milton Keynes: Open University Press.

Wise, J. MacGregor. (1997). *Exploring Technology and Social Space*. London and New Delhi: Sage Publications.

———. "Intelligent Agency." *Cultural Studies* 12:3 (1998): 410–428.

———. "Home: Territory and Identity." *Cultural Studies* 14:2 (2000): 295–310.

World Wide Web Consortium. "Character Entity References in HTML 4." World Wide Web Consortium. <http://www.w3.org/TR/REC-html40/sgml/entities.html>.

Yahoo. "Yahoo!" Yahoo! Inc. <http://www.yahoo.com/>.

Chapter 12

Difference and the Internet: When Ethnic Community Goes On-line

Joel Weiss, Vera Nincic, and Jason Nolan

The idea of virtual community is embedded in a deep matrix of McLuhan's Global Village and the dominant Western cultural influence. Although there is space on-line for an infinite number of virtual communities, they tend to reflect real-world groupings and organizations based on notions of difference. In this context, difference can be seen as perceived variation based on dissimilar characteristics where groupings resemble communities in which members share at least one common interest. And it is this sense of difference that informs our exploration of "virtual ethnicity" (Poster, 1999) in an on-line environment we call Serbia.web. Ethnicity is one such common intersection that helps define a community. Ethnicity is often tied to bioregionality, common geographical colocation, and it is a struggle to maintain ethnic ties as groups spread across the globe under the influence of events such as those in the former Yugoslavia, and in Afghanistan. Since large movements of different ethnic groups around the world are almost commonplace for diasporic reasons, ethnic groups are often faced with the tension of assimilating to new regions and maintaining a sense of ethnic identity. Many groups cultivate on-line communities to ensure that their ethnic identity will not be lost by developing, and participating in, on-line communities.

Our example of how a geographically dispersed ethnic community's sense of difference is both challenged and maintained through Internet-mediated communication starts with a discussion about creating virtual community, and with comparisons between virtual and real-life communities (Rheingold, 1993). As educators we are interested in how a virtual community is a "space for pedagogy." We look at the transformative and contradictory elements contained within the creation and maintenance of the community. In particular, we look at the concept of difference as it relates to the tension between assimilation and ethnic identity. This tension is manifested along two dimensions: the use of the Internet to ensure some differences from the dominant community, and how the dominant language of the Net is resisted in order to reinforce this ethnic difference. The example allows us to consider how the virtual community is changed over time as a reaction to external events, ironically, a regional conflict that divided ethnic groups in one region of Europe.

The term "virtual community" has become so widespread in its use that there is a tendency to conflate all social activity into a single concept and not consider the diversity of virtual contexts. Another challenge is characterized by the debate about whether on-line groups can be termed "communities" at all. This debate focuses on the relationship between on-line and off-line communities. Baym (1999) believes there are two issues that should be considered in such a debate: "does on-line community really serve as a substitute for off-line community in any meaningful way?" and "what occurs on-line that leads some people to experience them as communities in the first place?" (pp. 37–38). In considering virtual communities, there are several issues or aspects to be taken up: member's backgrounds, role within the community, participatory style, structure of pedagogy associated with the space, resources for structuring the community, and of course, what is learned, shared, and experienced.

This suggests dimensions that Rheingold could not have anticipated when he suggested a definition of virtual community that predates the explosion of public involvement that came with the World Wide Web in 1994; "*Virtual communities* are social aggregations that emerge from the Net when enough people carry on . . . public discussions long enough, with sufficient human feeling, to form webs of personal relationships in cyberspace"(italics in original; Rheingold, 1993, p. 5). But, how do these virtual communities begin?

Baym (1998) has studied social uses for Computer Mediated Communication (CMC) and suggests that it is difficult to predict CMC patterns because of complexities of interactions among five factors: external contexts, temporal structure of the group, system infrastructure, group purposes, and participant characteristics. She does suggest that an understanding of a virtual *style* can be achieved by describing these interactions: participants strategically exploit the resources and rules those structures offer. The result is a dynamic set of systematic social meanings that enables participants to imagine themselves as a community. Most significant are the emergence of group-specific forms of expression, identities, relationships, and normative conventions (Baym, 1998).

Groups more associated with social purposes are sites for acquiring information, feeling a sense of community, as well as potential learnings associated with participating in a virtual space. On-line ethnic communities have become very important sites for the exploration of how ethnic affiliations are taken up and used as a basis for the creation of on-line communities. Internet technologies have become increasingly embedded in everyday life (Agre, 1999; Baym, 1998; Bell, 2001; Wellman and Gulia, 1999), prompting careful inquiry into cultural and social implications of on-line interactions. Several studies of ethnic on-line groups were undertaken (Hongladarom, 1998; Mitra, 1997; Stubbs, 1999) with the intention of understanding how the Internet technologies facilitate the creation of "communities of sentiment" (Appadurai, 1996) or computer-mediated "diasporic public spheres" (Appadurai, 1996; Stubbs, 1999). This is especially important in enabling individuals, who are physically cut off from their sense of "home," to develop common ground with others in the same position. In a sense, it offers the dual situation of emphasizing differences with the dominant cultural group while seeking the comfort of sameness with others.

Attempts to grasp the social and cultural implications of on-line interactions frequently emphasize the need to perceive computer technologies as one of the major supporters of the hegemonic process of globalization. There is an assumption that technologies emerge out of dynamic social processes influenced by, and also influencing the culture from which they came. This approach urges us to gain insight into the dynamic interplay between culture and technology by reflecting on the technology's "cultural background" (Coyne, 1999; Dodge and Kitchin, 2001; Noble, 1997). "Computer culture" could be used as a referent for the complex social, economical, and cultural matrix that computer technologies promote and encourage. The critical challenge of treating computer technologies as an important cultural force of globalization comes from several researchers (Pargman, 1998; Keniston, 1998; Voiskousky, 1998). They pointed out the potential embeddedness of cultural practices into computer hardware and software. Seen in that way, Internet technologies could shape and reconfigure off-line ethnic practices when participants move on-line. However, seeing the Internet network only through its globalization trends disregards the issue of active appropriation of cultural products (Appadurai, 1996)—how they are locally used, with what purpose, and how they are integrated in "local" cultural repertoire. That very struggle between the global and "local" cultural trends could be seen by closely viewing the daily life of ethnic on-line communities using that very globalizing technology for the creation, and maintenance, of their local cultural presence.

Serbia.web is a generalized pseudonym for a variety of virtual community locations operating for those interested in Serbian culture, language, and related issues. These locations of community are often dynamic forms of conflict as well as political struggle that reflect, if not mirror, the real-life environments from which the on-line groups find their members (Bell, 2001). Though the on-line Serbian community may be itself undertaking an important struggle for identity and cultural expression, this struggle is not without its own inherent challenges and dangers. The various on-line media that make up the collective discussion on Serbia, and issues important to diasporic Serbs, represent an example of a particular kind of on-line community. And there has been a great deal of attention given to diasporic community involvement in CMC environments centering on the "Wars of the Yugoslav Succession," which locates the on-line experiences of various diaspora from the region in a growing post-national cultural experience (Stubbs, 1998, 1999). It is both ethnic and cultural, and most importantly is an on-line manifestation of a community that transcends the boundaries of both real-life and virtual manifestations. Serbia.web represents an example of a virtual community that manifests itself across various on-line technologies such as web pages, Java-chat, IRC, and e-mail discussion lists. It is founded on an external cultural experience. As well, this community has grown in ways unanticipated by its founders as a result of external events and influences.

It could almost be said that the experience of Serbia.web is somewhat mundane, concerned with the same collective and individual matters that all on-line communities are faced with. That is, if it were not for the Kosovo crisis. The quantum leap in activity in and around the on-line community reflected the chaotic and kinetic nature of the real-world events playing themselves out. During the Kosovo Crisis (spring 1999) the number of the participants increased fantastically, averaging over 300–400 active participants, up from an average of 15 to 30. Some Internet statistics placed the community web site in the top 1,000 web sites on the Internet by number of hits during the crisis.

Real-life and death consequences were being taken up in a manner that just is not seen in most other virtual communities. The real need not only for information, or even sharing information, but to be able to *verify* information from a variety of sources, and bring together the variety of experiences and information from the members of the community was necessary for so many in order to develop the most coherent picture possible of what was actually going on half a world away. Once the real-life crisis ceased, the activity level decreased somewhat, but has since maintained itself at a level much higher than before the conflict, recognition of how communities coalesce around times of threat or stress to its members, and that the threads of a community may often go farther and deeper than is easily discernible on the surface.

Strongly reflecting real-life experiences, especially in times of stress such as war, Serbia.web could be an example that supports the argument by Fernback and Thompson (1995) that virtual communities "seem more likely to be formed or reinforced when action is needed, as when country goes to war, rather than through discourse alone." As an "ethnic virtual group" this on-line community is composed mostly of immigrants, coming from Yugoslavia, who emigrated within the last ten years. They are, to follow Mitra's (1997) suggestion—a "new wave" of immigrants, "scattered across the Western hemisphere, working in similar professions but spatially distanced from each other" (p. 57). The ethnic communities coming from less populated countries are especially vulnerable to cultural assimilation by host countries, not only due to their geographical dispersion, but due to also the impossibility of being meaningfully represented in the official host media. Used as an alternative media, the Internet allows immigrants to create a culturally specific space, to exchange information that could not be exchanged otherwise, and to create a social network that could offer relevant and understandable environment.

On the one hand, it could be argued that instead of accepting its passive social position of slow assimilation (additionally fostered by relative geographic distance of its members), the ethnic virtual group actively uses the Internet to meet a variety of cultural needs of its members in fostering and maintaining a sense of difference in terms of representation, language, and collective identity. The emotional investment of the people in community, the amount of time they spend communicating, offering each other comfort, sharing information, and organizing meetings off-line—all these practices suggest what we could think of as active moments in creating a relatively homogeneous community. On the other hand, participation in the ethnic community does not necessarily imply some fixed correspondence between feelings of belonging to real-life ethnic group and active participation in an on-line community, nor address the differences in how members feel about belonging to a specific real-life "ethnic" group. In some ways, "ethnicity" taken up in on-line environment could be seen as a "membership card" that Internet participants could use to gain entrance to a community as a way to resolve their off-line isolation, or feelings of difference from the dominant group. The complex relationship between real-life ethnic membership and virtual ethnic membership is additionally facilitated by the possibility of "passing" or performing as a member of an ethnic community by using the Serbian language as a marker of ethnicity. The ethnic performance is possible because many non-Serbians belonging to different ethnic groups from the former Yugoslavia region are able to use the Serbian language to actively participate in the virtual community even if they do not "actually" belong to real-life ethnic group. This highlights the potential range of differences in "ethnic" participation as to the actual intentions, needs, and feelings of on-line participants.

Another active moment where on-line community participants take up "ethnicity" is more closely related to the Internet medium itself. Many characteristics of the Internet and its related technologies for on-line communication should be seen as important mediators for conveying interactions of on-line community (Baym, 1998). In that sense, the communicative practices of the on-line community members are shaped by characteristics of, for example, the computer conference forums or IRC software—especially the software support for the Roman alphabet and the Roman characters used in the English language.

The issue of the English-based Internet software is becoming increasingly important when seen in the light of the constant increase in the number of on-line participants coming from non-English–speaking countries and recent immigrants settled in the English-speaking ones. It could be argued that the English-based Internet environment discourages or even disables communication in languages other than English (Nolan, in press). However, as the Serbia.web example suggests, the English-language prevalence on the Internet has been challenged on the local community level. This would have required a prior sophistication in the use of computers or a necessity for some to learn to make the adaptations. The community's members use the English-based software to communicate in Serbian, the language shared by all community members. Even if the majority of community participants probably know English (working and living in North America and Australia), many others in the community live in Yugoslavia, and elsewhere in Europe where English is not the dominant language. Though the written form of Serbian language uses the Cyrillic alphabet, the on-line community members can easily shift to its Roman character version (both written forms are taught in Yugoslavia), adapting the written form of the language to the environment. Political changes imposed upon the Serbian language after World War II required that both Cyrillic and Roman methods of writing the Serbian language be taught in schools. This means that the restrictive influences of the Internet and ASCII (American Standard Code for Information Interchange) character set have had on the writing of languages was not necessarily felt by the Serbian community because of the earlier change dictated by political influence.

By comparison with the English alphabet pool of letters, the written "Latin Serbian" requires five additional letters. To participate in the conference forums or use the IRC technology, Serbians use only the 25 letters Serbian and English share out of the 30 letters in Serbian. In that sense, the Internet communication technologies "force" the community members to exclude five letters in writing. Even if there is a possibility to change encoding and use, for example, the Cyrillic encoding in on-line asynchronous communication, this is not easily done because it requires the change of the font encoding settings by all participants. A similar tendency in using a "restricted" version of language other than English in the on-line environment suited for communication in English is suggested by Pargman (1998) in his study of a Swedish-speaking on-line community using MUDs (Multi-User Discourse) collaborative virtual environments.

It is important to note that on-line communication software requires the use of commands in English, because Serbians do not have the "localized versions" (Keniston, 1998) of software programs and operating systems in Serbian language. Consequently, for on-line participation in the community, the Serbia.web members simultaneously use the English-written commands with the on-line-adapted (Roman character set) Serbian. This interesting mixture of languages suggests the specific process of negotiation between the global and the local—seen here in the particular context of the on-line environment. The persistency of on-line participants in adapting the Internet technologies to their community's goals (in this case the use of Serbian language) suggests that this constructed language-hybrid environment is neither an obstacle to communication nor is seen as restricting the expression of cultural identity. The use of the Serbian language in this context is therefore not to be perceived as a gesture of isolation and deliberate segregation of the virtual group from other virtual groups. It can be argued that, by using the mother tongue of the participants as the major language of communication in the community, the virtual group creates a culturally inclusive space—to include all Serbian speakers, many of them living in non-English–speaking countries. In some contexts, Serbian is not a language of political and cultural choice, but rather the *only* language that participants share in common; in this context, English is just not an option if the goal is to be inclusive. And most importantly, it was this Serbian-based environment, especially during the Kosovo crisis, which offered the participants a version of "home" (Mitra, 1997, p. 70), and a "safe refuge." This allowed participants to share experiences of stress, fear, and anger with those, from the same country of origin, who are perceived as empathetic regarding events so far from the countries in which they now live. During the time of crisis, the virtual community served as an arena for verifying information, as well as for frequent emotional arguments fraught with nostalgia, and supported by anger, fear, and loneliness.

We would like to caution that it would be an oversimplification to perceive Serbia.web as a stable, homogeneous, and permanent community; a location where diasporic elements share their communal sense of difference from the external communities in which they reside. Though casual observers may see it in this manner, a closer look reveals that the appearance of stability is due to the well-defined community infrastructure, and not due to the homogeneity of thought or purpose. This infrastructure can be understood collectively as the set of on-line environments and tools that facilitate communication. This included the development of a set of rules, Netiquette, to be adhered to by all members, and sanctions for those who did not. Even the stability of infrastructure should be understood in relative terms— Serbia.web changed, albeit gradually.

The nonhomogeneous character of the Serbia.web is better revealed if the community is understood as the complex web of overlapping small communities, or as the network of interconnected on-line groups, many of them temporal, and only some relatively stable. From the insider perspective, the "ethnic" virtual community is a chaotic mix of Serbian speakers, residing in different countries, and "bringing" into community differences regarding knowledge of languages, beliefs, or attitudes, and social or economic backgrounds. All those off-line characteristics are played out on-line—frequently they are the basis for the further differentiation of Serbia.web into a variety of subcommunities. The great strength of this community is the diversity of new cultural experiences that the Serbian members have had in their new countries that inform and influence how they share, and make sense of, issues from "back home."

Existing as part of the broader Internet culture, the "local" character of the ethnic virtual community should be thought of in relative terms. As noted earlier, the Internet culture offers the local group the computer infrastructure with embedded practices of use, established meanings and forms of expressions, rules for on-line management and, the constant flux of new technologies that shape and change an already established community network. Even if organized locally and (self) excluded from other on-line communities by the language barrier, the local community experiences ongoing changes. The inclusion of new technologies for communication, the disappearance and emergence of subcommunities, the departure and arrival of community members—all suggest flexibility of the Internet environment for accommodating everyday challenges for cultural and linguistic expression.

This struggle is an active and constructive process that requires conscious attempts to initiate and sustain communication with members of one's own language and culture, versus being an attempt to *maintain* one's own heritage. It could be argued that this practice of "localization" could lead to the further ethnic segregation and even deeper marginalization of ethnic groups. However, taking into account the range of options that an ethnic group could possibly have, the active participation in the on-line community using the mother tongue in on-line communication may be the group's most proactive choice. This virtual community could offer, at various times for various participants, possibilities to build a "social net" and change the imposed position of a "submissive, silent, and isolated" immigrant.

Serbia.web reveals some of the tensions involved in the duality of assimilation/difference both between the dominant culture and the ethnic community, and also within virtual community itself. "Virtual" sites are seen here as created social contexts in which participants, drawing from different off-line and on-line resources (experience, cultural patterns, language, computer/Internet knowledge) explore and negotiate cultural meaning. Virtual ethnic community is thus perceived as a pedagogical location that "teaches" on-line participants—by its social organization, by its rules of on-line behavior, and by its modes of access.

And in this manner, the technology itself is a site of contestation in how a community tries to differentiate itself from the dominant cultures, virtual and real. The ability of digital networking technologies to serve a variety of social purposes, to be incorporated in a particular language environment, and to provide spaces for social organization suggests the importance of inquiring into virtual sites. These are points of intersection between IRL and virtual communities that have a bearing on the success of on-line community. Perhaps the important aspect in the community building of Serbia.web was technological knowledge and skills of community members, characteristic for the wave of professional immigrants in 1990s that enabled so many channels of communication to operate and to revise the technology to suit the community. What is needed is further inquiry into the activities of other virtual ethnic groups in order to understand how the on-line community provides a "space for pedagogy" in this duality of assimilation/difference between the dominant and ethnic communities.

Finally, it may be appropriate for us to comment upon the contribution that the study of virtual ethnic communities makes to the purposes of this volume, *Communities of Difference*. First, the inclusion of discourse on ethnic difference expands the categories of interest—race, class, gender, and sexuality. At the least, concentration on ethnicity expands the conversations about race. Second, in the hope of bridging the various theoretical orientations/positions (feminist pedagogies, critical pedagogies, antiracist or postcolonial pedagogies, and gay and lesbian pedagogies), one should consider theories and practices from cultural studies, popular culture, and virtual culture. At the least, virtual ethnic communities represent an additional layer for studying, and understanding, communities of difference.

Bibliography

Agre, P. (1999). "Life After Cyberspace." *EASST Review* 18 (2/3). Retrieved January 27, 2000 from the World Wide Web: http://www.chem.uva.nl/easst/easst993.html.

Appadurai, A. (1996). *Modernity at Large: Cultural Dimensions of Globalization.* Minneapolis: University of Minnesota Press.

Baym, N. (1999). "The Emergence of On-line Community." In *Cybersociety* 2.0, ed. S. Jones. London: Sage, pp. 35–68.

Bell, David. (2001). *An Introduction to Cybercultures.* New York: Routledge.

Coyne, Richard. (1999). *Technoromanticism: Digital Narrative, Holism, and the Romance of the Real.* Cambridge, MA: MIT Press.

Dodge, Martin and Rob Kitchin. (2001). *Mapping Cyberspace.* New York: Routledge.

Fernback, J. and B. Thompson. (1995). "Virtual Communities: Abort, Retry, Failure?" Retrieved March 11, 1998 from the World Wide Web: http://www.well.com/user/hlr/texts/Vccivil.html.

Ford, Peter. (2001). "Need Software in, say, Icelandic? Call the Irish." [html]. *Christian Science Monitor*, February 6, 2001 [cited October 15, 2001]. Available from http://www.csmonitor.com/durable/2001/02/06/fp1s3-csm.shtml.

Hardin, Garret. "The Tragedy of the Commons." *Science* 162 (1968): 1243–1248.

Hongladarom, S. (1998). "Global Culture, Local Cultures, and the Internet." In *Proceedings Cultural Attitudes Towards Communication and Technology '98*, ed. C. Ess and F. Sudweeks. Australia: University of Sydney, pp. 231–245.

Keniston, K. (1998). "Politics, Culture, and Software." Available at: http://web.mit.edu/kken/Public/papers2.htm.

Kollock, Peter. "Design Principles for Online Communities." *PC Update* 15:5 (1998): 58–60.

Mitra, A. (1997). "Virtual Commonality: Looking for India on the Internet." In *Virtual Culture,* ed. S. Jones. London: Sage, pp. 55–79.

Noble, David. (1997). *The Religion of Technology: The Divinity of Man and the Spirit of Invention.* New York: Knopf.

Ostrom, Elinor. (1990). "Governing the Commons: The Evolution of Institutions for Collective Action." In *The Political Economy of Institutions and Decisions,* ed. J. Alt and D. North. Cambridge: Cambridge University Press.

Pargman, D. (1998). "Reflections on Cultural Bias and Adaptation." In *Proceedings Cultural Attitudes Towards Communication and Technology '98*, ed. C. Ess and F. Sudweeks. Australia: University of Sydney, pp. 81–99.

Poster, M. (1999). "Virtual Ethnicity: Tribal Identity in an Age of Global Communications." In *Cybersociety* 2.0, ed. S. Jones. London: Sage, pp. 184–211.

Rheingold, H. (1993). *Virtual Communities.* Reading, MA: Addison-Wesley.

Stubbs, P. (1998). "Conflict and Co-operation in the Virtual Community: Email and the Wars of the Yugoslav Succession." *Sociological Research Online* 3:3, retrieved July 7, 1999 from the World Wide Web: http://www.socresonline.org.uk/socresonline/3/3/7.html.

———. (1999). "Virtual Diaspora? Imagining Croatia On-Line." *Sociological Research Online*, 4:2, retrieved July 14, 1999 from the World Wide Web: http://www.socresonline.org.uk/socresonline/4/2/stubbs.html.

Voiskousky, A. (1998). "Internet: Culture Diversity and Unification." In *Proceedings Cultural Attitudes Towards Communication and Technology '98*, ed. C. Ess and F. Sudweeks. Australia: University of Sydney, pp. 100–115.

Wellman, B. and M. Gulia. (1999). "Virtual Communities as Communities: Net Surfers don't Ride Alone." In *Communities in Cyberspace*, ed. M. Smith and P. Kollock. London: Routledge, pp. 167–194.

Chapter 13

Learning the Real, Theorizing the Virtual I: Toward a Postmodern Techno-Epistemology

Peter Pericles Trifonas and Paulo Ghiraldelli Jr.

Experience, Reason, and Education

How do we characterize the phenomena of virtual learning and its environments when we look at its theoretical presuppositions, its pragmatics, and technologies through a contemporary philosophical perspective on experience and education?

Early on in the twentieth century, John Dewey told us that the most important philosophical notion for education was "experience." According to the pragmatic focus of his doctrine, experience was deemed to be not just a relation between consciousness and "the real world," but a living, learning environment—a contextualization of educational phenomena generated from the relation between elements of the Universe, that included subjects and objects. Experience, for Dewey, was the central point in his real and virtual cosmology of education and constituted the nature of learning environments. This empirical epistemology posited that knowledge was possible because we *were* our experiences, and education—as the pragmatic ability to solve problems—was a simple job of discovering the dimensions of reality and making meaning from it for ourselves. Dewey was firm in the belief that we should "reload" our experience with diversity, thus enabling us to give life and living new meaning, leading from one experience to another experience at breakneck speed via the epistemological curiosity of the subject. And so, to new kinds of new experience. The regeneration of experience from experience itself constitues a never-ending cycle of learning and an infinite resource for education. Sometimes, Dewey's philosophy showed an odd equation: experience = life = education. Education as a concept and process was grounded in "the real" world of nature not "the virtual" world of cyberspace. The institutional context of learning would constitute schooling as an artificial educational environment. Dewey's "philosophy of experience" was undergirded by a theory of social reconstructionism and ethics that focused the pragmatics of education as discovery learning for a moral purpose. He viewed education and schooling as a way to the self-actualization of the subject as a critical citizen with the ability to change society for the better and uphold democracy for morality and justice. Consequently, John Dewey has been called "the philosopher of the Democracy." Education and democracy created a special environment for public discussion that was not "virtual" or removed from experience through any technological means, but grounded in experience and therefore, meaningful in the subjective formations of reality as a meaningful context for learning. The authenticity of the real experiences was thought to generate socially conscious subjects able to interpret and evaluate natural and social phenomena for the purpose of informed discussion in the public sphere. Dewey showed us how the sustained exchange of the diversity of perspectives upon experience, with luck, can create the dissemination of new ideas to generate a better world.

After Dewey and the high period of American Pragmatism, two schools of philosophy questioned the belief that we could take the truth of our experiences at face value. Modernity ushered in the age of technological development and industrialization that created learning environments rooted in the economic division of classes by the systems of production and labor. The Frankfurt School tried to persuade us that in the Modern Period objective reflection on experience was impossible. Empirical reality linked reason to the senses. Thus, the effects of nature on the subject could only be measured in relation to experimental procedures that gauged the cause-and-effect relations between phenomena as percieved by a self-conscious ego. Using the Marxist notion of reproduction theory, social interest, and false consciousness, the Frankfurt School drew a picture of Modernity that showed the relation between the subject and real-world phenomena as inevitably ideological and based in the means of production and the class struggles that structured the institutions and social foundations of all capitalist societies. Karl Marx talked about the power of commodification and economic self-interest to influence the formation of subjectivity, but the Frankfurtian philosophers used reproduction theory to further critique the closed nature of the learning process prominent in capitalist and socialist societies. Reproduction Theory was governed by a notion of reason as instrumental—or a calculus for limiting meaning to finite interpretations. Reason defined in this way does not permit a questioning of the ground of subjectivity and the interpretative structure of educational environments. The transparent relationship posited between words or signs and natural phenomena renders the truth an object indisputable. The relationship between words and objects provides the philosophical cover of reason and its claims to truth. The Frankfurt School exploded the idea of reason as "disinterested" and therefore questioned its validity as a basis for pedagogical action, consequently highlighting the need for the creation of effective learning environments that involved thinking rather than the reproduction of acceptable ideas. They critiqued Dewey's notion that all experience was a pragmatic experiment, on the part of the subject, involving interaction, relation, and movement in nature and cultural history. The Frankfurt philosophers defined a special kind of experience. In German, the word "Erlebniz" describes psychological experience and "Erfahrung" refers to historical and social experience. For the Frankfurt School, Dewey's notion of "pragmatic experimentalism" would not adequately conceptualize the idea of "experience." In the *Eclipse of Reason* (1946), Max Horkheimer charged that Dewey seemed to be reducing thinking to instrumental method. Horkheimer objected to the fixed notion of reality and the universal picture of the world that Dewey advocated via a process of reification with problematic trajectories for securing social justice, if the world were to emerge for the epistemic subject through an "instrumental rationality." According to the Frankfurtian philosophers, "instrumental reason" was an objective rendering of reason arriving *after* a social transformation made by Modernity and its technological mastery of nature by human ingenuity. Theodore Adorno and Herbert Marcuse argued that subjects should strive for social and intellectual emancipation from the circumstance of political and economic domination enshrined by the powers-that-be. This core Marxian tenet applied to the concept of reason promoted by the status quo of the State and its ideology. The Frankfurtian philosophers sought to maximize the subject's capacity for a revolutionary move to a state of freedom and the possibility of self-actualization without external cohersion or force. This meant analyzing the ideological conditions for exploitation and how reason exuded the potential for an interpretative plurality within hegemonic discourses and called for an illumination of the structural conditions of oppression, power, and its working through the educational institution and its apparatus. A negative critique of reason was aimed at derailing the effects of false consciousness on the rendering of the subjective world of experience and learning. This estrangement of the incorporate shell of subjective identity was thought to be a fundamental step to the individual's emancipation from the hegemony of ideology infusing the site of unabashed exploitation. A counter-hegemonic practice well versed in the nuances of negative critique is the intellectual instrument for a sustained resistance to the imposition of meaning from ideologically overdetermined sources outside the self. To liberate subjectivity, in this sense, does not mean to deny self-identity, but to assert independence and control over the homeostatic effects of ideology that enslave the subject to a living-through of the interests and desires of the system.

So, for the Frankfurt School, Dewey's philosophy was a mirror of Modernity and not a reflection of the *rational life* per se. Dewey's conception of experience, it was argued, constructed an empty relation between the subject and reality using a positivist perspective on science to forge artificial links between the consciousness and the external environment in relation to class structures and the economic power base of the status quo. The objection to Dewey that comes from Horkheimer and the Frankfurt School forms the basis for an insurrection against the potential tyranny of learning environments constructed through a blind obedience to technological rationalism. The Frankfurt School was influenced by the meditations of Martin Heidegger on technology and the principle of reason.

Heidegger argued that in the principle of reason there is an element of accountability (*Rechenschaft*) for the "truth-value" of representation (*Vorstellung*). That is, the judgments made about an object placed and positioned *before* a subject—an ego who sure of its self, thinks "I" (*sum*) am. The justification (*Rechtfertigen*) of the certainty of such a self-grounding of knowledge yielded of the *cogitation* rests on the security of demonstrating the proof of the "evident correctness" of an explanation. The logic of perception, Heidegger explained, is set back on the source of the response (e.g., the subjective consciousness) as mental instructions directed by language. Reason is sufficiently rendered, "given back," and *it has to be* for the determinacy of the *ens rationis* (intellect) to piece together an *idea of reality*. If and when a "representation that judges" reality can display the "truth" of its propositional outcomes by re-directing the ground of the "connection" between subject and predicate—the "what" of "is"— back to a cogitating "I." This structure of repetition orders the chain of consequence and organizes the syntagm of language in the coming-back of its returning of presence to the "double effigy" of the sign/picture for concept (*Begriff*). It has the function of "holding" or "keeping" the world of beings firmly fixed (*fest-gestellt*) in the bright light of "objectivity" (*Gegenständlichkeit*), over and against, the underlying filter of the projecting self-consciousness of the "knowing self" as *subjectum* or *hypokeimenon*, "that-which-lies-before" (*qua* prior).[1] Heidegger showed how the firmament of the truth of experience depicted as such bears an anthropocentric foundation and the unmistakable mark of a *metaphysical humanism*. To expand in a slightly different way—on the one hand, the productive reflexivity of the ego sustains the "purity" of the ground of its reasoning. Simply put, its "power-of-bringing-back-to-presence" the self-presence of itself, ensures the *truth of representation* from within the abiding swells of an inwardly spectating imago of the mind. But this is not enough. On the other, a collective form of the responsibility to *give an account of reason* (*logon didonai*) is co-affirmed outright by the *auto-poietic* reflexivity—a self-consciousness of self and self-*hood*. It disengages itself from empirical reality to set apart the Sub-ject from Ob-ject, the Self from Other. It subordinates nature to itself and mortgages its foreclosure in a nature that is always ready-to-hand (*das Zuhanden*). Taking these together: the sense of *ratio* understood in the affirmative form of the principle of reason, *Omnes ens habet rationem* (Every being has a reason), is interpretable as a reckoning to account *for* the calculability (*Berechenbarkeit*) of entities (*Seinden*). The subject thus precedes the object in and ensuing the Cartesian age of modernity. Thus, the ground for the predictable equationing of reason convenes the primacy of calculation as the fate of Western thought and rationality.

The *techne* of this amenability of a reductive reason that we have outlined is the characterizing feature of the historical evolution of "philosophy" to "science" that after the epistemological trailblazing of the early Greeks (not the pre-Socratics) stimulates the ontogenesis of modern "TECHNO-science." The method of "Reason" as the "closure" of representation is not, nor could it ever be, outside the *scope of technology and learning environments,* but rather is a precursor of, and, moreover, integral to, *the necessity for a critical questioning of the grounding of the foundation of the institutional frameworking of knowledge.* Mainly because the metaphysical (logocentric) assumptions behind the objective setting of the value of truth are reductive, autarchical, and protective, of the *practical ends of the task of thinking. Reason and the technologies of Reason are not without interest, not without ground or a grounded grounding that withdraws, refracts, is concealed.*

The issue of the "properness" of response becomes more radical after the Franfurt School and Heidegger in conjunction with what has become a *post*modern "crisis of representation," a suspiciousness of reference and referentiality formed as a question of the "*Question of Reason*" and its "must" in the space of a virtual signifier?

Knowledge and Techno-Epistemology: The Rise of the
Virtual Teaching Machines

Postindustrial society exhibits signs of postmodern culture, Jean-François Lyotard explains.[2] A little more than 20 years after the appearance of *The Postmodern Condition*, we are coursing through the vicissitudes of a new millennium where epistemological certainty is no longer taken for granted, and yet, we must still have some empirical and conceptual foundations upon which to build knowledge. These knowledge structures of science as "moments of learning" are the minimal parameters of *what we know* that legitimize knowledge. Not only because the reality of a temporal disjunction engenders liminal perspectives on knowedge, but because the nature of episteme becomes redefined in accordance with the "problems of translation" (*PC* 3) between repositories of knowledge and their technologies of archiving. *The Postmodern Condition* is a turning point for understanding virtual spaces of learning because it is a philosophical meditation that looks toward a future *yet-to-come* and settles around the problem of *what it means to know* in relation to the epistemological field of technology, the crisis of legitimation after modernism, and the rule of language games.

A question we must always ask in education and research is: Can truth be reduced to an archive? Is it possible? Yes. Knowledge is nothing if it is not grounded upon the possibility of a permanent record of physical data that can then be used to establish "laws of science" as the demonstrable evidence of the self-certainty of the truth of research. Culture depends upon the feasibility of referring to relatively archives of meaning to endow expressions of understanding with the evidence of empirical value and predictive power. The failings of conscious memory require the continuing, demonstrable proof of a past and a future to secure the possibility of a genealogical rendering of human experience.

Language intervenes nevertheless to question the validity of laws as denotative statements based on the power of the archive to stabilize the ground of meaning-making. The signs of knowledge thus exteriorized are transformed into the more general category of "information"—its "use-value" not withstanding the effects of representation that mediate for the limitations of human understanding by giving way to the instrumentality of technological reason. Lyotard states that "Scientific knowledge is a kind of discourse" (*PC* 3). A postmodern proclamation. Knowledge is not a technology in itself. The *a posteriori* of practice is lacking. Knowledge as discourse need not be instrumental. Commands can be disobey and disavowed, consciously or unconsciously. We must consider the significance of Lyotard's statement regarding scientific knowledge with respect to language and technology—the two sides of a postmodern techno-epistemological understanding of real-world phenomena through information and communications media (e.g., the computer).

Postmodern epistemological doubt settles in between the apparatus used for the technical manipulation of information and its archival containment of data as virtual signs of understanding. The need for a techno-epistemology—or a view of virtual knowledge that takes into account the influences of technological mediation upon the sources of its production and perception—arises out of the lack of faith in the truth of science. Representation deforms, denatures, and supplements the originary eidetic structures of conceptual formations. Technology redeems a postmodern epistemological doubt by quelling it in the practice of facilitating pragmatic ends through the supplementation of human weakness. Despite ineptitude. Lyotard isolates the origins of technology in prosthetics, or devices which are "aids for the human organs or as physiological systems whose function it is to receive data or condition the context" (*PC* 44). Such a post-Darwinian supplementation of nature readily follows the "principle of optimal performance" (*PC* 44), whereby God given deficiencies are minimized and one purposeful action "expends less energy than another" (*PC* 44). Technology presupposes the need for the proof of the efficacy of research "as the pragmatics of scientific knowledge replaces traditional knowledge or knowledge based on revelation" (*PC* 44). The concreteness of its manifest structures and operations objectify the union of thought and action. Instrumental reason is born when the root of technology becomes competence rather than invention or *poiesis*, utility rather than creativity or art. Lyotard refers to the fact that after the sixteenth and seventeenth centuries, but especially during the Industrial Revolution, the quest for "technical apparatus require[d] an investment" (*PC* 45) of capital and energy predicated on the promise of optimizing efficiency for greater productivity, which in turn gave it a "surplus-value derived from this improved performance" (*PC* 45). The economizing of reason as "instrumental," of course, has commercial implications for the production of knowledge by promoting the logic of end-oriented research. The point is to add to the cultural archive of information for social profit. A lack of ecological and intellectual altruism directs the reason of technology toward capital incentives rather than educational imperatives and puts it to use for the benefit of private interests that guide the progress of science and the production of knowledge, regardless of the public good. We do not need to give examples; we live them and know them.

The dubious talent of *homo faber* as researcher is revealed in how the raw materiality of the human world can be used as "standing-reserve" (*Bestand*) for material production. That is, a resource always present-at-hand (*Vorhandenheit*) and ready to be used for the artificiality of a ready-made "techno-ecology," whereby nature is brought to a standstill by the enframing (*Gestell*) of a pre-fabricated world picture (*Weltbild*). Like Heidegger, for Lyotard, techno-science contributes to a postmodern spirit of pessimism caused by feelings of alienation and homelessness (*Unheimlichkeit*).

Technology and capital can coexist; and they do, one supporting the other and vice versa through collaborations and partnerships. However, the epistemological legitimacy of knowledge suffers when the ethics of research are compromised for a "learning circulating along the same lines as money" (*PC* 6). And research becomes tied to funding and science to capital for specific outcomes related to application. The economic terms of the exchange then result in what Lyotard calls "payment knowledge" and "investment knowledge" (*PC* 6), whose first priority is not ideological or "communicational transparency" (*PC* 6). The philosophical and ethical disinterestedness of "higher learning" that Kant champions becomes redundant relative to the economic viability of sustaining publicly supported educational institutions.[3] A new academic responsibility toward the production of applied knowledge is thus consecrated in the context of the total subjugation of educational institutions to the technologies of

informatization or data creation. A cross-contamination occurs between the "instrumental" and the *poietic* aims of research, where and when the specificity of the goals or
purposes of knowledge is blurred by economic interests. Education cannot but
become the site of modern TECHNO-SCIENCE, Lyotard tells us, although not
without a cost to basic research within the university. The amenability of reason to
technology is the characterizing feature of the institutional evolution of knowledge
from "philosophy" to "science," from theory to practice, and the necessity for the
empirical justification of knowledge. The application of reason as the structure and
end of research is not, nor could it ever be, outside the scope of a critical questioning
of the grounding of the foundation of the institutional frameworking of knowledge.
For Lyotard, the metaphysical assumptions behind the attempts made at an objective
setting of the values of truth are reductive, autarchical, and protective of the practical
modality of a teleological thinking. Reason and the use of technologies of Reason in
the process of research and teaching cannot be legitimated without interest—without
the power of a subjective ground of logic—an ideologically grounded grounding that
withdraws, refracts, is concealed by the self-sustaining logic of a closed system exemplified by the epistemological hierarchy of disciplines. In this articulation is reflected
the arbitrary structure of social interests actualized via the institutional hierarchy of
the disciplines as the practice of knowledge generation gets worked out through the
"crossing-over" of science from theoria to praxis. Normative criteria come to govern
the optimal performance of "ideas in action" for the purpose of subordinating the
quality of information to the augmenting effects of technological performativity.
Lyotard calls this accretion of the power of truth—its principle of reinforcing reality
through a supplementation of the deficiencies of reality—"the best possible input/out-
put equation" (*PC* 46). This techno-epistemological cultivation of efficient representations of phenomena both prefigures and supports the existence of metanarratives of
academic responsibility that appeal to narrowly defined ethical standards of research
for the purpose of authenticating and legitimating the means used for the production
of practical knowledge. Technology propels the work of science toward the facilitation
of an instrumental rationality outside the scope and interests of intellectual inquiry *in*
and *of* itself. According to Lyotard, the "rising complexity" of proof becomes the goal
for the axiomatic demonstration of truth. Techno-epistemological claims to knowledge require the mysticism of an "other" language of science reconcilable only to the
binary logic of its own expression of decidability. The limits of truth are programmatic
and incommensurable to the presence of otherness within the interpretative frameworking of a system that constructs meaning according to the "principle of a universal
metalanguage" (*PC* 43). Techno-epistemology facilitates the proof of science by modeling the laws of reality as a simulation of real phenomena. It produces a simulacrum
of experience faithful to the conceptual structures of experience. Reality is heightened
by the virtual expression of empirical knowledge. Technology, it can be said, is more
than just to the principle of verification required for the legitimacy of research.
Scientific proof has power through the performativity of "good verdicts" (*PC* 47) that
concretely represent the meaning of experience. Technology "reinforces" science,
Lyotard maintains, because "one's chances of being just and right [about a knowledge
of reality] increase accordingly" (*PC* 47) through efficient research applications. There
is another side to it nevertheless.

Technology cannot bridge the difference between reality and experience, because it is predicated on principles of practice governing the consistent production of instrumental reason that mimics verisimilitude. And yet, technology also functions as a difference engine, creating "a plurality of formal and axiomatic systems capable of arguing the truth of denotative statements" (*PC* 43), but unable to show how empirical proofs support the logic of conclusions. Techno-epistemology illustrates the postmodern paradox of science as applied research when the status of reality is questioned and academic responsibility is at stake. For Lyotard, "proof is problematical since proof needs to be proven" (*PC* 44). Technology does not compute (for) interptretative alterity, and so, unwittingly augments the unlikely probability of its commensurability or the conceptual reduction of difference via a paradigmatic rendering of the full presence of the other within the possibility of a mechanized reproduction of the same. Ironically, the result of techno-epistemology is a crisis of legitimation in the postmodern age of science. The rapid proliferation of paradoxical theorems and conflicting findings undermine the power of the grand masternarratives to persuade research communities to reach a consensus of meaning. The principles of techno-epistemology create a performativity of simulations that offer a substitute for empirical proof. For the purposes of legitimation, the outcomes of applied research practices come to determine the effectivity of scientific inquiry. Technology, however, exacerbates the postmodern condition of incommensurability between the metanarratives of science because it "cannot fail to influence the truth criterion" (*PC* 46). The paradoxes of techno-epistemology are produced by the proliferation of competing interpretations that threaten the credibility and legitimacy of claims to knowledge. Science surrenders to paralogy: the game of language played from within the axiological framework of a system of meaning-making to undermine the self-certain truth of research.

Legitimation Crisis and Language Games

It is not difficult to ascertain why Lyotard cautions against adopting the principles of techno-epistemology without reservation. He believes that the instrumental aims of corporate and government funding of research for the purpose of orienting the efficiency of scientific performativity "subordinate the institutions of higher learning to the existing powers" (*PC* 50). The pursuit of a techno-epistemological justification of knowledge is not necessarily a "bad" thing. That is, if it is just one more available method of testing, among others, to query the validity of scientific protocol. The desire to implement a system of research based on the logic of performativity is however misguided. An "imperative of performance" placed upon the "task of science" to generate usable information supports the " 'organic' connection between technology and profit" (*PC* 45). This is true. Although to be fair, the application of knowledge can be ethical whether it is originally directed or not. Free will is involved. And Lyotard does leave room for the power of the imagination and aesthetic inspiration to shape scientific discovery as an intangible influence upon the limitations of instrumental reason. But, if the point of research is to improve the performance of the social system through a techno-epistemological rendering of science, then what can learning be tied to other than the creation of "skills that are indispensable to that system"? (*PC* 48).

Here again in Lyotard's postmodern futurology are echoes of our contemporary dilemma, especially in the higher echelons of the education machine. Now, more than ever, the surplus-value of knowledge is molded through the use-value of technology because global competition requires the citizen to be capable of supporting the economic mission of the nation-state on an international scale. On the one hand, Lyotard predicts that there will therefore be a "growth in demand for experts and high and middle management executives" (*PC* 48) in "any discipline with applicability to training in 'telematics' (computer scientists, cyberneticists, linguists, mathematicians, logicians. . . .)" (*PC* 48). We most certainly have seen this to be the case with the explosion of the World Wide Web and the Internet and the rapid rise of a new global economy of virtual proportions. The architecture of technology itself is not the obstacle to intellectual and economic self-actualization now as much accessibility to it is. On the other hand, Lyotard sees the delegitimization of liberal education and a discrediting of its "emancipation narrative" (*PC* 48) that has informed the disciplinary construction of knowledge within institutions of higher learning since the beginnings of the modern university in Prussia under the guidance of Wilhelm von Humboldt. The need to create citizen-subjects "with the skills [to fulfill] society's own needs" (*PC* 48) diminishes the necessity for dabbling in philosophical ideals, so there are only so many doctors, so many teachers in a given discipline, so many engineers, so many administrators, etc. The transmission of knowledge is no longer designed to train an elite capable of guiding the nation toward its emancipation, but to supply the system with players capable of acceptably fufilling their roles at the pragmatic posts required by its institutions (*PC* 48).

Learning in the postindustrial age promotes the development of skills, for competence and productivity, not the value of speculation, for invention and discovery. No interest is taken in science for its own sake. The principles of "liberal humanism" no longer ground the model of an emancipatory education through which autonomous self-actualization is attainable. Occupational horizons and careerism do. Consequently, the professionalization of work is informed by the ethical imperative of gathering the situational knowledge needed to perform and excel at a job skill as opposed to engaging in the speculative production of knowledge for general inquiry. Functionalism overtakes learning. But this could not happen without the delegitimation of philosophy and science in light of the distinction between theory and practice that collapses under the weight of an interdisciplinary questioning the universal premises of truth. Postmodernism can be held accountable here, if it is as Lyotard states, "an incredulity toward metanarratives" (*PC* xxiv) or legitimating stories that seek to explain the meaning of experience. To quell epistemological doubt and control the transmission of established knowledges, didactics takes over learning after the ground of certainty has disappeared under it.[4] Method supercedes for the reproduction of a cultural archive and its paradigmatic and self-conscious teachings. The result after postmodernism is that philosophy and science are no more capable of extrapolating truth than any other disciplines, since the decline of the grand narrative, "whether it is a speculative narrative or a narrative of emancipation" (*PC* 37), reduces knowledge to a method of language games.

It is crucial to recognize the semantic elision that Lyotard makes—but does not specifically state—between the archiving of knowledge and the constitutive means and methods of doing so, that delegitimize grand narratives and create a crisis of meaning. The paradigmatic shift from discourse to technology changes the social and epistemological definitions of research and truth. Not to mention the cognitive and affective preconditions of teaching and learning. The speculative dimension of reason comes into question after the instrumental push of technology to recode human experience according to its own nature is made. And yet, teaching and learning requires creativity and imagination. It is moved forward by epistemological curiosity— the quest for infinite human progress—and not the inculcation of procedural outcomes that render subjectivity as the products of coded instructions performed via electronic commands. Lyotard is enamored neither by the prospects of a "cyborg subjectivity"—and the potential it foresees for a new information society of techno-automatons—nor, by the vision of a learning culture that prioritizes the ethical value of the digital enterprising of knowledge. He details how research in such a techno-epistemological milieu will begin to be legitimated according to the power of information as a commodity to be used by nation-states "in the world wide competition for power" (*PC* 5). Lyotard's predictions about the future of knowledge in an economic globalization here are uncanny—"the breakdown of the hegemony of American capitalism, the decline of the socialist alternative, a probable opening of the Chinese market" (*PC* 6). Furthermore, he envisions the influence of the digital age on higher education. He anticipates the miniaturization of technology and the increase in computing power through which "learning is translated into quantities of information" (*PC* 4). These "bytes of knowledge"—channeled by finite systems of translation with discreet programmable languages—will produce highly directed areas of inquiry. Consequently, the legitimacy of research is determined in accordance with its potential viability to serve "industrial and commercial strategies on the one hand, and the political and military strategies on the other" (*PC* 5). The field of scientific inquiry narrows drastically when it is tied to the circulation of capital. Basic or fundamental research becomes shaped in relation to the interests of multinational corporations and nation-states vying for control of information.

In a postindustrial, postmodern age, where knowledge is reinterpreted as information—and its value is determined by the capacity to incite profitable exchanges between social actors—Lyotard explains how learning is also commodified in the public sphere. Education no longer becomes the sole "purview of the State" (*PC* 5), but is determined through the socioeconomic and ideologico-political forces that structure and mercantilize knowledge. An information society and its "new economy" is predicated to grow through the open exchange of information on a global scale. Lyotard was perhaps the first modern philosopher after Martin Heidegger to predict the future impact of technology on knowledge without referring to more recent inventions such as the World Wide Web and the Internet. The need for the flow of information supercedes and overrides the necessity to censor the quality of the information made available. *All information is created equal.* That is the motto of the new information age and its pseudo-intellectual economy. Lyotard outlines the implications of what this contemporary perspective proselytizes. The hidden significance of information is posed as a future problem of equitable access to data: "who will know?" (*PC* 6). Ideology is now joined to the question of the status of knowledge. Another more personal question arises: "Why should I know?" Quite simply, because the telematic system of communication and its open exchanging of messages that techno-epistemology has effectualized, now obliges a citizenry to be responsible for the dissemination and growth of information. And of course, the obligation extends to the direction of the language games of science that are played in the public sphere. Ignorance of technology no longer contitutes an excuse when the stakes for a way of life and living are high.

Language is the foundation of technology and of science. Narrative constitutes the source of subjectivity. Postmodern doubt complicates the self-certainty of identity from which the empirical value of science as a discourse of truthful knowledge is constructed vis-à-vis the Greek *logos*. Lyotard appropriates the Wittgensteinian concept of "language games"—the rules of expression governing the constative and performative instances of utterance within the field of communication—to articulate the paradoxical essence of knowledge under the influence of a postindustrial techno-epistemology. Narration is antagonistic to "hard science" because it exposes data to an interpretative modality of analysis that in effect cannot be controlled. For Lyotard, narrative creates an *agonistics*, whereby a community of truth is transformed into a community of dissensus through *paralogy*, or the proliferation of paradoxical discourses that contradict meaning though the games played with the rules of science via language. At least, this is Lyotard's hypothesis. The problem with language games— and all "games theory" in general—is the supposition that each "move" both incites and merits a "counter-move" to offset the structure of the system, to keep it in balance. The binary madality of the logic is totalizing as well as simplistic: if there are no rules, there is no game; if there is a move, it requires a response. This is not necessarily the case. Sometimes a game only has one player who knows the game is being played. Technology renders the use-value of knowledge incalculable as new information is produced, publicly archived, and made accessible at a faster rate than ever before in history. Interpretability is open. Information can be recoded into existing systems of knowledge and can be used to build new structures and frameworks of understanding. Language enables the constant changing of rules that characterize the validity of a denotative or prescriptive statement referring to a state of knowledge or knowing. So, it is essential for those in the private and public domains who may well benefit from it the most to attempt to stimulate the circulation of messages that are "rich in information and easy to decode" (*PC* 5). Technology allows a future manipulation of research to occur with subtlety under the capitalistic guise of sustaining democracy.

The Virtual Future?

Expanding the question of the status of knowledge to include a generalized overview of postindustrial, postmodern virtual learning environments brings to light how the location and the nature of learning are being integrated with the practices of everyday life. Lyotard does not address the consequences of the intellectual engagement of virtual archives as a cultural practice. He prefers to concentrate on the use-value of knowledge in relation to its performative commodification through technology. The "computerization of society" (*PC* 7) instantiates a "legitimation crisis" according to Lyotard. Although, not in the Habermasian sense of a community reacting to iconoclastic attitudes that question the validity of scientific truths. A digitally driven information society inheres the relation of knowledge to power and the ideological underpinnings of claims to reason. The focus of postmodern theory on discourse instantiates, after Dewey, a critique of the principle of reason that governs the philosophical genealogy of the Western epistemological tradition and its privileging of a naïve concept of representation.[5] What distinguishes a postmodern vision of a computerized information society is the recognition of the ethico-political dimension of knowledge that an instrumental rendering of science and research technologies diminishes. Five or ten years ago we heard people talking about the Internet as a kind of mass media and telecommunications system. They assimilated its reliance on language and images conceptually into the familiar real-time landscapes of the media— newspaper, TV, radio, phone, magazines, and so on. It was thought that the Internet could not be a teaching and learning machine of virtual information. But the Internet is not a communication channel. It is a complex environment. And it is not just any environment; it is *a virtual* environment. The virtual environment has its proper time, space, coordinates—and semantics! It is *almost* a kind of new dimension without boundaries. It has the cache of being a universe of infinite possibility and yet it could also be a fictional construction of space. But if we invoke it as a fiction, we can say: it is a special kind of fabrication, since it produces fiction and reality without boundary. This is its power. It is a postmodern feature highlighting the virtual education that Lyotard's perspective took in almost thirty years ago when he wrote *The Postmodern Condition*. In questioning modern philosophy and its closed epistemology we are breaking down blind hierarchies between fields of knowledge and their metadiscusrive rationality. Mathematics is not more true than Literature, or Music is not less scientific if compared to Physics. The Internet is an educational situation that breaks down hierarchies within a virtual learning environment inasmuch as it upholds them. So, the old discussion about who is against the possibility of "experience" or who defends the notion of experience is rather pointless. What happens between a computer user and the virtual web is not what Dewey called "experience" or what Horheimer and Heidegger denied could be "real." *Between* virtual web and learner we have a unique relation   a virtual one. We do not have an interaction. We have just a unique fiction of symbiotic union between human beings and machines that covers the reason of both. The computer user is a virtual learner and the computer a piece of technology, but you cannot think of the two parts separately when the virtual environment starts to work. When we realize what the specificity of the environment entails we cannot imagine an "inside" and an "outside." That fiction creates the *ether* or the *web* of connectivity and virtual space—the web is not "inside" or "outside." The web is a new way station to knowledge and meaning creation—it is knowledge in process but it is not an "experience of reality" or the discovery of new meaning from experience. The Deweyan cosmological model does not work here. We do not see subject or object because the web is not constructed by *one*, and it is not *there* like an object fixed by a subject. It keeps itself growing and improving like an auto-generative plasma, but a plasma without an arterial system. It is not possible to know what is in *the* learner's brain. The cognitive apparatus does not stay *on* the web and govern its manifestations. "On line" is an English word, but in the rest of the planet it is a metaphor, maybe a bad metaphor. The cognitive apparatus does not stay *in* the web. We can spell "*Internet*" looking for a meaning, but you would not find a satisfactory meaning covering the multiplicity of conceptions associated with the word. Virtual learning and teaching does not happen in the virtual camp, but it *is* the virtual camp, that is, the web, the virtual environment working fast and suggesting that we are living in a special dimension. It does not stop. It does not have a break when someone turns off a computer. And maybe what we call "the real world" breaks down if the web stops for even just one second.

And yet, the archiving of information is not benign, but subject to the governance of the means of representation by external forces, mechanical and ideological, though ultimately grounded in the logic of cultural practices. The translatability of messages and other sensory data (visual, auditory, haptic) permeating the virtual public sphere remains greatly under the power of controlling forces who shape their form according to the reason of exposition. But given that the field of interpretation may be open to aberrant codings and responses, the power of information is undecidable. Intentionality is factored into representation, but cannot control it. Signs are not autogenic, therefore virtual. Responsibility is involved in representation. The desire for technological determinism characterizes the reason of "the most highly developed societies" (*PC* 7). Cybernetics becomes the terrain for the struggle over knowledge that manifests itself according to the Occidental passion for decidability and appropriation. Justice is not an issue when nature is fixed as experience. A community of learning grows from a commensurability of perspectives wherein truth is qualified by the adherence to traditions of inquiry. Certain discourses are accepted, while others are not. Censorship comes by way of a paradigmatic modality of knowledge. The masternarratives that are generated to support the ideology of the system of representation are in need of excavating to explore the truth of reason in the virtual realm of learning environments. That is, if we are to question the ethics of techno-epistemology and the democratic status of knowledge in the information age after postmodernism and the rise of education machines.

Notes

1. See Martin Heidegger, *The Question Concerning Technology and Other Essays*, trans. William Lovitt (New York: Harper & Row Publishers, 1977) for the discussion of technology as a mode of *aletheuein*, revealing—the essence of technology being nothing "technological" but *poietic*. Also Martin Heidegger, *The Principle of Reason*, trans. Reginald Lilly (Bloomington, IN: Indiana University Press, 1991). We can follow trail that leads from the transformation of the pre-Socratic notion of Being as *physis* and *aletheia* into the conception of Being as *eidos* and *idea* from Plato to Being as humanity's idea to technology.

2. Jean-François Lyotard, *The Postmodern Condition: A Report on Knowledge*. Originally published in France in 1979. All further reference to this work in the text are to the English translation by Geoff Bennington and Brian Massumi (Minneapolis: University of Minnesota Press, 1984).

3. See Immanuel Kant, *Critique of Practical Reason*, trans. Lewis White Beck (New York: Macmillan Publishing Company, 1956) and Immanuel Kant, *The Conflict of the Faculties/Der Streit der Fakultäten*, trans. Mary J. Gregor (New York: Abaris Books, 1979). See also Jacques Derrida, "Mochlos; or, The Conflict of the Faculties,"

trans. Richard Rand and Amy Wygant, in *Logomachia: The Conflict of the Faculties*, ed. Richard Rand (Lincoln: University of Nebraska Press, 1992).

4. See Jacques Derrida, "On a Newly Arisen Apocalytic Tone in Philosophy," trans. John P. Leavey, Jr., in *Raising the Tone of Philosophy: Late Essays by Immanuel Kant, Transformative Critique by Jacques Derrida*, ed. Peter Fenves (Baltimore: Johns Hopkins University Press, 1993), pp. 117–171.

5. Gianni Vattimo, *The End of Modernity: Nihilism and Hermeneutics in Postmodern Culture*, trans. Jon R. Snyder (Baltimore: Johns Hopkins University Press, 1988) gives an excellent rendering of the crisis of meaning after the questioning of representation.

Index ∼